Learning to Think Strategically

New Frontiers in Learning

The **New Frontiers in Learning Series** features books presenting cutting edge developments in learning practices that drive performance in organizations. Particular attention is given to strategically focused linkages between learning and performance. However, the focal point of each book in the series will be on learning processes and performance outcomes at the individual, team, and/or organizational level. The theme that unifies the books in the series is learning solutions that add value in highly competitive environments, including both the non-profit and for-profit sectors.

Titles in the series:

LEARNING TO THINK STRATEGICALLY

Julia Sloan

ELSEVIER

AMSTERDAM • BOSTON • HEIDELBERG • LONDON
NEW YORK • OXFORD • PARIS • SAN DIEGO
SAN FRANCISCO • SINGAPORE • SYDNEY • TOKYO

Butterworth-Heinemann is an imprint of Elsevier

Butterworth–Heinemann is an imprint of Elsevier
30 Corporate Drive, Suite 400, Burlington, MA 01803, USA
Linacre House, Jordan Hill, Oxford OX2 8DP, UK

∞ Recognizing the importance of preserving what has been written, Elsevier prints its books on acid-free paper whenever possible.

Library of Congress Cataloging-in-Publication Data
Sloan, Julia.
  Learning to think strategically / Julia Sloan.
    p.   cm.
  Includes bibliographical references and index.
  ISBN-13: 978-0-7506-7879-7   ISBN-10: 0-7506-7879-8 (alk. paper)
    1. Strategic planning.   I. Title.
HD30.28.S53 2006
658.4′012 — dc22   2006040907

British Library Cataloguing-in-Publication Data
A catalogue record for this book is available from the British Library.

ISBN 13: 978-0-7506-7879-7
ISBN 10: 0-7506-7879-8

For information on all Butterworth–Heinemann publications
visit our Web site at www.books.elsevier.com

Printed in the United States of America
08 09 10   10 9 8 7 6 5 4 3 2

Contents

Preface

Right before our wedding, my husband invited me to join him for an international balloon competition in Umbria, Italy. A certified international balloon pilot, he often travels to Europe to participate in various balloon races and fiestas. I stow away for the sheer pleasure, and I take special delight as an unofficial observer in the balloon. At that time I was toiling over research for my doctoral dissertation on learning strategy. Flying through blue skies over the sunflower fields of Umbria, watching the other balloons and observing the maneuvers of my husband, I couldn't help but notice how his piloting a balloon in a race mirrored the findings of the data that I was in the midst of analyzing. Ballooning was a metaphor to making global strategy.

Balloon flying is a very special kind of sport. Pilots have minimal control over their environment, and, to a high degree, it is unpredictable, uncontrollable, and risky; and a race is all about winning. A pilot can control only the vertical movement of the balloon by using a propane burner to warm up the air inside the balloon envelope. The inertia of the huge balloon is a critical factor; it takes several minutes before it responds to any effort. And pilots are at the mercy of Providence and the weather—especially the winds. Balloons can go horizontally only if taken by the wind; and at different heights, the winds gust, shifting direction without warning. Sure, there is some data from the weatherman, but trusting the weatherman with your life is like swimming into a whale's mouth!

A good balloon pilot is a strategist "par excellence." I noticed that my husband ascended to a space far above the other balloons and, from this panoramic vantage point, calculatingly assessed the "big picture": What balloon at what height is taken by the wind in which direction at what speed? Instruments and gauges are available, but they compete with time and are no substitute for "knowing." As other pilots were burning propane, bobbing up and down seeking the right wind to take them in the right direction, he suspended motion, carefully observed and quickly decided his course. He "knew" when to ascend and descend ever so slightly. He had a "feel" for the subtleties and nuances required and trusted his judgment learned from past experiences. Watching him pilot was like watching him perform an intimate dance with his balloon.

I was struck by how much this sport reflected making global strategy—watching the competition and learning from their successes and failures, rather than imitating the successes, making or repeating their mistakes. Though I didn't think to mention the metaphor at the time, I was reminded of it several years later, in a conversation with my husband about how he proceeds with making strategy in his international business. He started by recounting how many of the strategic lessons he learned came from his ballooning experience. Recalling this metaphor, and the similar stories of so many clients, made me ever more curious to understand how successful strategists *learn* to think strategically. This was the research knot I needed to untie.

It wasn't strategy formation or strategy implementation that compelled me to launch a systematic inquiry into strategic learning; it was my intense desire to understand what happens *before* strategy is made, about which I was truly curious. I wanted to find out how successful strategists *learned* to think strategically. I wanted to explore and to understand the first link in the strategy chain—*learning* how strategic thinking occurs.

Based on more than a decade of experience working as an international consultant with key corporate and public-sector executives responsible for making global strategy, I came to the simple conclusion that there were executives who were able to think strategically and those who were not. Given the impressive educational credentials and the equally impressive strategy budgets of the key strategy makers with whom I worked, it became clear that learning to think strategically was sufficiently more complex than being adept at problem solving, applying a model, or operationalizing a vision. These instrumental cognitive functions were skills the executives had mastered, with little effect on the success of their actual strategy making.

There was something curiously common about the thinking process of the successful key strategists with whom I worked in Asia, Africa, Eastern Europe, the Middle East, Western Europe, and North America, regardless of their respective cultural backgrounds. I couldn't help noticing a pattern among the successful strategists—something seemed to inform their thinking process. Having lived and worked abroad myself for much of my career, and being well versed in cross-cultural theory, I sensed that this transcended culture.

It appeared that those who were able to make and remake successful strategy in very different circumstances, had a particular way of thinking. I wanted to know what that particular thinking process was. My quest was to learn how the successful strategists actually *learned* to think strategically, and I wanted to understand it from the perspective of the executives' own self-reports.

This book is my journey on the road to understanding how the successful strategists learned to think strategically. In this book, I offer a synthesis of findings from several years of qualitative research in pursuit of a single question: How do successful executives *learn* to think strategically? As part of an interpretive case study, I conducted in-depth interviews with nine successful executives in Japan, Poland, China, Germany, the United States, and Hong Kong to pursue this inquiry. I visited the executives in their work environments to see what their worlds were like, to ask questions, to listen, and to observe.

Early on, I decided that to understand how these executives learn, I should ask them directly. So I did. The personal interviews paint an entirely different picture from the kind of information that is derived from a large-scale, checkbox-style quantitative survey study. While there are many circumstances in which statistical quantitative surveys are an outstanding format for gathering data, for this particular research I believed personal interviews offered a special depth and richness that no check-box questionnaire, however well designed, could deliver.

Personal interviews are loaded with details. It is one thing for an executive to check off a box indicating that a particular experience or event had an impact on his thinking. It is far more powerful and useful to understand *why* this experience had such power, how it occurred, and whether other executives can benefit in their work from the story. The more illustrations and quotations an executive can offer to buttress a point, the better and more helpful that point is for others.

Each executive in the study had a story to tell. Collectively, their stories reveal certain common themes. Their stories emphasize the critical role of informal learning and the identification of five essential attributes required for learning to think strategically: imagination, broad perspective, "juggle," no control over, and desire to win. It is striking that their learning was so similar in nature, given the diversity of backgrounds, industries, and histories.

I was impressed by the powerful, heartfelt, passionate stories about the subject: learning strategic thinking. Interviewing these executives was a special pleasure for me. They had strong viewpoints and high expectations and were enthusiastic and productive. The best part was that all of them had suggestions for improving academic and business aspects of facilitating learning to think strategically. They constantly question what they do, and how to do it better.

All the findings in this book came from in-depth interviews. Every executive participated in several interviews, each lasting four to five hours. Analzying responses to each question of the in-depth interviews was a long, tedious, and fascinating process. Slowly but steadily I developed a process for categorizing experience, coding the rich stories told by real executives. It was not the numbers and the statistical tests that told the truth of this research—it was the stories. The lessons of their experiences were vivid, emotional, and anything but objective.

Strong findings emerged that have influenced my professional practice of consulting, teaching, training, and coaching, and I hope it will do the same for readers. Do these findings generalize? This is just a single interpretive qualitative research study on a handful of successful global executives. My visits and work with other companies and organizations around the world have convinced me that the findings in this book apply broadly. But this is up to the readers to decide. Is it their story as well?

I am struck by how much of what executives in other organizations say is similar to what the executives I interviewed for the study said. Maybe a select few findings won't generalize, but it is clear to me that most do so quite well. I know that enormous differences exist among organizations and individual executives. Yet nearly all of them have a wish to enhance learning, to improve learning development initiatives, and to organize their businesses in such a way that they can make a positive contribution to the learning of others. If the findings I present here help readers take a few steps toward achieving these outcomes, I will consider this book a great satisfaction.

Acknowledgements

I have been the beneficiary of the generous assistance, advice, encouragement, love, and caring support of so many people from around the world—most of whose names do not appear in this book, but whose contributions are embedded in the ideas and examples within the text and forever in my memory.

No book emerges as the sole manifestation of its author. Over the years many business clients, academics, and students have strongly influenced my thinking. Many people and circumstances have shaped the insights and experience I have gained, and I owe an immense intellectual debt of gratitude to these special clients, colleagues, and friends. I could not have written this book without the dedicated assistance of so many people.

I am deeply indebted to Michael Petty for technology assistance and graphics. Much of this book was written in airports and enroute to and from various countries—Michael made himself available around the clock and across time zones. He has been astonishingly generous with his willingness to help and relentless in his enthusiasm and support. I owe much to his imagination, indefatigable organization, and uncanny ability to read my mind and convert my messy sketches into intelligible figures and tables.

My sincere appreciation also goes to Annemarie Leyden who graciously reviewed the early manuscript and readily contributed many suggestions. Her expertise of the subject has been an enormous asset as has her willingness to help. I also want to thank Marie Volpe for her generous contributions to my thinking and for her encouragement to persist through the up's and down's of the writing process.

My deep gratitude to Eileen Capone who read the initial draft and was perceptive and tactful in her suggestions for major revisions. Her wonderful energy and intellectual acumen prompted constructive changes that the reader will surely appreciate. I also wish to thank John Gillespie who provided expert advice, a grounded perspective, and encouragement from conception to completion.

Jason Rardin has been another source of extremely valuable input as he conscientiously labored over a preliminary draft of the book and had the good sense to recommend numerous cuts and offer suggestions as to the chapter sequence. His incisive questions led to possibilities I had previously not considered.

There were numerous people who volunteered to do anonymous "blind reads" of the manuscript at various stages. I would like to extend my deep appreciation to each of them for their candid, precise, and helpful suggestions.

Clients have been great teachers in the conceptualization, content, and examples within this book, bringing with them a sense of genuine interest and willingness to share what is important and what is not relevant in their learning experience with strategy. They have taken a keen interest in my research and provided me with an understanding of their thinking, feeling, and the practices of their respective organizations. From them I have gleaned a tremendous collection of cases, examples, and stories. I am most grateful to them for sharing their time and experiences and hope I have represented them well. Many people graciously agreed to be part of projects, experiments, and interviews; this has added great value to my research and book. I owe them all a debt of thanks for their rich and generous contributions.

I would also like to extend my appreciation to the series editors, Lyle Yorks and Carol Gorelick, who recognized the potential of a book on learning to think strategically and kindly invited me to contribute to their series.

The professional team at Butterworth-Heinemann has been the best of the best to work with. Their confidence and encouragement during the editorial process have been tremendously supportive. The book would never have reached its present form without the enthusiasm, dedication, and integrity of the editorial team.

My great appreciation to Ailsa Marks, whose expert advice, efficiency, and quick wit were encouraging from start to finish and whose broad perspective served to maintain momentum for the project. I am also very grateful to Dennis McGonagle for his energy, enthusiasm, and his prompt and patient explanation of details to a novice author. He helped to keep deadlines in check, track progress, and redeem morale throughout. And my genuine thanks to the experienced eye and meticulous mind of Jeff Freeland and the other staff who navigated the production process. Their scrupulous attention to detail has been invaluable and greatly improved the readability of the book.

I am profoundly grateful to my many friends who have been loyal, patient, and most generous in their encouragement: Linda Masterson and Vic Van-Ballenberghe, Amita Gupta, Sally Dunn, Patricia Bouta, William Chen, Susan Gold, and Louis Michnowsky.

Many thanks to my extended and very dear family for their sideline cheers and persistent telephone calls and emails requesting progress reports on the book. Their encouragement and support nudged me to persevere.

Finally, there is my husband Oleg, who has been a pillar of support and understanding. Writing a book, I've discovered, is an all-consuming endeavor—it takes on a life of its own that is both isolating and invigorating. I literally closed the door on him for countless days, most weekends, and far too many holidays. Without his encouragement, humor, sacrifice, candid insights, intellectual rigor, and love the effort would have been nearly impossible to sustain. His affection and patience have endeared and inspired me.

Introduction

Learning to Think Strategically is structured around three key questions: (1) How do successful executives learn to think strategically? (Is it something they are taught? Where? By whom? How?) (2) What learning approaches are used by successful executive strategists? (3) What is most essential to their learning to think strategically?

One of the most frequent and impassioned requests I hear from executive leadership, regardless of nationality, industry, or size, is "How can I develop my people to think strategically?" As we discuss their observations, wants, and needs, these executives deftly identify their need as being able, repeatedly and rapidly, to shift course and to have more strategic thinkers in the "pipeline." Their want, however, is to have a quick and easy, step-by-step model so that they can sit down and produce a fool-proof strategic plan, once and for all.

Learning to Think Strategically is intended for organizational leaders and professionals who are serious about increasing their capacity to think strategically in order to create, re-create, and sustain strategic effectiveness. It is also aimed at those who are committed to and tasked with developing and sustaining the "pipeline" of strategic thinkers in their organizations:

Executives
Chief learning officers
Chief knowledge officers
HRD and OD department managers and staff
Senior line manager partners
Internal and external consultants
Professors and Students

Furthermore, it is intended for anyone else who is interested in leveraging learning to enhance strategic performance.

Paramount among the challenges facing the leadership of all organizations is how to get their organizations continually to adapt and change in new directions and to generate the momentum needed to propel innovation. This is quite different and much more difficult than orchestrating a single massive change.

Strategic organizational learning is becoming increasingly critical for sustaining high-level organizational performance in a world that is becoming ever more turbulent and characterized by rapid technological innovation, shifting political alliances, and emerging economies. Global organizations have responded by becoming increasingly reliant on decentralized value chains comprising networks and alliances. A critical organizational asset in this rapidly changing world is having a "pipeline" of strategic leaders who can think strategically and ensure the competitive positioning of the company.

Traditional strategic thinking models tend to be premised on linear and rational concepts of problem solving, decision making, and planning. Conventional approaches to thinking strategically tend to focus on the teaching/training function, and they use some variation of a planning model that results in a "product"—a master plan supported by incremental action plans. While there is nothing wrong with planning—it brings plenty of benefit—it is only one side of the strategy coin. Learning to think strategically involves different functions, different processes, and very different performance outcomes.

University faculty and strategy consultants have become intent on the teaching aspect of strategic thinking, without first addressing the underlying *learning* supposition of thinking strategically—something that is nonlinear and far more independent than the traditional teaching approach. Executives want to teach and be taught with the brevity of bullet points and sound bites, without the hassle of acquiring the necessary insight of understanding how we *learn* what we need to know. We want to "produce" a strategy rather than generate or create a learning process for sustainable, innovative re-creation capability.

As you will discover, this is not a how-to book. Learning to think strategically is hardly a quick, easy, or step-by-step learning process. Rather, the process rubs against the conventional grain and raises questions about much of what most of us have learned and been taught in traditional strategy courses. Yet the long-term return on investing in the learning process (versus a specific planning model) pays dividends by creating sustainable, innovative, and adaptive organizational strategic capacity that creates and re-creates winning strategies.

Executives, consultants, and executive development professionals have succumbed to the business culture myth of simple and short with regard to strategy thinking, seeking a quick how-to approach for even the most complex of problems. Our unchallenged mantra is fast, faster, fastest equals good, better, best! The lure of the myth has enticed us to deny or ignore the complexity, ambiguity, paradoxes, and contradictions that are inherent in the learning process required for thinking strategically.

Executives talk about wanting to develop organizational strategic capability that is sustainable and competitive, and they recognize internal strategic capability as the most valuable "human" capital asset; yet these same executives cling to their habit of wanting to learn strategy as a "fast fix" planning model. Efficiency in the "production" of strategic thinking is rewarded and perpetuated in most business schools and organizational development programs, over a mucky, unpredictable *learning process* that creates a sustainable competitive advantage. We are dismissive and avoidant of the extraordinarily complex factors of everyday business reality—voluminous data, contradictory and complex information, laser-speed decision making—which require a very different approach to factors of time, problem solving, discipline, and decision making.

It is well recognized that thinking strategically has everything to do with business performance, resulting in survival at worst and blasting the competition at best. We tend to recognize who is able to think strategically and who is not. Yet a gaping hole in the literature and in practice is that we have not examined how the strategic thinkers *learned* to think that way; therefore, it is difficult to support the development of strategic thinking. The literature and practice are overwhelmingly focused on what strategic thinkers *do*, but not on how they *learn* to think strategically.

Based on my experience consulting and advising executives on making strategy, I assumed that the learning process is more tacit and informal rather than a structured and systematic process. For many decades, much of learning to make strategy was assumed to occur formally, through executive development courses, strategy workshops, and so forth that focused on the learning event rather than on the learning process. Therefore, an enormous collection of literature on best practices of formal learning has emerged, but scant references regarding the literature on informal learning are available.

The literature on strategy, management, adult learning, and organizational behavior demonstrates that there is little empirical support linking formal strategic thinking processes *per se* to performance. The process of creating strategy through critical reflection and dialogue in a continuous cycle of learning is what links it to excellent performance. It is the quality of this reflection and dialogue that makes a significant difference in the quality of strategic performance. The knowledge, skills, and ability of those participating in the strategic conversation determine, in large part, the quality of those dialogues and ultimately the quality of strategic performance. This book provides a theoretical framework and research to support this position and relates learning, strategic thinking, and performance in the chapters that follow.

Organization of the Book

This book is organized to reflect the informal and dynamic perspective that I take toward the facilitation of learning to think strategically. Ten parts comprise the book in its entirety, with each part consisting of several chapters. Part I sets the framework by presenting a historical overview of strategy perspectives. Part II posits informal learning as the primary learning approach, while Part III illustrates a three-stage informal learning process.

Part IV explores the concept of learning domains; Part V expands on the deeper learning domain by introducing the role of critical dialogue and inquiry. Part VI positions intuition as a vital complement to analysis in learning to think strategically. The reflective processes of framing, shattering, and reframing are described as methods that help to make meaning of experience. Part VII links the roles of intuition and analysis with regard to strategic decision making.

Part VIII discusses socio-national culture as a factor of influence in learning to think strategically. Part IX identifies five essential attributes for learning to think strategically that emerged from the research findings. And finally, Part X puts forth some of the recommendations that I use to support the development of strategic thinking on the individual and organizational levels. Involvement in a creative endeavor and action learning are the two learning processes suggested. The recommendations are not prescriptive, formal, or structured in nature, but rather broad and flexible in scope and in depth, reflecting my professional belief that strategic thinking is a long-term informal development process, best learned from experiences outside the work environment and supported and processed inside the work environment.

Two features distinguish this book from others. First, its focus is on the *learning* aspect of thinking strategically, in contrast to an emphasis on formulating and implementing strategy. The second point of differentiation is that this book invites the reader to select a strategy development approach that is based on an informal, nonlinear *learning process* rather than on a traditional approach that is structured according to a linear, planning model.

There is a profound and urgent need to have an understanding and a picture of a practical strategic learning process so that we can facilitate our own and others' strategic development. It is my goal that *Learning to Think Strategically* provides just this. I hope that reading this book will generate questions and ideas that the reader can use to create alternative ways of facilitating his or her own strategic development and contribute to the learning experience of others. My intention is for this book to be a starting point for exploring ways of learning to think strategically.

HOW DID WE GET TO
THIS POINT?

Back to the Future:
A Historical Overview of Strategy

All men can see these tactics whereby I conquer,
but what none can see is the strategy out of which victory is evolved.

Sun-tzu
(4th century B.C.) Chinese military strategist

Chronology of Strategy

Developing organizational capability for strategic thinking can be one of the most significant contributions executives and managers can make to organizational performance. By developing a "pipeline" of strategic thinkers within the organization, companies can truly begin to realize human capital as a strategic asset and build sustainable organizational strategic capability.

Prior to discussing the learning aspect of strategic thinking, we will pause briefly to recollect notions of strategy from our past. Although this book focuses on the learning aspect of thinking strategically, this preliminary overview of strategy is provided in order to familiarize readers with an historical backdrop against which Western strategy evolved. The learning dimension of strategic thinking is vital to address because learning is generative in nature and it enables us to be adaptive and innovative. In turn, this leads to organizational sustainability and, ultimately, has the potential of creating winning strategies.

Part I frames organizational strategy within a historical context, focusing on a learning perspective. Curiously, we'll see that everything old is new again—or at least current trends in organizational strategy thinking are not incompatible with strategy concepts of ancient Western civilization. Current views of strategy are not so much new as they are strikingly similar to veins in the past. Knowing a bit about ancient strategy history can make the present strategic debate less perplexing and inform current decisions. Most often discussions about the history of business strategy start with the 1950s. Chapter 1, however, starts by tracing strategy from ancient Western civilization to the present. Chapter 2 discusses contemporary competing views of strategy. And Chapter 3 acknowledges some of the implications of strategy history for strategic learning.

Although the term *strategy* is commonly and conveniently used, its meaning is far from shared. Essentially, its meaning depends on whether we are looking toward the future or into the past. For those who look into the past, it is a repeated pattern on the path to a success; and to those who look toward the future, strategy is a broad framework for actions that will culminate in a win. Within Western civilization, the term *strategos* can be traced back to the ancient Greeks, for whom it meant "a chief magistrate and military commander-in-chief responsible for employing the science and art of the political, economic, psychological and military forces . . . to afford the maximum support to adopted policies in peace or war."[1]

Throughout history the concept of strategy has been closely associated with the military. The military analogy became popular within a business context during the 1950s, as operational plans called for companies to attack the competitor, conquer markets, win product wars, and so on. The imagery has changed for those who believe business strategy is about creating competitive sustainable development. There are volumes of strategy books on the shelves, ranging from Clausevitz and Bismarck to Winnie the Pooh, Dilbert, and Zen.

Despite volumes of academic research on the topic, there is remarkably little agreement on what strategy is. While its complexity defies simple description, its basic characteristics can be agreed on. Regardless of the particular definition, all definitions imply a will to win, an element of competition, a process or framework to win, an extended time horizon, determination of a broad and major aim, unifying intent, and decisions about resource allocation.

Those responsible for facilitating the strategic learning within organizations have a particularly important role to play. This brief strategy overview offers insight that will hopefully generate new ideas about facilitating the development of strategic thinking—a historical perspective against which new thinking and applications can be tested.

Ancient Greek Concept of Strategy

The ancient Greeks, whose view of strategy influenced Western civilization, likened a military or political strategist to helmsmen on seafaring vessels. These early strategists had to construe their maps and their understanding of the prevailing currents with their journey's purpose and their own skill with a rudder. The Greeks regarded strategic wisdom as oscillating between different positions and perspectives toward a particular purpose.[2]

The concept of premodern strategy emphasized the personal and relational rather than the objective and rational qualities of spatial order. Subsequently, premodern maps were evolving and "organic," in the sense that they could be added to, reinterpreted, and modified according to a particular traveler's experiences. A depiction of mountains, valleys, or other important milestones and particular indicators of progress could easily be added to the maps.[3] This subjective relativism had a significant influence on the ancient Greeks' concept of strategy.

While this view may be attributed to what is now called a lack of knowledge perspective, it was also due to a different worldview and way of conceiving people's relationship with the world. Rather than the prevailing modern Western worldview of ascertaining objective knowledge from a detached perspective over and above particular events, the ancient Greeks saw the world subjectively. In other words, their relation with things *was* knowledge. Because they saw the individual human being as a *microcosm* of the universal *macrocosm*, the ancient Greeks sought knowledge by finding certain characteristics in themselves before going on to create relationships with other things by seeing analogical connections. Thus, they viewed plants, animals, and land as intelligent organisms with particular "personalities" and purposes. Over time, this view was extended and associated with the stories related to and attributed to particular gods.

Within a global context, there are cultures and societies today that hold a similar worldview to varying degrees — cultures that are highly relational, contextual, subjective, and fatalistic in their perspective. If an executive assumes this worldview, it can be a struggle to conform to a contemporary Western view of strategy as detached, rational, and objective. While the frameworks and worldviews that influence the conception of strategy can be very different, this way of thinking is not inferior in any way. The different worldviews are, however, manifested and exacerbated during strategy conversations when conceptual expectations become explicit. I find that understanding the learning process that supports strategic thinking can mitigate fundamental differences in concepts.

Given the subjective, interpretative, and unfolding nature of knowing, wisdom was also perceived differently by the ancient Greeks. Their foundation myths and belief in many personable gods and goddesses, each of whom had particular likings and likenesses, were quite unlike the omnipresent and omnipotential unitary Judeo-Christian deity. Furthermore, the ancient Greeks assumed an unresolvable tension between and mutuality of chaos and *cosmos* (order). While we have learned to see paradox and contradiction as an obstruction to strategy making today, they saw paradox, ambivalence, and contradiction as natural.

Consequently, the Greeks did not see wisdom as being able to represent the order of things with objective certainty for the purpose of bringing predictability and control, but rather as *metos*. *Metos* referred to the ability to oscillate or steer a course between the world of order (cosmos), of forms and laws, and to deal with the world of chaos, which included the multiple, the unstable, and the unlimited nature of affairs, in order to engage in mapping a prudent course.

As explained by Stephen Cummings in *Images of Strategy*, this *metos* feature of the ancient Greek concept of strategy was characterized by an ability to bring to bear a number of different frameworks with which to confront particular situations at any given moment and move quickly between these two realms of order and chaos. A strategist had to be sufficiently wily to bend his course of action and be able to go in many different directions as needed.[4]

In keeping with this concept of *metos*, strategy was about moving between order and uncertainty. It was about detached long-term forethought, planning, and ordering in advance of action. At the same time, because the frontlines were the best place to get a feel for the "becoming" of events, to implement plans or to adapt and change plans as events emerged, strategists understood that strategy making also happened here. They were expected to be at or connected to the points where action took place in order to reinterpret things.[5]

Moreover, given that the organizational form operated on many different fronts at once, depending on particular circumstances, strategy had to "become" according to the form that the organization took at a particular point in time. Therefore, strategy occurred at all levels and parts of what we would see as the organizational hierarchy, as a blend of what we might now call strategy, tactics, and operations.

Given this concept, the ancient Greeks would have had difficulty comprehending the current debate between the top-down design and bottom-up emergence schools of thought. Premodern strategy was about the interplay of seeming paradoxes and apparent contradictions, playing off one another and balancing the strategic thinking process. Design and emergence were both embraced, and *metos* required oscillating between cosmos and chaos and between structure and circumstance.

20th Century Corporate Strategy

Corporate strategy, as we tend to understand it today, came about in the late 19th century, at the height of the scientific, technical, rational, or modernist optimism era and the second industrial revolution. The concept of strategy during this period, which is influential today, is clearly a reflection of this context.

According to the model of technical rationality—the late 19th century view of professional knowledge that has most powerfully shaped both our thinking about the professions and the institutional relations of research, education, and business strategy—professional activity consists of instrumental problem solving made rigorous by the application of scientific theory and technique.

Where does this dominant view of professional knowledge as the application of scientific theory and instrumental knowledge come from? It comes from the last 300 years of the history of Western ideas and institutions. The term *technical rationality* is the legacy of positivism, the powerful philosophical doctrine that dawned in the 19th century as a result of the rise of science and technology and as a social movement aimed at employing the achievements of science and technology to the prosperity of humanity. Technical rationality became institutionalized in the modern university, founded in the late 19th century, when positivism was at its height, and in the professional schools that anchored their place in the university in the early 20th century. There are many excellent sources that detail this era elsewhere, so I will only mention a few key points here as they relate to shaping our notion of strategy.

The systematic knowledge base of a profession is thought to have four essential properties according to the technical rational school of thought: It is specialized, firmly bounded, scientific, and standardized. This last point is particularly important with regard to our conception of strategy, because it explains the current analytic obsession of strategy that many executives continue to have and to hold.

Contemporary strategy making is grounded in systematic, fundamental knowledge, of which scientific knowledge is the prototype. But what happens when the industry and business environment are unstable or ambiguous? Rigidly or unknowingly adhering to an outmoded framework only becomes a part of an already complex problem. The ability to make successful strategy requires a new framework.

The first industrial revolution (mid-1700s to mid-1800s), driven largely by the development of international trade in a few commodities such as cotton, witnessed intense competition among industrial firms.[6] Yet most private companies did not have the potential to affect the outcome of competition. The political and economic instability of the period led economists such as Adam Smith to describe market forces as an "invisible hand" that was perceived as largely beyond the control of individual companies. The word *strategy* in a business context dates only to the 20th century, and it has been used in a competitive context only since the second half of the 20th century.

The second industrial revolution (late 1800s) saw the emergence of large-scale investment to exploit economies of scale in production and economies of scope and distribution.[7] In the United States, the construction of the railroads after 1850 made it possible to build mass markets for the first time. A new type of vertically integrated firm began to emerge, first in the United States and then in Europe. These multidivisional corporations made large investments in manufacturing and marketing and in management hierarchies to coordinate those functions. Together with improved access to capital and credit, the emergence of mass markets encouraged companies to consider strategy as a way to control market forces and shape the competitive environment.

Additionally, the second industrial revolution triggered the establishment of several elite business schools in the United States in response to the demand for trained managers, beginning with the founding of the Wharton School in 1881. It was the Harvard Business School, founded in 1908, that was one of the first to promote the notion that managers should be trained to think strategically and not just act as functional administrators.[8]

Two decades later in the business arena, top executives of these multidivisional corporations first articulated the need for a formal approach to corporate strategy. In the 1930s, Chester Barnard, a senior executive at AT&T, argued that managers should pay especially close attention to "strategic factors" that depend on "personal or organizational action."[9]

The organizational challenges associated with fighting two world wars in the first half of the 20th century provided a vital stimulus to the field of strategic development. The need to allocate scarce resources across an entire economy in wartime led to the use of quantitative analysis in formal strategic planning. The concept of the *learning curve* (later termed the *experience curve*) was first put forth in the military aircraft industry in the 1920s and 1930s, where it was noticed that direct labor costs tended to decrease by a constant percentage as the cumulative quantity of aircraft produced doubled. Learning, as a factor of operational impact, figured prominently in subsequent wartime production planning efforts.

The wartime disruption of foreign, non-U.S. multinational businesses and European and Asian companies and markets enabled U.S. companies to profit from the post–World War II boom without effective competitors in many industries. Insights into the nature of strategy gleaned during World War II — that by consciously using formal planning, an organization could exert some positive control over market forces—remained undeveloped until the early 1960s, when many large multinational corporations were forced to consider global competition as a factor in planning.

Strategy and the Academy

On the academic front in the late 1950s, Harvard professor Kenneth Andrews, argued that "every business organization, every subunit of an organization, and even every individual [ought to] have a clearly defined set of purposes or goals which keeps it moving in a deliberately chosen direction and prevents its drifting in undesired directions."[10] This became the banner under which the proponents of the design school of strategy operated and under which businesses and consulting firms have rallied since the 1950s.

Design School

The design school, the most influential strategy concept since the 1960s, has provided the basis of business school courses on strategy, corporate strategy approach, and consulting. Remnants of the design school can be found in each of the subsequent schools of strategy that have developed, and its imprint has profoundly influenced business school curricula, consulting firm propositions, and corporate strategy development approaches.

Two sources credited with the thinking underlying this design school of strategy were Philip Selznick's 1957 book *Leadership in Administration* (University of California, Berkeley) and Alfred Chandler's 1962 volume *Strategy and Structure* (MIT). The idea of *distinctive competence* was introduced by Selznick, who highlighted the need to bring together the organization's "internal state" with its "external expectations."[11] By the 1960s, academic discussions focused on identifying the strengths, weaknesses, opportunities, and threats (SWOT) that a company faced in the market. This approach has continued ever since, with an explicit strategy aim of making a "fit" between external and internal factors that are assumed to be controllable. Selznick also argued for building "policy into the organization's social structure,"[12] which later was termed *implementation*. The idea of strategy formation and implementation as separate and sequential segments was born of this belief.

A few years later, Alfred Chandler added to the design school the notion of business strategy and its relationship to structure. Chandler's classic 1962 definition of strategy focused on the determination of basic long-term goals and objectives of an enterprise. Chandler saw strategy as having "two specific characteristics: many distinct operating units, managed by a hierarchy of salaried executives."[13]

Distinctive of the design school is a singular foundation of economics. The case study became entrenched as a primary strategy development technique —a highly structured descriptive–prescriptive tool, it uses secondhand experience as a focus for analysis and implies following a "best" example. The design school provided the basis for the development of subsequent strategy tangents such as the planning and positioning schools. Ideas from the design school were extrapolated, elaborated, and rearranged around various other assumptions underlying the strategy process. But the premise of the design school dominated strategy even into the new millennium.

The real momentum behind the design school thinking was from the Harvard Business School. As Kenneth Andrews, eminent proponent of the design school, noted, the ensuing "establishment of business schools provided the basis for the education of strategic managers and the division-alized structure of organizations provided the form for them to work within."[14]

The 1959 Carnegie and Ford studies on the curricula of business schools concluded that "in order to counter the disparate 'organic' growth of programs with differing contributing 'specialisms,' it had to be realized that economics has traditionally provided the only theoretical framework for the study of business."[15] Economics then became the central stem to which other courses in a management degree would be connected. Having outlined this premise, it was used as a basis on which to determine a proper array of contributing subjects. The Carnegie and Ford studies advocated the standardization of the curricula's top level, or *sharp end*. They recommended *capstone courses* that would allow students to culminate what they learned in the separate business fields. This tip of the educational triangle became courses in corporate strategy.

The Carnegie and Ford Foundation reports on the curricula of business schools consolidated an image of companies as triangular hierarchies— Ansoff and Chandler's image of organizations was also that of a triangle. This "tip-of-the-triangle" mental model was consistent with the design school notion that those at the top of an organization know best, an idea that many organizations and business schools continue to base strategy thinking on even today with capstone courses.

The contextual background of the 1960s–1970s was conducive to such strategy schools as the design and planning schools. The overall trend in business school education, corporate strategy development, and government was formal learning, formal training, formal analysis, metrics, and numbers as a substitute for dialogue. Strategy was the responsibility of a select cadre of highly educated planners at the tip of the corporate triangle. Professional conferences and industry consulting firms were enlisted for the purpose of promulgating strategic "how-to" planning approaches.

Planning School

Simultaneous to the dawn of the design school, was the rise of the planning school, spearheaded by Igor Ansoff. Ansoff defined strategy as "a rule for making decisions pertaining to a firm's match to its environment" and set out to "enrich the theoretical conception of the firm."[16] Ansoff's seminal work in 1965, *Corporate Strategy*, identified a gap between increasingly complex business environments and the activities of multibusiness firms. He suggested that this combination of factors positioned companies to use foresight in order to exploit environmental change and offered a theory based on the prevailing microeconomic conception of a business.

Proponents of the planning school detailed the differentiation between definitions for goals, objectives, values, and so on and developed extensive procedures for construing elaborate quantitative metrics and methodical explanations. Exhaustive checklists and techniques for each procedural step and tightly crafted diagrams ensured an ability to control internal and external factors. Hundreds of forecasting as well as audit analysis techniques and control measures have been developed to assess the hundreds of strategic planning models.

The planning school overlaps most areas of the design school, but it requires a considerably more formal and systematic process—a nearly mechanical methodology premised on beliefs from the industrial era. MIT strategy theorist Henry Mintzberg noted that the strategic planning process is based on the machine assumption, to "produce each of the component parts as specified, assemble them according to the blueprint, and the end product (strategy) will result."[17]

A recent outgrowth of the planning school has been scenario planning and strategic control as part of a risk management portfolio. Scenario planning is based on the idea that if the future cannot be totally planned, then at least by planning several futures we increase the likelihood that the right one will be selected. In addition to formal quantitative analysis, scenario planning expands analysis to incorporate the insight gained from analyzing various factors in different scenarios. Strategic control is an extension of planning that is intended to review, test, and control the strategy that was planned. In short, if it wasn't planned and if it can't be measured, then it doesn't count.

This planning view saw organizations as simply turning resources into outputs through a production function and assumed that managers just manipulated the factors under their control to maximize profits. It offered managers little decision-making guidance as to how they could take different positions. The "people at the top" are assumed to carry out strategy—those best placed to have an objective global view, to forecast and represent changes in the environment, and to position and control corporate development accordingly. To this day, strategy is subsequently presented in textbooks and by proponents of traditional strategy development as a process occurring at the highest and most detached level of the organization.

Strategy and Consultancies

The 1960s and 1970s saw the rise of strategy consulting practices. The Boston Consulting Group (BCG), in particular, had a major impact on the field by applying quantitative research to problems of business and corporate strategy. BCG founder Bruce Henderson's underlying premise was that "good strategy must be based primarily on logic, not . . . on experience derived from intuition."[18] Henderson was convinced that a quantitative approach would someday lead to a set of universal rules for strategy development.

McKinsey & Company introduced a strategy planning system during the same period that divides a company into *natural business units*, later called *strategic business units* (*SBUs*). They also presented an approach to portfolio planning called the Profit Impact of Market Strategies, or PIM, program.

By the 1970s virtually every major American consulting firm applied some type of quantitative analysis to strategy making, pushing strategic thinking "down the line" to managers closer to the particular industry and its competitive conditions.[19] In 1965–66, BCG had developed a version of the learning curve—labeled the *experience curve*—which implied that for a given product segment, "the producer ... who has made the most units should have the lowest costs and the highest profits."[20] A second BCG tool, Portfolio Analysis, compared the relative potential for investment of a diversified company's business units by plotting their experience curves on a grid.

The design and planning schools of strategy were highly influential and provided an ideal platform for consulting firms. The emphasis on quantitative measures produced an enormous inventory of analytical tools, models, and metrics for predicting, monitoring, and measuring strategic planning.

Shift in Corporate Strategy Role

Strategy can be viewed from several perspectives, including organizational strategy, hierarchical levels, structural and infrastructural strategy. The focus here is on the shift of the corporate strategy role in organizational strategy.

Three themes that emerge from the strategy literature amassed over the centuries have specific implications for the functional role of corporate planning. First, no approach or school of thought, however sound, applies to all organizations at all times under all circumstances. Successful strategy reflects both a specific and a broad context. Second, each school of strategy has limitations when carried to extremes or used in exclusivity. Specific strategy schools appear to run a natural course, coming into and out of favor, and tend to be self-corrective either by blending into other schools or by transforming to accommodate the context. Third, successful strategy across the centuries has proven to be dynamic and generative, not static and finite. These three themes imply that organizational strategies need to be adaptable and open in order to be successful.

As we have seen from the literature, throughout the mid-20th century, formal models of strategic planning gave rise to the creation of corporate planning staff functions in large organizations in keeping with the design and planning concept of corporate strategy. Beginning in the 1980s, many companies reconsidered the value of these functions and replaced them by tasking business units with planning responsibilities. The strategy concept continued to be planning, but the responsibility was diffused.

At the same time the role of corporate planning changed—from formulating strategy to supporting strategy by providing technical input and analysis. This trend has recently accelerated and has been further modified as companies move toward "intra-preneurial" and "entrepreneurial" business models—less vertically integrated structures that function more as internal market economies rather than as planned economies.

An interest in strategy as thinking rather than strategy as planning has gradually begun to surface. A few organizations are beginning to realize that they must have a strategy thinking process that encourages routine challenging, testing, and imagining for strategic thinking to occur. This process must include critical inquiry as a best practice as well as theories and models of dialogue and debate, rather than simply models and theories that result in strategic imitation or the limitation of planning.

It is no longer a strategic advantage to be a bit better than the competition. This notion is radical for executives who were groomed to believe that incremental gains were strategic successes. In order to be strategically competitive today, executives must be able to critically reexamine data and perceive information in novel ways, to dramatically shift perspectives, and to re-create and adapt instantly. Around the globe, I have noticed that forward-thinking strategists are taking an interest in strategy thinking rather than conventional strategy planning—and by extension are intensely curious to understand how people learn to think strategically.

Organizational Strategy

Simply stated, organizational strategy is strategy applied specifically to organizations—which this book considers as corporate or nonprofit entities—rather than to political, military, or other institutions. In terms of organizational strategy, business author C. A. DeKluyver offers a conceptual strategy definition in his book *Strategic Thinking: An Executive Perspective*, which suggests, "Strategy is about positioning an organization for sustainable competitive advantage. It involves making choices about which industries to participate in, what products and services to offer, and how to allocate corporate resources to achieve such a sustainable advantage."[21]

Professors C. K. Prahalad and Gary Hamel have put forth another conceptual definition of organizational strategy called *strategic intent*.[22] Strategic intent is a central idea that anchors the organization over the long haul; it guides the organization in making decisions in the face of emerging options, choices, and alternatives. Strategic intent refers to a leadership position created in relation to a firm's competitors, and it presents a specific criterion against which the company can mark progress.

2

Contemporary Competing Views of Strategy: Two Sides Face Off

As we consider the traditional approaches to thinking about strategy from 1960 forward, it may be useful to characterize them according to the Sloan School of Management's ten major schools of thought[23] (see Table 2.1). The following major strategic schools are commonly referred to in the strategy literature due to their influence on practice. While these ten schools depict fundamentally different aspects across similar strategy-making processes, they can be channeled into the two basic perspectives: the design strategy viewpoint, which we have already outlined, and the emergent viewpoint, which is mentioned later in this chapter.

The ten schools of strategy represent a line of chronology through history, but not as a descent by replacement. The planning school, for example, may be a predecessor of the positioning school, but it has not disappeared. There is a tendency for previous schools of strategy to contribute to newer schools in complicated and often subtle ways. All of the schools continue to coexist today in practice, infiltrating newer frameworks under various guises and different circumstances.

The big contemporary uproar from the 1980s through the present within the academic, business, and consulting fields has been whether companies select and design good strategies through rational thought or whether good strategies actually emerge through a process of experimentation and intuition.

Technical Rational Influence

On one side of the argument is the design strategy perspective, which we discussed in Chapter 1. Heavily influenced by the technical rational period of

TABLE 2.1 Ten Schools of Strategy Making*

	Sources	Base Discipline	Advocates	Intended Message	Realized Message
Design	Selznick; Andrews	None (architecture as metaphor)	Case study teachers (especially Harvard), leadership advocates (especially U.S.)	Fit	Think (strategy making as case study)
Planning	Ansoff	Links to urban planning, systems theory and cybernetics	"Professional" managers, MBAs, consultants and government controllers (especially France and U.S.)	Formalize	Program (rather than formulate)
Positioning	Porter; Purdue University (Schendel, Hatten)	Economics (industrial organization) and military history	Planning schools, consulting "boutiques," military writers (especially U.S.)	Analyze	Calculate (rather than create or commit)
Entrepreneurial	Schumpeter; Cole	None (early writings from economists)	Popular business press, small businesses (especially Latin America and overseas Chinese)	Envision	Centralize (then hope)
Cognitive	Simon and March	Cognitive psychology	People with a psychological bent (pessimists and optimists—in opposite camps)	Cope or create	Worry (being unable to cope in either case)
Learning	Lindblom; Cyert and March; Weick; Quinn; Hamel and Prahalad	Some links to learning theory. Chaos theory in mathematics	People inclined to experimentation, ambiguity, adaptability (especially Japan and Scandinavia)	Learn	Play (rather than pursue)

Power	Alison; Pfeffer and Salancik; Astley	Political science	People who like power, politics, and conspiracy (especially France)	Promote	Hoard (rather than share)
Cultural	Rhenman; Normann	Anthropology	People who like the social, the spiritual, the collective (especially Scandinavia and Japan)	Coalesce	Perpetuate (rather than change)
Environmental	Hannan and Freeman; Pugh, et al.	Biology	Population ecologists, some organization theorists, splitters, and positivists (especially Anglo-Saxon countries)	React	Capitulate (rather than confront)
Configuration	Chandler; Mintzberg; Miller and Friesen; Miles and Snow	History	Lumpers and integrators, change agents. (Configuration popular in Netherlands, transformation popular in U.S.)	Integrate, transform	Lump (rather than split, adapt)

thought prevalent in the early 19th century and continuing through today, this strategy perspective is anchored to principles of industrialism. This perspective reflects one of modernity's key tenets—*objective representationalism*, the idea that the purpose of knowledge is to represent, without logical contradiction, the "way things really are," or the linear, functional causes of actions.

The design school has had a profound influence on the concept of strategy within the government, corporations, and nonprofit organizations. Strategy within this framework is commonly perceived as separate from and overseeing, organizational action in a linear and hierarchical manner. The design perspective is about developing the most accurate and objective construction model of the environment possible and then positioning the company and formulating rational plans as to where the company will move in the future.[24] Traditional ideas of rationality—diagnosis, prescription, and finally action, underlie the technical rational school of thought. Logic, control, and linear thinking support the strategic assumptions, and thinking is considered to be a separate function from action.

Emergent Theory Influence

On the other side of the strategy argument is the emergent, a more intuitive strategy perspective. It was the technical rational triangular-hierarchical view of strategy as a top-down affair that strategy theorist Henry Mintzberg challenged in the early 1990s. Mintzberg's research found that managers were far less rational and foresightful strategy makers than the literature of management supposed. This led the way in proposing a more "organic" view of organizations.[25]

Mintzberg's challenge to the classical design view of strategy argues that the perspective of Ansoff and others were dependent on "the fallacy of detachment," the belief that thinking and doing are separate. Managers, according to Mintzberg, are not rational, logical directors—their agendas and actions are influenced by politics, history, and human patterns of behavior over time.

Consequently, Mintzberg found that the interaction crucial to strategy does not occur between top executives and the environment—it happens where employees at the operational level of the organization interact with one another (at the coffee bar or snack machine) and react to or anticipate customer needs and wants. Over time, the informal strategy making that organically occurs within various parts of the organization may create patterns of behavior that filter up the apex to be formalized in plans; but strategy does not come from the top. Mintzberg and other emergent theorists subsequently argued that "real strategy" emerges bottom-up.

Ansoff was equally adamant that the evidence he was continuing to gather supported the planning view of how strategy really develops. This school of thought was adopted by Michael Porter, whose models are constructed on the premises of microeconomics and the design school and are among the most popular strategy tools today.

The debate between what became known as the emergent school and the design school of strategy became increasingly polarized in the first half of the 1990s. By the late 1990s this debate had become colossal and a fundamental factor in the conceptual development of strategy. In his 1998 book *Strategy Safari*, Mintzberg (along with Ashland and Lampel) outlines many different strategy approaches and concludes that no one is better than the others.[26]

Comparative Discussion

I suggest taking the strategy debate back to the premodern perspective as a point of reference. If we trace strategy back to its ancient base, we see the course of the design-versus-emergent debate rather differently. Instead of being viewed as two diametrically opposed schools of thought, each in competition with the other, the design and emergent schools, when taken together, represent a well-developed version that mirrors the elemental strategy conception of the ancient Greeks. If they continue to be perceived in opposition to each other, businesses themselves stand ultimately to sacrifice strategically; but if they are viewed as two parts of a whole, strategy takes on an expanded and constructive role. We may further be served by viewing this inclusive approach to strategy as one that establishes a natural synchronous movement between these two realms as being essential to thinking strategically—so strategy can be continuously re-created.

Certainly, the ancient Greek concept of strategy is not incompatible with the direction of strategy thinking that is required today. The ancient worldview is sometimes misconstrued as a less refined, unsophisticated, less educated version of our own, and, therefore, the strategy concept is unfairly disparaged as a simple and irrelevant version. While our knowledge and perspective base has dramatically expanded due to cumulative advances in information technology over the centuries, the basic nature of our complex reality suggests a need for inclusion, dealing with paradox and contradiction and incomplete information, and being able to juggle many different things at once. This complex reality represents the same basic nature as the reality confronted by the ancient Greeks.

Complexity Theory

Another indication that contemporary strategy is gradually moving toward a more inclusive, holistic, and integrated approach is the extension of interest into a concept of natural science, *complexity theory*. The current interest in complexity theory is not new thinking, but it is a new application to strategic thinking. In a nutshell, complexity theory focuses on the apparent random, disparate, and discontinuous nature of change. It compares the nature of organizations to that of other living organisms through a behaviorist and a Darwinian lens, referring to such naturally occurring organizations as "complex adaptive systems."

Complexity theory presumes that such systems inherently tend toward order rather than randomness and that this kind of nonlinear world is characterized more by discontinuities than by incremental changes. Complexity theorists purport that when it comes to continuous adaptation, nature is the best teacher. They argue that it is almost impossible to forecast the future. Therefore, according to complexity theory, the idea that companies can plan ahead is fundamentally an illusion, a waste of time and resources, and an exercise in futility.

Given that adaptation is inherent in sound strategy, complexity theory looks to the world of nature for cues to creating successful strategy. Accordingly, an oversimplification is that nature is constantly conducting a massive set of experiments through the genetic process known as natural variation. These variations, presumed to be random in nature, test various survival strategies, such as changes in color, size, shape, food preferences, and mating behaviors. Most of these variations are failures, but a few of them succeed. As in nature, the rules of survival in global business are Darwinian—we must keep moving. We must continually develop advantageous variations in business—or risk extinction.

Foremost among the leaders of complexity theory is the Santa Fe Institute; eminent thinkers include Steve Kaufman, James Gleick, Roger Lewin, Ralph Stacey, and Margaret Wheatley, among others. This group of theorists believes that human organizations are also complex adaptive systems that instinctively "know" how to act "strategically," if left to their own devices. The role of a corporate leader is to create conditions that will allow strategy to emerge—

naturally. This process is what complexity theorists refer to as *self-organization*. Work conditions that encourage this kind of self-organization include decentralization, individual expression, and even chaos. An abundance of top-down controls are believed ultimately to doom the organization to failure. Complexity theorists suggest that virtually all controls should be eradicated, allowing a multitude of minds to contribute new ideas.

Although complexity theorists insist that chaos is essential for ideas to flourish, I suggest a responsive and flexible process must be established for chaos to emerge, one that encourages regular input, learning, and creativity throughout the organization. Creativity, we know from current research, requires a subtle balance between chaos and order. To foster this, it is necessary to support an atmosphere that encourages novel insights, unusual perspectives, contrarian opinions, and an abundance of data to surface and be recognized.

The learning theorists and the complexity theorists agree that our current competitive, unpredictable, and inconsistent business environment places unprecedented demands on our capacity to re-create clever and resilient strategy. Drawing on Darwinism, we know that it is not the largest, the strongest, or even the most intelligent of species that survive—but the most adaptable to change.

It is interesting to overlay complexity theory onto corporations, which are artificially constructed organizations comprising humans—organisms of the highest level. While there are of course parallels, there are also points of diversion, namely that humans have the capacity to reflect, to think, and to feel. Although nature is extraordinarily creative and adaptive, it nonetheless has a vital flaw: Nature is unable to understand why it succeeds or fails.

Eighteenth century German philosopher Kant noted the dubious fact that "Man is the only creature which must be educated." Fortunately, being at the top of Mother Nature's pecking order enables us to critically reflect and learn from our experiences. As Columbia University professor Willie Pietersen notes in *Reinventing Strategy*, "[An] adaptive enterprise is one with the built-in ability to renew itself over and over again."[27]

I find it interesting to note the renewed interest in natural order, in ancient history, and in other cultures with regard to learning to think strategically. I think it points to an implicit need to explore beyond the means we currently use to define strategy making and hints at a willingness to extend our search for making meaning within a broader strategic context. We seem to have "outgrown" the technical rational scientific model as an exclusive model for making strategy.

Chaos Theory

Another contemporary, high-anxiety view of strategy is to perceive the future as totally unpredictable, uncontrollable, and chaotic. The chaos concept appeared first within the field of meteorology in the 1960s, when founder Edward Lorenz (MIT) was working on a project to simulate weather patterns on a computer. Contrary to the technical rational school of thought, which has deluded executives into believing that strategy is a means of controlling the future, chaos theory refers to whether or not it is possible to make long-term predictions of any system if the initial conditions are unknown to a high degree.

Essentially, chaos theory contends that because the universe is chaotic and an unpredictable place, it is nearly impossible to predict what is going to happen at any given time and place, because everything within a given system is ultimately connected. Therefore, an action in one place can have an effect in another place. Although chaotic systems appear to be random, theorists claim they are not. Beneath random behavior, patterns emerge that suggest an order. Oddly enough, chaotic systems develop in a way that appears to be smooth and ordered.

Acknowledging that the stock market is a nonlinear, dynamic, and chaotic system, chaos theory can be applied in order to determine the pattern behind the nature of market prices. Aspects of chaos appear everywhere around the world. The mathematical equations for predicting how a system will act have been applied to other highly complex systems, such as ecological systems, biological systems, population growth, and epidemics, and experimented with in human organizational systems. Chaos theory is really about making order from apparently random data.

From a scientific perspective it is seen as ultimately understandable and sensible. From a human organizational perspective, it can foster alienation and a feeling of powerlessness. There is, however, a certain perverted fatalism that is appealing from a strategic perspective: Why bother if things are going to unravel and unfold with or without my help?

Why is chaos theory relevant to our discussion of strategic thinking? One reason for its popularity in business strategy relates to the postmodern worldview of social change. The ancient Greeks believed life proceeded in cycles; in the 19th and 20th centuries, social theorists believed life moved forward in stages; and current thinking has tended to swing in the direction of believing the world is inherently a gamble, largely left to luck. Strategically, this future phobia of chaos theory manifests itself through executive avoidance tactics such as overanalyzing ("Let's conduct just one more study"), through incrementalizing ("Let's just 'tweak' our existing strategy"), and through overplanning the minute details ("Let's place each subphase of the timeline under the microscope lens").

Another reason for chaos theory's relevance to strategy has to do with a shift in the approach to which businesses view the future. When the future was seen as a variation or a projection of the past, it was predictable; it was within an organization's strategic initiative to determine and to control any significant diversion from the past. In recent years, political and social events have shifted dramatically and rapidly—beyond imagination and comprehension. This has given rise among business executives to feelings of unpredictability, vulnerability, and some degree of powerlessness. Curiously, there is some comfort in perceiving one's company as being subject to the whims of chaos: If the future is the convergence of chaotic forces, then it is impossible to predict and control. So why try? There is a natural reassurance that comes from being absolved of responsibility for an unknowable and uncontrollable future of an organization.

Among the corporate clients with whom I work, I have noticed a diminishing emphasis on strategy whenever there is a major economic hurdle in the road. Executives tend to shift their focus from the strategic success to myopic, short-term operational success. In many companies the CEO has actually stepped back from the strategic responsibility in an effort to perform operational triage. The emphasis on emergency cost cutting and short-term results and an obsession with short-term financial strength eventually sever the companies' lifeline to a competitive future.

Furthermore, I typically see corporate strategic horizons as being one to two years rather than the five- to ten-year span of the mid-1990s. Given such a time frame, it is necessary to ask whether strategy is really "strategic" in nature or whether we have succumbed to the belief that anything beyond the scope of a year or two is outside the realm of predictability and, therefore, responsibility. Can we attribute this to executives' resistance to prepare their companies for what they see as a chaotic future?

If the past is considered to be a less reliable predictor of the future than previously believed, then chance or chaos becomes an appealing and relevant alternative explanation to strategic planning—but not to strategic thinking. Strategic thinking is a proposition that says we can affect the future through a strategic learning process that positions strategists as adaptive influencers in this ominously unpredictable environment rather than as victims or controllers.

Dealing with natural contradictions, paradoxes, and polarities is a central part of strategic thinking within a global environment. Within the framework of the natural order, ancient history, and other cultures, contradictions, para-doxes, and polarities are not regarded as opposites with an objective to conquer, crush, or cancel the other factor. Rather, they are perceived as a delicate yet durable whole that is necessary for a natural balance. The tension that is inherent in uncertainty and ambivalence is a constructive component for avoiding stagnation and maintaining a dynamic process. This same tension supports strategic thinking through its emphasis on learning, creativity, adapt-ability, and sustainability.

Strategic thinking is the key to successful adaptation. If we learn from our experiences, we will avoid a process of strategy by default. We can build the capability to continuously challenge, astutely choose, and perpetually increase our chance to re-create innovative strategy.

Strategic Planning and Strategic Thinking: Two Sides of the Coin

The changes in the corporate strategy function and role have implications for those responsible for facilitating strategic thinking and learning within orga-nizations and for line managers who are increasingly involved in strategic thinking. The highly analytical data-based strategy decisions need to be strengthened with a process of challenge and testing that shifts from a linear planning to a thinking model. Table 2.2 highlights key strategy factors and compares a strategic planning perspective to a strategic thinking perspective. The key factors include the concept of strategy, key dimensions, the academic discipline that anchors strategy, who formulates strategy, performance mea-sures, and how analysis is regarded.

While strategic thinking is most often described through linear models as something that is logical, sequential, and analytical, in real life it is typically more emergent and messy—an outgrowth of experimentation and a response to trends, the result of intense dialogue or confrontation.

Many strategy concept models, including Porter's five forces and the BCG Growth Share Matrix among the most common, can promote relevant analy-sis and focus the direction of strategy thinking by providing a structure for further thinking and dialogue. However, successful strategy is not all about data. When paired with the subsequent process of challenge and refinement, the data gradually lead to broader, more creative, and deeper insight. There is nothing wrong with any of the current models; they are just insufficient for strategic thinking, unless they ride in tandem with a process of critical inquiry.

TABLE 2.2 Contrast of Strategic Planning and Strategic Thinking

Factor	Strategic Planning	Strategic Thinking

Concept	A "product"
	Analysis, metrics, numbers
	Successful strategy is present
	  tense and future tense
	Convergent
		A "process" that is renewable,
		  re-creative, generative,
		  adaptable
		Insight, innovation, ideas
		Successful strategy is past tense
		Divergent

Key dimensions
Anchor strategy
	Financial
	Singular, exclusive
	Economics
		Financial, social contribution,
		  individual development, risk
		  assessment, business, integrity
		Multiple, inclusive
		Economics, sociology, history,
		  politics, science, arts, humanities

Formulation	Executive committee Corporate management team VPs Business unit heads	Corporate management team Business unit heads Functional heads "Pipeline" of strategists
Performance measures	Financial Money as asset Static Quantitative	Comprehensive Relationships are assets Dynamic Qualitative and quantitative
Analysis	Convergent Quantitative Neutral Objective	Quantitative and qualitative Relationships Contextual Objective and subjective
People and organization development	Cost/expense Profitability	Investment/asset Sustainable growth

Feuding Factions

The design-versus-emergent school debate between Ansoff and Mintzberg further intensified late in the 1990s and continues today. Mintzberg eventually framed the difference between the emergent approach that he advocates and Ansoff's analytical and formal approach as "strategy as learning" versus "strategy as planning."

Ansoff immediately countered by reframing his position with a declaration that the differences are about two contrasting views of strategy as learning. This takes the process of learning within the planning school from being implicit to explicit and opens the debate to new possibilities. Their debate is now between strategy as a process of learning through hypothesis generation and revision in accordance with the view of the design school, and strategy as a process of learning through exploration and discovery from the perspective of the emergent school.

Mintzberg does not berate the value of formal planning. Instead, he now argues that strategic planning is analysis, as opposed to strategic thinking—something that is considerably more.[28] Mintzberg purports that the role of planners is to support strategy formation by supplying the data and analyses for strategic thinking in order to expand the issues considered during strategic discussions, not to discover the correct choice. He furthers his argument by pointing out that strategy making does not happen in isolation from the workings of the organization. Rather, it involves the totality of everything that is involved with the business.

3

Implications of Strategy History for Strategic Learning

So what does our understanding of the history of strategy have to say about learning to think strategically? Interdisciplinary thinking (i.e., management, science, mathematics, education, anthropology, philosophy) offers a degree of convergence about the current direction of learning and strategy. Although learning has always been implied in the strategy literature, the human resource development literature has increasingly emphasized the role of strategy and the concept of learning as well. The pendulum appears to be moving toward a more integrated, inclusive, holistic approach to strategy as a balance to the highly analytic, rational, linear approach that has dominated the field since the modern industrial era of the early 1900s.

As we have seen from modern strategy history, learning figured prominently in U.S. wartime production planning efforts. The U.S. military financed studies and subsequently developed instructional approaches to strategy development based on the current strategy concept—economic efficiency—which translated into operational efficiency for the military. Therefore, many of the strategy approaches to learning born of the U.S. military are based in the analytical, rational concept of strategy making and have eventually been modified within the corporate sector.

Organizational strategy history has shown that learning became explicit with the development of the "experience curve" by the BCG in the 1970s. Learning models such as the BCG's Growth Share Matrix implied continuous learning based on market share analysis. Porter's influential five forces model of strategic positioning emphasized the need for learning to search for strategic opportunities. Both models were outgrowths of the highly structured formal school of strategic planning that considered strategic issues as complex problems to be solved—the learning assumption was that a best answer exists for "the problem." The instructional development response that supported this learning assumption was the development of a multitude of skills-based problem-solving approaches and analysis techniques for various levels and types of problems, extensively and almost exclusively used today.

Although the acceptance of strategic thinking as an emergent process is gradually gaining momentum among academics and consulting firms and within the organizational development field, most textbooks, business school courses, and corporate development approaches do not differentiate between strategic planning and strategic thinking. Highly linear, rational, and analytic approaches continue to be presented, to the exclusion of almost anything else. Emergent strategy is aligned with a learning belief that strategy-making problems have no single correct answer—only action that is somewhat better or worse.[29]

Realignment of Strategy Approaches

The schism between strategic planning and strategic thinking is an important conceptual distinction for executives and those seeking to advocate a learning approach to strategy making for their organization. Those responsible for facilitating strategic learning can draw from the history of strategy a precautionary warning against being swept away by the next new approach or trend. Perhaps the jargon has changed and the formula is updated, but it is doubtful that the premise is dramatically new.

Furthermore, historical themes suggest that we needn't be afraid to integrate and realign bits and pieces from the various strategy approaches and to imagine new configurations and experiment with possibilities. As previously mentioned, schools of strategy come into and out of favor, and strategy making is a dynamic and messy process. Intricate models, complex jargon, and scientific formulas have a way of creating false security and an aura of precision within the realm of strategy. New strategies are often a recasting of the old. In a sense, old strategic ideas never disappear entirely. They go underground and infiltrate new practices covertly.

While risk analysis is imperative to the strategy-making process, a singular obsession with rational, logical, analytical, linear thinking essentially runs counter to the whole of human nature—overrationalizing and overcontrolling those things we do not understand or are unable to choose "between." On the contrary, as recalled from the ancient Greek concept of strategy, balancing "among" opposing and contradictory things is inherent to the complexity of being human in nature.

The complexities of making strategy today have brought us to a critical juncture: We recognize that the strategy approach we are using is not generating what we need, but we fear the unknown. We are stuck in a logical, rational planning framework, which keeps us spinning in a cycle.

If successful strategy thinking is regarded as a process of continuously asking questions and critically and creatively thinking through the issues, then correctly constructing and responding to questions may be more important to long-term, innovative, and generative strategic thinking than finding the "solution." Accordingly, understanding the learning process for strategic thinking is now a competitive business imperative.

HOW DO WE LEARN TO THINK STRATEGICALLY?

Formal Learning Takes a Backseat: It's All About Informal Learning

We receive three educations,
One from our parents,
One from our school-masters,
and
One from the world.
The third contradicts
All that the first two teach us.

Charles Louis de Secondat, Baron de Montesquieu (1689–1755),
French political philosopher

4

Informal and Formal
Learning Defined

How do we actually learn to think strategically? "It's not so simple as step by step. It [strategy] is not a formula or a simple pattern. It is a complex, constantly developing process; it is not an ordered process. Making strategy is not a straight line—I don't sit at my desk and just build it like a model," claimed the CEO of a leading privately owned Polish manufacturing company when asked to describe his thinking when he makes strategy. A Japanese financial executive declared, "I don't even like the word *strategy*. It seems to mean that it is a model or . . . fixed steps to follow. To be frank, I think all the models and theories, they are only complicated planning ideas. Strategy is not so orderly."

Throughout this book, informal learning is highlighted and contrasted to formal learning, because, as noted, it is the informal learning approach, rather than the formal one, that successful strategists credit as influencing their own learning to think strategically. These thoughts were echoed by the CEO of an American technology company who matter-of-factly stated, "It's a hard thing to describe—I wouldn't say it's at all step by step. It's more like a ball or something that's spinning. It's not even a single thing. And nothing truly strategic has ever occurred to me in the office. Never."

Another president of a manufacturing company endorsed strategic thinking as an informal process by noting, "It's not this kind of problem solving, formula, straight-line thinking—it's more about just opening up—seeing what kinds of opinions you can draw on. How many different perspectives can you find? What precedent has been set? Is there a new twist you can give? It's not very linear."

As stated in previous chapters, strategic thinking is nonlinear and a-rational and does not occur within a prescribed time and place. According to the findings of the interviews I conducted with successful corporate strategists, we learn strategic thinking informally. In discussions about strategic thinking, *learning* is generally not the first word to pop up. Yet learning is an essential link to connect with strategic thinking if we are to have any hope of developing innovative, competitive, adaptive, and sustainable strategic capacity within organizations. In order to make this happen, we need an understanding of what informal learning is and how it applies to thinking strategically.

Informal Learning

Informal learning warrants particular attention when it comes to understanding how successful executives learn to think strategically, for the strategy and learning literature concur that it is informal learning, rather than formal learning, that is most influential on thinking strategically. The current strategic development practice, however, has not necessarily caught up with this notion.

As informal learning has come into vogue during recent years, the term has sometimes been used to refer loosely to any "accidental" behavior outside predicted or anticipated norms—related to learning or not. Day-to-day workplace banter makes little differentiation between informal and formal learning, and the word *informal* is becoming a convenient catchall term within circles of human development practitioners. This chapter establishes informal learning as the predominant learning approach used to think strategically. The next chapter presents the reflections of successful strategists on the impact of formal learning. The final chapter of this part discusses the factors of context and transfer on the strategic thinking process.

Several definitions are offered as a simple way of differentiating formal and informal learning. Informal learning is regarded as learning that is predominantly unstructured, unplanned, experiential, noninstitutional, and nonroutine. It takes place as people go about their daily activities at work or in other areas of life. By contrast, formal learning is considered to be structured, planned, preprogrammed, and institutionally sponsored or classroom-based learning where a trainer, teacher, manager, professor, or some other "education agent" is responsible for planning, implementing, and evaluating the learning that occurs.

Let's not forget that we human beings are, by our very nature, learning beings. We learn all the time by identifying and solving problems, observing other people, asking questions of friends and colleagues, requesting advice and help, and accessing records of human experience, such as stories, books, and online information. Although many people associate learning with their educational experiences, most learning actually occurs outside any formal educational environment as we struggle with the challenges of our daily life and work.

A Hong Kong technology executive explained that strategy "is not really a step-by-step process. It's not that black and white. It's more ongoing and not really a structured sort of thing. There isn't anything methodical or scientific about it. I don't think strategically in a meeting. It's just where I state my thinking — if I'm lucky!"

According to adult learning theorists Victoria Marsick and Karen Watkins, informal learning is "predominantly experiential and noninstitutional, nonroutine, and often tacit."[1] By its nature, informal learning cannot be fully preprogrammed. It arises spontaneously within the context of people following interests as they arise. Informal learning can be planned or unplanned and involves some degree of conscious awareness that learning is taking place. Informal learning is driven by our everyday preferences, choices, and intentions. Self-directed learning, social learning, mentoring, coaching, networking, learning from mistakes, and trial and error are some common kinds of informal learning.

Incidental and Intentional Learning

Two subcategories of informal learning are particularly relevant to strategic thinking: intentional and incidental learning. Intentional learning is what we expect or anticipate we will learn. For example, if I have a phone conversation with the company's finance director to discuss a currency valuation formula and I learn a new currency valuation formula, then intentional learning has occurred.

> *Much of the learning involved in thinking strategically is informal — either incidental or intentional in nature.*

On the other hand, incidental informal learning is "a byproduct of some other activity, such as task accomplishment, interpersonal interaction, sensing the organization, trial-and-error experimentation, or even formal learning," as defined by adult learning researchers Karen Watkins and Victoria Marsick.[2] In our preceding example, I may incidentally learn not to trust the finance director's department because I also learned during the conversation that they have a very high staff turnover rate. I may become suspicious of the department because longevity signifies stability and trust in my belief system.

Incidental learning is unintentional and unexpected, and we are almost never conscious of its happening. It includes learning by doing, from mistakes, and learning through a series of covert interpersonal experiments. This type of learning is tacit, taken for granted, and implicit in its assumptions and actions.

As we will see in this chapter and the next, much of the learning involved in thinking strategically is informal—either incidental or intentional in nature. Table 4.1 outlines types of informal learning and describes some of the characteristics and examples of each type.[3]

In my practice, I notice that strategic thinking can be greatly enhanced by an awareness of the concepts of intentional and incidental learning. Both influence the perceptions we hold of situations that are part of strategic discussions. A heightened awareness of intentional and incidental learning can help wipe away our blind spots and lead to seeing new strategic possibilities.

TABLE 4.1 Description of Informal—Intentional and Incidental—Learning*

| | Types of Informal Learning | |
	Intentional	Incidental
Characteristics	Experiential Noninstitutional Controlled by learner Somewhat planned, but may not be a primary aim Expect learning outcomes, but they may differ from those expected Nonclassroom site Fair predictability of outcomes	Experiential Not planned Not intentional By-product of other activities Unclear, unpredictable outcomes
Examples	Self-directed learning Coaching Networking Personal study Mentoring Distance learning Feedback Performance planning Experimentation Research Trial and Error	Involvement Mistakes Assumptions Beliefs, values Attributions Hidden curricula in formal learning

*Modified from Marsick and Watkins.

Education theorist Peter Jarvis distinguishes formal, nonformal, and informal education by stating that "formal situations are bureaucratic, nonformal are organized but not necessarily in a bureaucratic environment, and informal situations are ones where there are no prespecified environments, although there are always covert, procedures of interaction."[4]

The executives whom I interviewed described some examples of incidental learning as they were engaged in making strategy. The Hong Kong technology executive implied incidental learning in the process of information gathering when he explained:

What's happened to me a lot is—when I go for regulatory data or legal data, it's easy to get—straightforward. You know exactly what you need. Then I talk about it and play out different impact scenarios with people here, and also with counsel, and expert advisors . . . and honestly, I've been burned a lot (laughter). And what I've really learned in looking back is that I can't trust anybody when it comes to data—not the analysts, not the publishers, not even my advisors or mates here. You just can't trust people with data. You have to look behind the curtain.

His intentional learning was retrieval of accurate data; what he learned incidentally through his experiences of gathering information was that he could not trust people involved in the data-collection process.

Interestingly, while we often intend to learn factual data from information we gather, we also learn some "other stuff" incidentally. In the case of the executives who were interviewed, they learned incidentally not to trust the media that publish the data, or the data itself sometimes. They also incidentally learned to gauge boundaries among competitors and learned to weigh trust levels with colleagues and rivals—primarily through experiences having to do with personal interactions and industry culture mores as they attended trade shows, conferences, and meetings.

Thinking strategically does not tend to happen in meetings or at work—it occurs informally outside work in a very nonlinear manner.

Intentional learning is also experiential and driven by the learner, though it may or may not be the primary aim of the action or learning. Coaching,

TABLE 4.2 Intended and Incidental Learning Acquired from Information Gathering

Learning Source	Approach	Intended Learning	Incidental/Actual Learning

Self-study	Journals
	Publications
	Newsletters
	Newspapers
	Professional
	  papers
	Reports
		Technical information
		Legal
		Demographics
		Regulations
		Trends
		Projections
		Statistical data
			Technical and professional
			  information
			Not to trust all data or sources
			Inaccurate/misleading information
			Contradictions
			Hidden motive to publications
			Need to verify data

Professional
  meetings
	Conferences
	Conventions
	Trade shows
	Lectures
	Government
	  meetings
	Financial
	Currency
	  meetings
		Competitor reports
		Financial reports
		Industry standards
		Industry projections
		Regulatory policies
		Legal information
			New ideas
			Different products and inventions
			Inside information/gossip
			"Political" savvy
			Need to withhold information
			Realistic data
			Intellectual stimulation
			Credibility "testing" of competitors
			Not to trust all official data
			One's position can create dangerous
			  distance from reality—and skew
			  projections

Colleagues	CEO President CFO COO	Specific information New ideas Different perspectives	Intellectual stimulation Reactions New ideas Different perspectives Gossip/agendas/hidden motives

Professional
  associates
	Journalists
	Experts
	Other business
	  leaders
	Government
	  officials
	Politicians
		New ideas
		Different information
			Intellectual stimulation
			Challenge
			Testing
			New ideas
			Different perspectives

Strangers	Students
	Airline passengers
	Friends of friends
	People in stores
	People in coffee
	  shops
		Opinions
		Ideas
		Reactions
		Feedback
			Reality check
			Different perspective
			New names of inventors/
			  innovators/products
			New ideas
			Different, informal data
			Good questions
			Opinions
			Intellectual stimulation

feedback, networking, and personal study are some common forms of intentional learning. The incidental learning of the executives in the study is apparent in the differences in the responses indicated under intended and incidental learning presented in Table 4.2.[5]

5

Formal Learning Refuted

What role do all the strategy courses and consulting seminars play in learning to think strategically? A seemingly weak and unconvincing role. Again, it is important to differentiate between learning to think strategically and learning to plan systematically. As noted earlier, thinking strategically does not tend to happen in meetings or at work—it occurs informally outside work in a very nonlinear manner. This is an interesting point to note for those responsible for strategic development. Thinking strategically is a considerably more holistic, conceptual, and complex exercise than sequential and linear planning.

When senior executives were asked a series of questions about how they learned to make strategy, none referenced any formal learning approaches (e.g., courses, models, schools of thought, and theory), except through negative connotation. The executives were asked to identify background factors, particular people, or circumstances that influenced them and to name things they pay particular attention to when thinking strategically. Not only were the executives negative in their recollections of formal strategy-making approaches, they either discredited it or noted it as a factor of noninfluence regarding how they really learned to think strategically.

Formal approaches to learning were rejected in favor of an informal approach that referred primarily to experience. The formal education and training that the executives received were dismissed outright as being irrelevant to their actual learning to make good strategy. Therefore, formal education for developing strategy making appears to have been neither a facilitator nor an impediment to their learning—just irrelevant. This is a sobering thought if we consider the budgets that are targeted for strategy courses.

A Japanese financial executive concluded, "Most of what I learned in courses was only technique—like a nice craft." And a German manufacturing executive said, "I tell them [junior executives] they must talk to many people and read everything. And I tell them not to worry about learning about the models of strategy (laughter)." When asked to explain more about this, she continued:

> You know, I have taken strategy courses in Germany from American consulting firms and I have read many books on how to make strategy. So I understand you have so many models to choose from. But they are not accurate to what really happens if you must be responsible for good strategy — because it [strategy thinking] is not systematic.

This specter of doubt regarding the contribution of formal learning was further reflected by a young president of a U.S. technology company who said:

> I learned about strategy when I was getting my MBA, but it was mostly about, umm, you know, umm, well see, I can't even remember! (laughter) I think it was mostly just theories and models for analysis and whatever. This is not about thinking strategically. Maybe they're okay for planning.
>
> I will be honest with you, I haven't used any of it [the models]. I don't think what I learned — all of these different models and theories — is practical. It's maybe okay for planning, but strategy is so much bigger, and I don't think this way. You know, I think it's much better — much better, to just teach people to talk to each other and to think in a hard way.

When asked to name the most important points to include if he were teaching a course on making strategy, this same executive responded by saying, "I don't think I'd teach strategy as a separate course, I think that's a mistake. I'd want to use a more integrative approach — teach thinking and world affairs — that's how you get people to start thinking strategically."

Traditional approaches to developing strategic thinking have largely been formal and ineffective — ritualistic and mechanistic, with a lopsided emphasis on the analytical aspect. While this is indeed critical, it is only one side of the coin. A reaction to the failure is the growing interest in informal learning. However, just because formal learning has been refuted and been disregarded as being influential to learning to think strategically, we need not discard it from strategy development. In other words, there is no need to throw the baby out with the bath water. It is, however, an invitation to reconsider what is working and what is not with regard to the learning and development disconnection.

If one of the fundamental assumptions about "teaching" is that it supports learning, we need to better understand how we learn to think strategically if we are going to "teach" or facilitate learning to that end. It is essential that those responsible for facilitating strategic thinking leverage individual learning and organizational learning in order to build capacity for sustainable, innovative, long-term strategic performance.

Learning alone does not produce such an outcome. Learning itself is not the end result of thinking strategically. Only when learning is specifically targeted toward the creation of an innovative, adaptable, and winning strategy does learning to think strategically contribute real value to an organization.

The traditional approach to developing strategic thinking is most often premised on the concept of a planning model rather than as a process based on learning and creation. The planning model of strategic thinking offers very little emphasis on creative thinking, long-term thinking, critical reflection, dialogue, challenge, or testing. And the planning approach rarely results in a long-term competitive strategy, nor does it generate an innovative or sustainable strategy. It is imperative to regard strategic thinking as a continuous learning process rather than as a sequence of steps ending in a strategy "product."

Formal learning was consistently refuted among the successful strategists as a primary source of influence on learning to think strategically. Reflecting on the factors that were most influential to his learning to think strategically, an executive of a Hong Kong technology company described the way he learned to think strategically:

> I think I had a pretty good education, I went to Harvard for my MBA, studied in France—so that was probably good for basic education. But to be honest, I don't remember much about strategic thinking. (laughter) Maybe I just don't remember specifics—but I've learned the most important things traveling and living in a different country. These are the things that really contribute to enriching your thinking—you know, you get to see all kinds of things and hear things. And most of it doesn't make sense at the time. But that—knowing how to make sense of things—that's what's required, I think, for learning to think strategically.

This point of making sense of things brings us to the notion that knowledge is not always the outcome of learning. Rather, the learning outcome is the experience itself and the meaning that individuals give to the experience, according to learning theorists Peter Jarvis[6] and Jack Mezirow.[7] In terms of learning, Mezirow sees learning as "the social process of construing and appropriating a new or revised interpretation of the meaning of one's experience as a guide to action. The learning process, as meaning making, is therefore focused, shaped, and delimited by our frames of references."[8]

Travel was a dominant theme among the executives interviewed as they described influential factors on their learning to think strategically. For example, when probed about the role that traveling and working in a foreign country specifically contributed to his learning to make strategy, this same technology executive explained, "You're constantly working with mounds of information that seem unrelated, and so much data, and a lot of unknown variables . . . so it's a game. You're always working with an incomplete entity —it's frustrating, but also exciting in a way. That's what it's like to make strategy!"

The oldest executive in the study, a 61-year-old CEO of a Polish manufacturing company, noted

> *As I continue to travel, I learn more about different ways of looking at things, and that's a certain kind of experience too, and it's valuable—I'd say critical to making strategy. Experience, I say, is like the answer book to your new questions. I don't really think that being young or being old is an advantage per se. I'm still learning, and I think experience is probably the best teacher.*

> *Learning occurs when our situation is one of imbalance, for learning is the process of seeking balance.*

The connection between travel and experience goes back centuries, as indicated in the following observation from more than a few years back: "Experience, travel—these are an education in themselves" (Euripides, *Andromache* (c. 426 B.C.). The experience of travel offers us an environment in which to challenge our own and others assumptions and core belief systems, to expand our perspectives, to test and to imagine new possibilities. We see new connections and different relationships between and among objects, people, and values. Sometimes we are forced to break our comfortable habits and use new patterns—we either adopt something new, adapt, or retain our original frameworks.

Accordingly, learning occurs when our situation is one of imbalance, for learning is the process of seeking balance. Travel is the quintessential metaphor for strategic learning. When we travel, we are striving to create balance in a highly imbalanced context; therefore, we are in a constant state of learning. For example, when we intend to take a trip, we make plans. But we experience continuous imbalance when the ticket gets misprinted, we arrive only to find the hotel reservation is inadvertently canceled, we get food poisoning, we address a meeting where our language is not fully understood, our objectives are misinterpreted, and we assess financial reports that have been "fudged for foreigners." The success of our travel depends on other people and things we cannot control. The same is true of strategy making. What is strategic thinking if not an attempt to balance our imperfect, incomplete, and infinitely complex world?

As discussed in Part I, strategy theorist Henry Mintzberg has made the role of learning explicit in his research, demonstrating the emergent character of much of the real strategy of organizations. In his book *The Rise and Fall of Strategic Planning*, Mintzberg deciphered the "code" of how strategy is really made. His well-publicized study reported that 90% of the projected outcomes in most companies' formal strategic planning processes never actually materialize. Only 10% of most companies' actions arise out of their strategic planning (i.e., *realized strategy*).[9] The source of the other 90% of what companies do Mintzberg calls *emergent strategy*. This is the accumulation of day-to-day decisions, disjointed initiatives, and actions taken by managers in response to everyday work demands, without any grand master plan or comprehensive strategic concept. When everything is taken into account, this is the real strategy that most companies follow. Emergent strategy is based on the notion that strategy thinking is a nonlinear and informal learning process.

Why should we bother developing strategic thinkers if their strategy is just going to "emerge" anyway? While "chance" strategy or "accidental" strategy will happen—for better or worse—the aim of strategy development is to increase the odds of positive and generative strategic thinking, not to produce a string of happenstance, serendipity, or lucky events. We need to understand what is required, pay attention to what works, and have a process that supports successful repetition.

6

Context and Transfer as Factors in the Strategic Thinking Process

The role of context as a factor of informal learning cannot be understated or ignored. Context has been found to have a significant influence on the quality of dialogue required in learning to think strategically. An awareness and sensitivity to signals from the environment is essential for determining whether learning occurs, for it provides an ability to construct and reconstruct frameworks and patterns for questioning assumptions grounded in past experiences.

The importance of context with regard to thinking strategically is widely known. But what was particularly surprising in the study was the highly diverse, nonwork context all of the executives credited with their learning to think strategically and subsequently used as their anchor experience against which to test their strategic thinking. All of the executives I interviewed described how they learned to think strategically in nonwork environments and then transferred their strategic thinking process into a work context. They "saw" sameness in the strategic thinking process, whether they were painting or expanding global financial markets.

The vastly different contexts of the executives' prior successful strategic thinking experiences (e.g., painting, auto racing, farming, sculpting) actually supported the learning transfer into a global business context for the executives in this study by providing a successful strategy-making experience on which they could draw. In other words, how learning occurred is what the executives anchored to, not what or who was involved. The executives were aware of and mitigated contextual factors that then allowed the informal learning process to remain constant, regardless of the context. The enormously diverse contexts from which they learned and successfully transferred their strategic thinking calls into question the role of context and the function of transfer in the informal learning process.

The place in which the executives' prior successful life experience occurred (e.g., studio, race track, farm) was strikingly different from the global business environment in which they currently work, but the broader context was similar in a surprising respect. The context in each nonwork case provided executives the opportunity to learn to frame, reframe, and make meaning of an environment that was incomplete, unpredictable, uncontrollable, and demanding—precisely the environment in which they currently make global business strategy. These executives immediately identified these broader contextual factors as having a similar pattern, and the current situational specifics presented an opportunity to learn. This instant pattern recognition, ability to reframe, and ability to transfer relevant segments across contexts is what the executives credited as being critical to their learning to think strategically.

> *It is the ability to transfer that allows lessons to transcend context variables such as time, history, place, and people. We "get it" precisely because we are able to transfer learning.*

Learning to interact in ways that succeed over a broad range of situations requires reflective process ability. This is further supported by learning theorist Donald Schon's explanation: "It is this entire process of reflection-in-action which is central to the 'art' by which practitioners sometimes deal well with situations of uncertainty, instability, uniqueness, and value conflict."[10]

The ability to transfer across vastly different contexts is what enables us to hear a story, see a play, watch an episode, connect to a cartoon, or relate to an illustration that occurs in a totally different setting than the one we are experiencing and still "get it." We can transfer either the particulars or the generalities across context and learn from this kind of secondhand or peripheral experience, because we are able to make the transfer. The story or picture makes sense, even though the context is different. It is the ability to transfer that allows lessons to transcend context variables such as time, history, place, and people. We "get it" precisely because we are able to transfer learning.

What is required for contextual transfer is a degree of reflective processing ability, something that is teachable and learnable. The literal transfer of experience involves instrumental learning and an absence of the use of reflective processing. In other words, if the illustration or example is "not just like where I work," then frequently no learning transfer is made. "Customizing" learning aides, such as videos, case studies, examples, and simulations, are examples involving instrumental transfer. In fact, in many situations, this is a form of "dumbing down" the learning process because it assumes we cannot transfer our learning across contexts. It may be more effective to developing strategic thinking if we set expectations of transfer by deliberately using examples that appear to be "irrelevant"—examples that stretch the imagination and require divergent thinking by forging new connections. Surprisingly, people make the seemingly unrelated connections very easily.

"Customizing" learning aides and simulated experiences is often a waste of money and time for strategic thinking development initiatives if we do not understand or acknowledge the truth, that adults can and do transfer learning across contexts. We transfer our learning across vastly different contexts all the time in our day-to-day lives as well as in our business lives. Unfortunately, we often do not give adults credit for the ability to transfer. If a strategy works in an industry that is different from our own, we often dismiss it as an irrelevant case from which we cannot learn and insist that it be customized in order to learn. Not only is this kind of "customizing" unnecessary for learning to occur, it can actually weaken our learning opportunity because it does not set an expectation or provide an opportunity to use reflective processes. We are taking away an opportunity to make connections and use a reflective learning process that we possess.

Part II has posited informal learning as a requirement for strategic thinking in hopes that development initiatives to support the learning aspect of thinking strategically will be seriously addressed. Part III looks at the three-stage informal learning process that the executives we studied used to think strategically.

WHAT DOES LEARNING TO THINK STRATEGICALLY LOOK LIKE?

A Murky but Miraculous Process: Three-Stage Informal Learning Process

Experience is not what happens to you; it is what you do with what happens to you.

Aldous Huxley (1894–1963), English author and critic

7

Preparation Stage

Part II discussed informal learning as the way in which we actually learn to think strategically. In this part we examine a three-stage informal learning process that describes how we progress through the informal learning process of thinking strategically. The three stages of the informal learning process (Figure 7.1) are:

- Preparation
- Experience
- Re-evaluation

It is important to recognize that although we are referring to three stages of the informal learning process, in reality the process is iterative; that is, we move back and forth between stages. Next we describe each of the three stages of the informal learning process.

The *preparation* stage of strategy is difficult to identify because it can happen at any time and any place. Yet we need to be able to recognize what happens in this stage if we want to facilitate learning to think strategically. The Polish CEO explained how he "begins" to think about strategy:

You need a reason to begin. Sometimes the reason is only to survive. Sometimes the reason is to fulfill a dream or an idea you cannot let go of. Sometimes the reason is to avoid a punishment or you are afraid something terrible will happen. But the reason must be a powerful one, or you will not really make strategy; it will only be a simple plan.

Planning can be step by step, but strategy is not. You must have a very strong reason. And you must feel and believe this reason deeply.

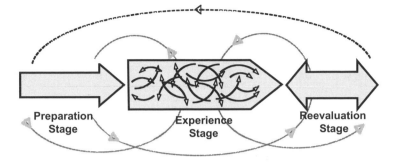

FIGURE 7.1   Three-Stage Model of Informal Learning Process used for Strategic Thinking.[1]

Otherwise, you have no motivation to look for the bigger picture, and the work of thinking and searching will be too exhausting and difficult. So it must be something you feel very strong about.

To build a strategy requires inspiration, you must want something very deeply. If that happens, then you must think carefully to yourself about why this is worth so much trouble, because I tell you—you will lose sleep, who knows, maybe friends over this!

You know, I said that strategy is not so simple. But you must continue no matter how tedious or troublesome. Because if you really believe something, it will need to have a strategy—you must see a very broad picture without a frame—it has no limit.

There are two aspects to the preparation stage: an *affective* component, which is a kind of emotional readiness during which the intensity of a must-win attitude is tested, and a *cognitive* component, during which information is gathered and data examined. These two components serve as preparation for action by enabling us to assess the situation, gather information, and initiate a retrieval of past knowledge and skills for adaptation and application in the strategic thinking process. The affective and cognitive components coexist and have a simultaneous interchange in this preparation stage.

Affective Component

The affective component of the preparation phase is often identified as the starting point, or as a strong urging we cannot let go. An American technology company executive illustrated this:

You have to have a gut-level reason or strong feeling for moving something ahead. I mean, you just don't make strategy for the sake of making it. I had this strong — this unbelievable drive, dreams, and piles and piles of plans about what I thought and really believed needed to happen with software production. I guess I couldn't let go.

According to the successful strategists interviewed, the pursuit of strategy starts with a relentless desire to win. The sources can be many and varied, but a must-win attitude, regardless of its origination, is essential. This competitive affective element is critical for learning to think strategically.

An American financial executive said, "I start with a desire to get things 'right' — to make something happen — to do something or go somewhere with an idea or a problem. Sometimes I suppose you could even have a disaster that gets you going. You don't have a choice but to clear it up."

A Japanese executive said:

Find something in your life that you love to do — and you are not making money on — (laughter) then you know you really love it — and not the money! Then, as I said, you will always want to protect it. This will be the most important lesson in learning to make successful strategy. Because you will be successful because [of] the fear of losing what you love.

One of the manufacturing executives succinctly stated: "Although I'm an engineer by training, I like the intellectual work of figuring out strategy — it's very emotional — and I like that."

An interesting and important part of the strategic thinking equation is how the tension within a situation manifests itself in the learning process. For example, the great American myth that learning must be fun to be effective profoundly impacts our approach to learning to think strategically. This deeply embedded American cultural belief needs to be revealed, challenged, and tested by those responsible for facilitating strategic thinking. Considerable research shows that the most significant strategic learning is a result of engaging in tough and difficult situations, not from "fun" situations.

Another point to consider is that challenge can be motivating and stimulating, the source of pleasure, satisfaction, and profound learning. It is not so much about fun or nonfun situations, but, rather, understanding that the affective component of strategic thinking is critical to the process itself: acknowledging negative feelings and experiences and deciding what to do with them. The executives interviewed strongly believed that good strategic learning often comes from the negative. In order to do this, a must-win attitude and highly developed reflective processing ability are necessary.

The affective component in the preparation stage is often expressed in terms of passion, conviction, and emotion acquired through past experience. This is particularly pronounced at the start, when we invoke a conscious self-check or a sort of readiness assessment to determine if we have the intense must-win attitude that will sustain the strategic thinking process. This emotional component is necessary to ensure that we are adequately prepared to move forward with good strategic thinking — not planning. The executives in the study seemed to believe that an absence of this emotional component would lead to a lack of stamina or drive necessary to pursue a truly good strategy.

A Swiss executive with whom I was supposed to meet cancelled a meeting not too long ago because of "mind fatigue." He took several days off to rejuvenate at a private mountain retreat because he was literally exhausted from "thinking very hard." This was just a couple of days after "fixing the strategy in his mind," and he knew he had to take some time off, or he wouldn't be able to continue into the next planning phase. This had happened to him several times before when he became so engrossed in thinking that he nearly collapsed of exhaustion. As we talked by phone, he said this is one of the lessons he tries to pass along to junior executives because they need to understand that "truly good strategy is an emotional experience; it is not just an exercise."

In addition to cognitive constraints, emotion itself plays a profound role in learning. It influences how we attend to a situation. The simple decision to mentally bring ourselves into or remove ourselves from the activities of a group or task is often done tacitly, yet this can dramatically impact what we learn from a situation. Furthermore, emotions and a deeply embedded cognitive process can construct defensive routines that prevent us from learning in situations. Without an awareness of our own personal tendencies, as well as the time to reflect on and learn from events, little effective and actionable knowledge can emerge from experience.

This move from feeling to action is not necessarily a predictable sequence. While a fiercely competitive must-win feeling can certainly be a powerful impetus to the learning process, it is also possible for new information, the cognitive aspect, to provide the impetus. Regardless, the affective and cognitive components are interconnected at the start of the informal learning process, though not necessarily moving in a stepwise progression.

*Traditionally, the role of the affective in
strategy development has been viewed
either as an inhibitor of learning due to
anxiety and stress or as something that can
be brought into conscious awareness as an
"object" for rational analysis.*

Frequently, traditional corporate and university strategic development approaches address only the cognitive component, that is, the planning, data-gathering, and analysis piece. The affective component is typically either ignored or recognized by structuring it into the "vision" part, on-demand affective learning that quickly shifts into a cognitive, linear learning progression. For example, we are asked to think passionately about our vision for the next hour. We are then asked to switch off the affective and get back to planning, the cognitive mode. While this common exercise may indeed be of noble intent and faintly recognize some affective requirement, it is rather oversimplified and misguided and rarely results in strategic thinking.

Traditionally, the role of the affective in strategy development has been viewed either as an inhibitor of learning due to anxiety and stress or as something that can be brought into conscious awareness as an "object" for rational analysis. The former has generated an emphasis on creating, safe learning environments for discussion; the latter has led to psychological and therapeutic approaches aimed at dissecting the issue so that strategic thinking can proceed.

Learning theorist David Boud has highlighted the role of feelings and emotions in the learning process, noting that they are often treated separately from the action of the task. Boud has observed that despite the fact that learning is experienced as a seamless whole, there is a cultural bias towards the cognitive aspects of learning in modern English-speaking societies. The development of affect is inhibited, . . . leading to a lack of emphasis on people as whole persons.[2]

Why are we so overly focused on the cognitive aspect of strategic thinking? Partly because our formal education habitually reinforces the cognitive learning aspect, often at the expense of the affective. The affective is much more the reserve of our informal learning. The cognitive is about the strategic planning and analysis that is easily structured into "teaching" material and a "teachable" approach—it is definitive, easily measured, linear, and largely instrumental and mechanistic. Although the affective is present, it can feel elusive and ambiguous and is not easily "taught" or articulated. Our formal learning often teaches us to ignore the affective learning dimension because it can get in the way of the cognitive learning.

When it comes to learning to think strategically, the affective component is tightly paired with the cognitive and is absolutely essential but largely invisible. We are not taught to be aware of it, to pay attention to it, or to value it as part of the strategic thinking process. We lack the confidence and ability to deal with it, so we ignore it. The affective deals with emotions and feelings and requires paying attention to intuition—taboos in the realm of strategy planning—imperatives in the process of strategy thinking. The affective aspect of strategic thinking is what enables the learning process to be highly nonlinear, unexplainable with words, not easily measured, and "felt."

Researchers David Boud and David Walker emphasize the importance of the affective component within the overall informal learning process:[3]

> *The heart offers more than simply feelings or inchoate impulses. Emotions do more than indicate crudely and vividly that something feels good or bad. A person's feelings can actually help make sense of an issue, give shape to it, and indicate what the stakes really are. In other words, the heart has reasons . . . [which] are written in a language different from the formal, explicit, logical one in which our minds operate. Discerning how one's instincts define a situation is a matter of translation. It is an interpretive art, and a difficult one.*

While theorists have long acknowledged the importance of the affective dimension on the learning process, the emphasis of learning within the strategy literature focuses on cognitive change, assimilating information, and acquiring behavioral skills. Increasingly the emotional aspect of learning is becoming explicitly incorporated into learning theory.

Cognitive Component

The cognitive aspect is also present in the preparation stage of the informal learning process, primarily in the form of information gathering and analysis. Traditionally we hone the cognitive—and this is all too often where we begin and end. To think strategically, of course we need to have specific information and clear analyses, and data needs to be gathered and tested on a continuous basis. This is the linear part of the strategy thinking process, the quantitative, and for many the most familiar and comfortable. It is an extremely important part, but it needs to be paired with the affective in order to be effective in the long haul.

Information gathering within a strategic thinking process is regarded as intentional learning and is used for four purposes:

1. To generate new possibilities
2. To verify an existing belief
3. To provide a new perspective within the framework of making strategy
4. To test other information

So what kind of information is important to gather when thinking strategically? It can range from highly analytical and quantitative to more qualitative data gathered through talking with other people. Interestingly, the executives interviewed indicated that they used conventional sources of data (e.g., reports, statistics, newsletters, publications, conferences) but relied on unconventional sources (e.g., talking to fellow airline passengers, listening to university students, coffee shop conversations, discussions with people outside the industry) to verify the data received from conventional sources. Some voiced humor and skepticism when talking about conventional methods of information gathering.

For example, an American technology company executive said:

Of course I read the same data everybody else does (laughter) . . . everybody reads the same things! But you know, one of the advantages to traveling is that you hear from people first-hand. We need to get out there and talk to people and think about things, and think about different things — what it could mean for us. Talking to people is kind of a check. Actually, it gives perspective and meaning to data, when everybody's reading the same stuff. It's just what I have to do — reading and going to places to hear other people, and I talk to a lot of people to see what they're thinking and learning. I think a big part of being able to make really good strategy is to constantly know what's going on all over the world.

Another technology company executive concurred:

And that's what I really like about strategy — you kind of bring everything into it. I mean, you need to know what's happening with federal regulations, state laws and what's happening with international

*laws, trademarks, patents, property rights — you need to keep up to
speed with inventions and distribution and all the laws around these.*

*And then there's economics, and how U.S. events and policies matter
to what's happening in other places. It's not enough to just pay attention
to forecasts and projections — anybody can print those things! We can't
rely on other people's numbers; we need to run our own. And the only
way to do that is to keep on top of things — all kinds of things.*

One of the financial executives from Japan stated: "I read economic forecasts
and financial market newsletters, but it's data people get paid to print! I think
traveling is a good way to check on this data and make a test of it. Otherwise,
it might not be true. And then your strategy won't work and you've been
fooled! (laughter) It's your own fault!"

As we can see, the preparation stage consists of both affective and cognitive learning components. The affective is most pronounced when we become aware of a compelling must-win attitude. This part of the learning process is propelled by our emotional drive — it is nearly overwhelming, for the desire to win must be satisfied. This affective component drives the strategic thinking process forward.

8

Experience Stage

Our own experience has the strongest influence on learning to think strategically. Specifically, we draw on two kinds of experience: current experience and prior successful life experiences. So how do we go from having an experience to learning to think strategically? In short, we engage with others in critical reflection and dialogue about our situations, and somehow, as a result, learning conversion and transfer occur.

> *Successful strategists learn to think*
> *strategically through informal learning,*
> *primarily from their own experience.*

In this chapter we first look at the two kinds of experience we use to process our experience, current and prior experience. Experiential learning is given particular attention in this chapter because it is the single area of informal learning considered most relevant to learning to think strategically. The application of prior experience to new situations is also discussed, in addition to the role reflection plays in making meaning of experience.

Experiential learning has come into its own over the past few years and is essential for understanding how we learn to think strategically. Successful strategists learn to think strategically through informal learning, primarily from their own experience.

John Dewey's assertions about the relationship between learning and experience inform many of the subsequent theorists' beliefs about learning from experience, including Chris Argryis, Donald Schon, Edgar Schein, Peter Jarvis,

Peter Senge, and Jack Mezirow, among others. For Dewey, it is the impulse of experience that gives ideas their moving force. Learning is a process of transforming concrete experience — the product of our interaction with our environment — into purposeful action.[4]

According to Dewey, we learn by confronting an error or problem, by observing surrounding conditions, developing and testing hypotheses about the problem through reflection, and then finally taking action. For Marsick and Watkins, learning from experience means how people make sense of situations in their daily lives. Learning theorist David Kolb presents the process of experience transformation as a four-stage learning cycle and argues that it is the foundation of all human adaptation.[5]

As we embark on a new strategy-making experience, we start with a conscious and compelling must-win attitude, proceed to information gathering, and then immediately move into an experiential learning mode during which we draw on either our current or our prior experience as a means of creating a challenge–test–reflection–refinement cycle. It is at this stage of the informal learning process that we make sense of our feelings and thoughts by integrating them into a perspective. By accessing our current experience or prior successful experiences we engage semiconsciously in a form of action-reflection. An appropriate recent or prior experience is recalled either intentionally or intuitively and serves as a pattern for transferring the learning to a new situation.

Current Experience

These current experiences come from many areas of life and, either directly or indirectly, influence our strategic thinking. In perceiving and responding to a situation, we draw on our previous experience and knowledge in an attempt to frame the situation and make sense of it in terms of what we already know and feel.

Prior Successful Life Experience

There is a point at which we unconsciously or consciously choose either a current experience or a prior successful life experience to test our new experience against; we frequently vacillate between the two. This process allows us to compare and test pattern validity. We often draw on and engage in a current experience initially and later tap into a prior successful life experience as another "check" or reference point for transferring learning—this time the experience is farther removed from the moment. Instead of testing vis-à-vis current circumstances, we refer back to a prior successful life experience as a baseline for assessment. Referring to a prior successful life experience provides us with both a familiar standard for acting and a place from which we can diverge with thinking and acting.

We very often use the prior experience as a metaphor for the current experience. Clients say things such as "This is like when I prepare for a photo exhibition," or, in the case of my husband, "This is like when I pilot a balloon in a race," or "This 'feels' like what happens when I'm in the middle of a sonata, and my string breaks—I have to figure it out on the spot."

How does this "test" happen? First, a quick reflection occurs during which we assess the similarities and differences of the new situation as compared to old experiences. The second form of reflection occurs when we decide on a course of action. And the third form of reflection occurs after the fact and enables a full reevaluation of the learning.

A prior successful life experience is the foundation on which we learn to make good strategy. It is the accumulation of experience that eventually becomes our "tacit" knowledge or our "autopilot" setting. Although the time, place, people, and circumstances can be very different in each prior successful life experience, the learning experience can transfer to a business context and consistently transfers over the course of time.

Interestingly, a prior successful experience was identified and described by each of the executives interviewed as being the most important experience that influenced their learning to make strategy. Furthermore, the prior life success experience that all executives described occurred in a nonbusiness context and was different from one executive to another.

The executives often referenced a current experience first and then reflected back on a particular earlier life experience to test against. Surprisingly, this earlier life experience was never work related, but, rather, was success related. These experiences were not single events; they were kind of "life interest" experiences that became an anchor for subsequent learning. This is striking because it attests to the ability to transfer learning from one context to another, something we often have great difficulty trusting.

One of the American financial company executives explained:

When I was thinking about whether to include consolidation of our new equities divisions, I bounced back to this experience about a year ago—looking for clues and troubleshooting problems. And then I—after a while—I thought I'd run it past my old days, about my farming—you know, I do that a lot when I'm thinking.

The Japanese CFO mentioned that he uses a similar pattern to test his thinking, but first by referring to a prior success experience of painting and then later to a current experience: "So it seems I always have a habit to check with my way of painting first." When asked to explain why this pattern contributes to strategic thinking, he continued, "It's because I see and know that my thinking is good then. And then I must examine it (laughter)—because I must try to find weak points in my thinking, and so I will next think about a recent experience—well, really, it's a little back and forth to make sure it's really a good way to think."

These executives created their own model of strategy making according to their prior successful life experience. For example, when the American finance executive was explaining the similarities between farming and learning to make strategy, he said that farming has become his model for thinking strategically. The Japanese executive continually referred to painting as his model for thinking strategically. Although their prior successful life experiences were very different, the learning process was the same—one that basically conformed to our three-stage process.

On the one hand, the prior success experience serves to intensify and solidify our commitment to a particular belief or way of thinking; it reinforces our frame of reference. On the other hand, it creates a curiosity and confidence that allows us to test and try new ways of thinking and acting.

We often reference a prior successful life experience in our "dress rehearsal" routine —playing through numerous scenarios before selecting one to act on.

Each executive compared and contrasted his or her own model against itself by actively and continuously testing the model using an informal "ritual" of reflective processes.

The model for learning through experience developed by Marsick and Watkins[6] begins with individuals facing a new experience and goes through eight phases:

1. Framing the experience based on past experiences
2. Diagnosing the new experience

3. Interpreting the context
4. Deciding on a solution
5. Drawing on or developing skills
6. Producing a solution
7. Assessing consequences
8. Drawing further conclusions

As noted, our prior successful life experience anchors our present-day thinking. The various testing methods, which include dialogue, debate, storytelling, and discussion, allow us to diverge in the safety of our mind before testing in real life. An example of this is the German CFO, who explained that every few months her executive group has debates and arguments about what various scenarios may mean to them; she called this a type of "dress rehearsal" before making a decision to act.

We often reference a prior successful life experience in our "dress rehearsal" routine—playing through numerous scenarios before selecting one to act on. This can occur instantly and intuitively or in slow, deliberate motion over the course of weeks, interrupted by more data, more dialogue, and more analysis. Drawing on a prior successful life experience is critical to our learning to make meaning in a new and different context.

When learning to think strategically, it is necessary to become aware of the importance of a prior success experience and to use it as a reference point from which to construct future successes. For example, the American banker continually made metaphoric reference to his farming experience in describing how he learned to make good strategy. In response to a question about how he fit strategy making into this farming experience, this executive said:

> It's just the same thing. Making strategy is not limited to corporations— sometimes I think it's narrowly presented that way. I mean people have made strategy forever—in all kinds of different settings. I never knew the word until I got my MBA, but I knew strategy making! I'd say probably better than just about anybody, and it came from my farming background. I'd been doing it for years—so I knew it.
>
> Well, of course I've tried a lot of different things and made a lot of mistakes in business, but I think where I've learned the most has been from applying what I've learned from my farming experience to a business setting. That [farming] experience has been the toughest teacher, and just invaluable to me. It's exactly the same as making corporate strategy, only the context is different.
>
> You've got to have some successful life experiences to draw from— these are the most important places to learn from anyhow. You know,

when we encounter new challenges, we have to learn somehow—and so we draw on these experiences. It's how we learn. Farming is a business, and you've got to figure out how to make damn good strategy, or you'll never survive. There's no better teacher—you learn. Period.

A technology company CEO said:

I think it's important to have these life experiences outside of a business context if you're going to be successful within a business setting. What I mean is, you need to have some successes—that's the experience that is so valuable for making really good strategy. And you're probably not going to get it in any company. They just don't give you the chance to learn. You'll get the boot.

This same CEO recalled his prior life success experience with sculpting as being influential in learning to make strategy: "I've studied sculpture. I think art is a good way for thinking about strategy." When asked to talk about how that is, he said:

You know, when you think, it's easy for your ideas to slip away. But when you're doing art, any kind, you record those ideas—sometimes in forms that only you recognize. But you can then go back to them and redo them, add on or change them or whatever. That's like making strategy, and I think that's why I like it.

He explained how his sculpting experience related to learning strategic thinking, continuing:

Maybe I've learned from my experience with art, sculpture, working with the clay. I think, for me, maybe, that's where I've learned the most. I think the most practical and valuable things we learn in real life, not in business. And like sculpture, most people would probably never think it relates to running a software company or anything (laughter), but it does for me! It's just not that different really, only the context is different —you know the people, the product, and the business. But the thinking and being able to see things and work with things differently, that's the art part.

When probed, all of the executives resisted the notion of learning from a past strategy-making experience *per se*. Instead, they "skipped back" over time and anchored and credited their new strategy-making experience to their prior successful life experience. This suggested a strong conviction on the part of the executives to the inherent value of an early life success experience.

A Japanese financial executive explained:

> I've learned to make good strategy mostly from unrelated experiences. Like I said before, when I [auto] race, I like to win. And I learned from my junior high school days that I could not just sit in my car and keep racing. I never really took any lessons or [had] a teacher who showed me how to race—it was just something I really wanted to do. And I learned by listening to older racers talk before and after races, and watched them on the television, and then just tried very hard. I think it is necessary to have early experience—a good experience. Then you learn to make strategy. Then you just do the same thing in a company. For me it was auto racing—and I just learned by practicing it.

Application of Prior Experience to New Situations

One way to apply past experience to new situations is to assess the gap between what we think we know, based on past experience, and what is unknown. By determining the gap between prior learning and the unknown, we are able to construe a learning process to fill the gap. Past experience brings technical expertise, understanding of people, and knowledge of processes. It also brings diagnostic capability to understand new situations more readily by asking the right questions and assessing against appropriate criteria. This learning through a transfer of experience begins with an early life success experience.

As one of the Japanese banking executives explained:

> I think it's most important to have one experience—anything—early in life that you are successful with. And then you just keep building on it for other situations. It's the foundation for learning something new. You must find something you enjoy very much to be inspired to think. And this is my painting experience—it is so good for me; it is exactly how I learned about making good strategy.

Further illustrating the importance of a prior success experience on present strategic situations, he explained: "I learned to love to paint, so I think it's natural that I take what I learned and had good enjoyment [with] and use it when I make strategy. And [I] just keep doing it in other areas of my life, not just banking. My painting background was very important to prepare me to make strategy. It was everything."

When asked how it helped him think strategically, he explained: "It taught me to be curious, and also that we will have many limitations in our thinking—so we must constantly acquire, add ideas. It's exactly the same as making corporate strategy, only the place and names are different. Everything else—it's the same."

Another financial executive described a similar belief:

> You know, strategy making is not at all like we're taught. In fact, I don't really know about all these courses and methodologies. You really need to find something you really care about, really love doing in your life—and you'll start to learn strategy from that. Because you don't ever want to give up something you care about, so you'll just naturally work on developing strategies to hold on to it because it's that important. That's why being a kid and finding out what you really enjoy and care about is important. You carry all that over into your life and will always draw on those experiences.

To echo the importance of a prior success experience, another executive noted:

> You do not begin to make strategy as an adult. It is a failure that way. You must continue to make strategy according to how you do it in another area of your life, for example, a hobby or some other sincere passion you have. Making strategy will come to you if you have a strong will to win at something. And then you do it the same way for business. It's exactly the same.

> *Certain aspects of an experience capture our attention and influence what we pay attention to, because our existing knowledge base shapes what patterns we see in a situation.*

Our experience provides us with an evolving source of self-reliance, confidence, skills, knowledge, and practice in using various conscious and unconscious reflective processes. It is a powerful and integral experience to which we automatically refer, and we use it as an anchor for subsequent strategy making over and over again. This provides consistency to our strategy making because we use a similar thinking process each time; yet we differentiate each experience due to context and by refining the reflective process each time.

What is learned from an experience is subjective and can often be fundamentally different from one person to the next, even when they experience the same event. Certain aspects of an experience capture our attention and influence what we pay attention to, because our existing knowledge base shapes what patterns we see in a situation. Furthermore, our interpretation of that same experience changes over time.

The current business goals we are committed to as well as the overall business climate and our personal belief systems shape the frames we use to discuss and decide strategic issues. This is why it is important to continuously include a wide variety of perspectives and opinions regarding finance, technology, integrity, risk assessment, and social contribution in strategy meetings and to invite challenge and testing as a means to ensure that our strategy is consistent and aligned with our values and beliefs. Without a concerted and committed effort to counter the subjectivity inherent in the interpretation of strategic events, what may be learned from an experience and passed on through the organization by way of stories or technical channels may be far removed from the actual event.

Role of Reflection in the Three-Stage Informal Learning Process

Reflection is one of the critical abilities for transforming experience into learning, and it is utilized in all three stages of the informal learning process. The literature is filled with references to reflection as an essential part of the learning process. Dewey's concept of reflection is set within the context of hypothetical-deductive problem solving.[7] Dewey defines reflective thought as "active persistent and careful consideration of any belief or supposed form of knowledge in the light of the grounds that support it and further conclusion to which it tends."[8]

The flux of terminology describing nuances of reflection can sometimes be confusing. Descriptions of what Chris Argyris calls *double loop learning*[9] and what Donald Schon has named *reflection-in-action*[10] and what Jack Mezirow refers to as *critical reflective learning*[11] occur as we attempt to learn from our experiences, firsthand or secondhand, current or prior experience. Suffice it to say that reflection-on-action is merely reflection after the fact, or looking back on an action or experience, as opposed to reflection-in-action, which reflects during or in the action or experience.

For Mezirow, reflection plays a key role in learning. It is the process of "critically assessing the content, process and premises of our effort to interpret and give meaning to our experiences."[12] The central function of reflection is validation of prior learning, or attending to the justification for our beliefs. Reflection may be used to examine the content or the description of a problem (*content reflection*); to question the problem itself (*process reflection*); or to look at the very premises — our belief systems or meaning schemes — on which the problem is founded (*premise reflection*).

Critical reflection assists in the ability to question presuppositions, routines, and patterns. A description that implied reflection was given by one of the Japanese financial company executives, who explained, "I've just learned [strategic thinking] from myself, just from experience and thinking and doing something and rethinking — and then I discuss matters with other people and I try, or test something I've been doing one way — it's good to do this, because you learn."

When asked to explain how he learns from this, he continued:

> *I learn because I have a habit that is good for me. I do something a certain way, and always somebody debates with me, or tells me I'm wrong, or to try it another way—and so I do. And then I must think, sometimes for a long time and in a serious way, about why did it work or not. And then I have more discussions or arguments (laughter) and I must think and try another new way—you know, it's a very good way to learn.*

Adult educator Stephen Brookfield notes that critical reflection "is the process to engage the learner in a continuous and alternating process of investigation and exploration, followed by action grounded in this exploration, followed by reflection on this action, followed by further action, and so on."[13]

The iterative and dynamic nature of informal learning was described in Marsick and Watkins' *Informal and Incidental Learning in the Workplace*:

> *Reflection is key to this learning, but it must be combined with action, else it becomes speculative. Through action, managers test out insights, but they also invite public examination of the problem, which leads to dialogue among themselves and the stakeholders of the problem. Action and reflection are not separate phases, although at times, managers may*

be doing more of one than the other. Action and reflection take place simultaneously or concurrently.[14]

The old adage that past success is a predictor of future success may hold true for learning to think strategically. Executives who can use reflective processes to connect a past experience to a future challenge—those who learn from their experiences—are likely to be successful at strategic thinking. When we engage in reflective processes, it enhances our ability to broaden perspective, activate the imagination, and ultimately allow us to think in ways that result in competitive strategy making.

9

Reevaluation Stage

The third stage is, in short, a reevaluation of an overall experience. Reflection, as we have mentioned, is a critical element of learning to think strategically, and it is utilized in all three stages of the informal learning process. Yet it plays a particular role at the end of the three-stage informal learning process. The primary function of reflection is validation of prior learning, or justification of our beliefs. Reflection in this third stage is critical and evaluative in nature, and it impacts our strategic decisions. Within this last stage of the informal learning process, reflection is used to "review" the action and decisions and to provide the rationale for those decisions created during the experience stage.

Reflective capacity is about much more than "going soft"; it is about our realizing that not everything can always be measured or controlled. Sometimes we have to trust and simply provide support by giving time to a situation for listening, critical questioning, and critical reflection. An essential ability for learning to think strategically is reflective capacity.

The reflective processes used in this reevaluation stage allow us to interpret and reinterpret experience by opening up different lines of thinking. The reevaluation stage is a combination of an act–think–talk–think–act cycle. Such a process allows us a strategic opportunity to experiment, imagine alternatives, refine, and decide.

The reevaluation stage is where new perspectives about priorities and relevance are generated. The earlier testing and validating ideas, expectations, and assumptions that were formulated during the experience stage are used as a "current experience" against which this new, reevaluative round of critical inquiry can be tested. Values are confirmed or reassessed during this process. Successful strategists incorporate reevaluation consciously, yet informally, into the strategic thinking process.

The executives interviewed consciously and deliberately included reevaluation after they took action and made a decision. For example, after the CEO of the financial company decided on a first phase of his strategy but before the actual delegation for implementation began, he consciously and critically examined it within the larger strategic context for "things he should do differently." He requested that not only his senior executive team "retest" the idea and underlying assumptions, but also the junior executives responsible for the implementation. Furthermore, he booked a four-stop flight, rather than his usual direct flight, to Europe in order to make time to "talk to a lot of totally uninformed strangers" about his first phase. He consciously engaged in an informal and intentional repetitive process of challenge–reflection–refinement in this reevaluation phase.

All of the executives interviewed described a holistic perspective to learning. They were comfortable with not having a finite task completion in the "cycle" of making strategy, because they believed that making strategy was a continuous process. This is similar to the ancient Greek notion of strategy, one that implied an expectation and assumption that there would be incomplete and inaccurate information, contradictions, and things that could not be rationalized. The ideas of *metos* and *cosmos*, previously described in Part I, are as relevant to strategic thinking today as in premodern times.

> *Emotions are facilitators to informal learning and are an integral part of the reflection process.*

The postreflection stage of reevaluation is a means for learning through the use of communication techniques and also through a more personal reflection process that enhances understanding and expands meaning perspective. Reflection during the reevaluation stage occurs when we identify the predisposition we held when we embarked on the strategy-making process and compare it with the perspective that emerges from the experience.

Emotions are facilitators to informal learning and are an integral part of the reflection process. Attending to feelings and reevaluating the experience are not definitively or consistently placed at the end of the process; rather, they

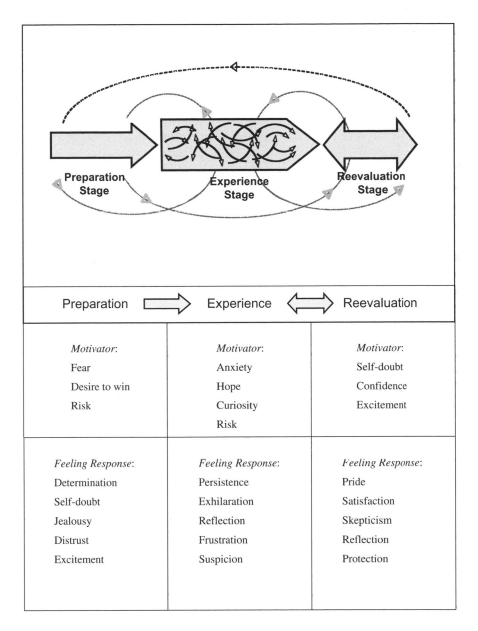

FIGURE 9.1   Affective Role Within the Three-Stage Model of Strategic Thinking.

are apparent and overlap within each stage. Reevaluation occurs in an iterative way—eventually connecting to the preparation phase, where the learning process recycles.

Figure 9.1 shows the three-stage model of informal learning used for thinking strategically that includes the affective component in each stage.[15] The executives I interviewed expressed an awareness of strong feelings in each of the three stages. It is interesting to see fear mentioned as the predominant feeling present in the preparation stage and the wide range and combination of emotions expressed throughout the strategic thinking process.

This three-stage cycle is critical to understand and to master if we wish to be able to re-create innovative strategy over and over in very different contexts. It is only by becoming conscious of this informal learning cycle that we can begin to use a disciplined approach to developing new habits of learning strategic thinking. By understanding and diligently practicing such a learning cycle, we can begin to develop a sustainable pipeline of strategic thinkers within organizations.

Reflective processes are essential for learning to make global strategy and are best learned through life experience. The executives in this study learned to make meaning of the complex, very unpredictable, ambivalent, and high-stakes international business environment from a prior successful, nonbusiness life experience.

IV

WHAT KIND OF LEARNING IS REQUIRED TO THINK STRATEGICALLY?

It's Your Choice: The Surf *and* Dive *Domains of Learning*

Though this be madness, yet there is method in it.

William Shakespeare (1564–1616), English dramatist and poet

10

Overview of Learning Domains Used for Strategic Thinking

In the course of my observation and facilitation of high-level strategy meetings, it quickly becomes apparent that the questioning, the responses, the interaction, and the process itself occur at lower levels than we might imagine at most companies. Although the position of the executives may be high-level, the quality of the conversations is most often variable at best. Many of these meetings consist mainly of an exchange of analytic data, summary findings, rapid-fire question–answer segments, possibly a brief brainstorming portion, and recommendations for a future course of action. Sometimes there is debate or perhaps discussion about the analysis, but I rarely encounter meaningful critical dialogue. Over the long haul this has a tremendous impact on the quality of the strategy that is made.

Some of this, of course, has to do with the political posturing and power games for which such meetings provide a forum, but much of it has to do with a lack of common understanding and a collective confusion about strategy meetings. Is the intent of the meeting strategy thinking, strategy planning, strategy implementation, or strategy assessment?

The key concept presented in this part is learning domains — specifically as the domains relate to thinking strategically. Part IV consists of two chapters. The first chapter differentiates between data, information, and knowledge and offers an overview of learning domains. It concludes with a presentation of three predecessors of learning domains. The second chapter discusses two specific domains of learning that are essential for facilitating strategic thinking, referred to throughout the book as the *surf* domain and the *dive* domain.

Through an understanding of the learning domains required for strategic thinking, we can greatly expand and enrich our learning because it gives focus to questions and responses. Working with clients in my consulting practice, I find it is essential for them to have information about learning domains in order to choose the domain appropriate to a particular strategic situation.

> *The dynamic process that is used to convert*
> *information into knowledge is learning.*

While there are many definitions of *learning*, the fundamental characteristic is that it involves some kind of change that is a reaction to an encounter, not just a function of a natural maturation process. This change can occur in domains of motor skills, intellectual skills, knowledge content, cognitive strategies, awareness, affect, or attitude.[1] The term *domain* refers here to an area of learning influence, similar to a taxonomy of learning activity.

Data, Information, and Knowledge

The starting point in any discussion about learning and strategic thinking is to distinguish between data, information, and knowledge. For the sake of simplicity, this book considers *data* to be neutral, static, and meaningless. *Information* is derived from data and is given meaning through the interpretation of facts or statistics. The aim of information is to construct knowledge using the surface domain of learning. *Knowledge* is information that is framed according to our (mostly) implicit belief systems. And finally, the dynamic process that is used to convert information into knowledge is *learning*.

An example of data is: A half million American adults living in nine states are not enrolled in any health insurance program. Information derived from this might be: The incomes of these adults rank in the lowest quartile and the states represent the nine poorest states; or this segment of the population is comprised of 75% nonnative English speakers; or these states have governors who rank near the bottom of an annual peer review poll. Knowledge gleaned from this information could include: Our social and medical system is at risk; or our political system is failing us; or the insurance business is an industry at fault.

Knowledge is the result of how the information has been interpreted within a context and the meaning it has been given. We interpret information automatically, according to frames of reference that we learn; and we relearn how to do this by slowing down the pace — pressing our "pause button" and engaging in critical reflection. Knowledge is most often tacit and is embedded within individuals and groups. It requires reflective learning, or what this book refers to as the *dive*, or deeper level of learning. As John Dewey noted, the aim of knowledge is reconstruction and meaning making, and this makes it heavily reliant on social interaction, dialogue, and critical inquiry.

In order to leverage knowledge into the learning required to make innovative, sustainable competitive strategy, we must "convert" the information and knowledge into strategic learning experiences through transfer. It is useful to understand the various learning domains in order to think about implications for developing strategic thinking.

Knowledge creation pioneers Ikujiro Nonaka and Hirotaka Takeuchi consider knowledge as a dynamic human process of justifying personal belief toward the truth. "Knowledge is about beliefs and commitments, . . . action and meaning."[2] Accordingly information is a stream of messages while knowledge is created by that very flow of information, anchored in the beliefs of the holder. This distinction is important to make in any discussion about learning to think strategically, because one of the fundamental requirements is that the information flow be consciously and routinely interrupted and that the knowledge base be challenged and rigorously tested against other anchors.

> *Strategists must be willing to seek out*
> *facts that might disconfirm a generally*
> *held belief and be willing to explore other*
> *possibilities.*

Although knowledge and learning are sometimes difficult to express, strategists should be encouraged and should encourage others to pursue an awareness and explicit means of expression of both knowledge and learning. Knowledge and learning are essential to challenging beliefs and assumptions, which is fundamental to innovative, adaptive, sustainable strategic capacity.

Strategists must be willing to seek out facts that might disconfirm a generally held belief and willing to explore other possibilities. Knowledge benefits strategic thinking when the perspectives of multiple sources of information, human experiences, reflective processes, creative thinking, dialogue, and supporting technologies are fully integrated. Those responsible for thinking strategically should be continuously encouraged to seek new and updated knowledge and to habitually challenge and be challenged as a means of testing professional strategic competence.

Knowledge sharing is facilitated through dialogue. Information technology systems can support this dialogue, at least partially, but they cannot store or transfer knowledge *per se*—only the record of the explicitly expressed knowledge. Technology systems only store and transfer data and information that has been or will be interpreted within the context of those who attempt to make sense of these data based on their own knowledge acquired from their past experiences.

SCENARIO

Margot, the CEO of a midsize software firm, panicked because her three-year winning strategy was failing. Her stockholders were complaining, the board was on her case, competition was on the rise, and her neck was on the line. Instead of opening up, she surrounded herself with people whom she considered to be loyalists, those who were like-minded and knew "where the lines were drawn." She fired her two top "antagonists" and refused to hire "outsiders" because they wouldn't know the company way and would bog down the process. She insisted that her global executive committee relocate back to Seattle for convenience and to help with "continuity" for some time. Fearful to shatter frames, Margot locked into her existing frames of reference. She was hoping to revive her strategy by simply extending her frames of reference—doing more of what didn't work! There are times when we need to be counterintuitive and not cling, but break, if we want to survive.

Three Predecessors to the Surf and Dive Learning Domains

In strategy-making courses I often hear executives say they have either a lot or a little "knowledge about" a certain topic. They distinguish that from what they really "know." As we will see in this section, theorists have differentiated these same domains of learning using various models and terminology. Prior to a discussion of what this book refers to as the *surf* and *dive* learning domains, it is useful to have some background on the thinking of several earlier theorists.

Knowledge About *and* Knowledge of Acquaintance

The distinction between the practical and abstract knowledge domains was first made by the philosopher William James at the turn of the 20th century, referencing them as *knowledge about* and *knowledge of acquaintance*. To learn knowledge about requires that we effectively transfer information and integrate that information into conceptual models and frameworks. With regard to strategy making, we commonly learn this way through instructional workshops, videos, lectures, reading, seminars, Web-based programs and other direct instruction methods designed for teaching various models of analysis, implementation methods, and so on. The meaning of such information is interpreted through the learners' frames of reference, though the rationale or framework of a particular theorist, professor, trainer, consulting firm, or school.

As the content becomes more complex, contradictory, or controversial, the ability to interact with others and critically question is required. This is what James referred to as *knowledge of acquaintance*.[3] Knowledge of acquaintance is learned through personal experience, and the essence of such knowledge is imbedded in decisions and actions and in our tacit knowledge. It can only be acquired through firsthand experience of the issue or situation in question — through practice, reflection, challenge, testing, and reaction. It can be learned through informal learning, incidentally through experience, and from structured activities, such as action-learning initiatives.

While the technical difference between *knowledge about* and *knowledge of acquaintance* is distinct, it is important to understand the relation between them. Knowledge about provides a framework against which practical experience can be tested. This framework can then be modified in practice and becomes knowledge of acquaintance. We do this when we apply analytical models, interpret the complex content, and make decisions about the implications of a meeting in order to make informed strategic decisions. This requires interaction between knowledge about and knowledge of acquaintance.

P *and* Q *Types of Learning*

Various authors have differentiated structured and unstructured problems within different domains of learning. Learning theorist Reg Revans refers to *P* and *Q* learning types as a way in which domains of learning are classified according to the structure of the problem. *P* learning refers to programmed learning or knowledge that has been codified in books, lectures, or analytical techniques. *P* learning is used to describe "puzzles," or problems for which a correct solution exists, even if it is hard to find.[4] An example is finding the best way to reduce the time or cost of some specific manufacturing operation. *P* learning is used for addressing problems of operational effectiveness. Discussion and debate are commonly used for this.

By contrast, *Q* learning typically represents "quandaries," difficulties or opportunities to which no solution clearly exists. An example is deciding the direction a company will take after a merger. This kind of *Q* learning can be supported through coaching individual executives and facilitating group meetings. It requires executives to reinterpret the meaning of current decisions and emerging trends, to challenge their assumptions, and to reframe their experience. Action learning programs, future search methods, lateral thinking, scenario planning, and introducing critical dialogue at all levels of the organization are ways of facilitating the *Q* domain of strategic learning. In relation to learning theorist Karl Weick's terminology, *P* learning correlates to problems of uncertainty and *Q* learning is equivalent to ambiguous problems that require judgment.

Clearly, strategic thinking involves both *P* and *Q* domains, but it is easy to get stuck into using *P* learning because it is easy to structure, moves quickly, is convenient to track, and has an end solution. *Q* learning involves questioning insight. Gaining strategic insight first requires asking discriminating questions and then combining data analysis with past experience and intuitive judgment to answer those questions. Each strategic decision requires a different combination of analysis, experience, and judgment. Obviously, there is no formula, because the variables in each situation are different.

Four Types of Learning

Another way strategic thinking can be perceived is according to the theory put forth by yet another learning theorist, Edward Cell. His model distinguishes learning by classifying it into four domains: response learning, situation learning, trans-situation learning, and transcendent learning. *Response learning* refers to a change in the way we respond in a particular situation; we respond with a prepared set of answers or techniques when handling a specific situation.[5] Response learning is studied by behaviorists in psychology and includes rote learning and what Skinner called *operant conditioning*.

This kind of learning can also require the learner to apply a sequence of skills or to match responses to options of varying complexity in situations, such as selecting the correct negotiating tactic from among many possibilities in the midst of a contentious negotiation. For example, a country manager learns to offer a set of appropriate responses when questioned by auditors investigating the profit picture. This type of repetitive learning is most effective for problems involving a low-level learning transfer to ensure that the skill set becomes an automatic baseline response. While this may be a useful type of learning for predictable circumstances such as security training, strategic thinking requires a different type of learning.

It is highly tempting to present strategic thinking as something that can be easily learned through a formula, an acronym, or a structured sequence. We are all too familiar with this learning approach and, unfortunately, have come to think of it as the best way to learn everything, simply because success comes quickly and easily with it. Not every problem or decision can be solved via such a linear process. It just doesn't pass the test as a learning method when faced with the complex issues involved in strategy.

Situation learning, the second kind of learning that Cell identifies, involves a change in how we organize our understanding of a situation. Cell notes that response learning is dependent on situation learning, since how we interpret a situation shapes our response to it.

Trans-situation learning, the third kind of learning, is learning how to change our interpretations of a situation. This is often called *learning to learn*. This kind of learning involves reflecting on the learning process and identifying and questioning the assumptions and attributions we are making about a situation, by using reflective inquiry for critical self-reflection.

Transcendent learning, Cell's fourth kind of learning, requires that we modify or create new concepts. Cell describes this kind of learning as providing possibilities, new tools, for interpreting individual situations. This is sometimes referred to as *transformational learning*.

11

The Surf and Dive Learning Domains

The complex, ambiguous, and paradoxical nature of the global strategy environment in which traditional linear, transaction-oriented, controlling executives now find themselves requires that they develop a range of thinking in order to make adaptive, sustainable, and innovative strategy. A down-to-earth board member of a British investment bank with whom I was working coined the terms *surf* and *dive* domains of learning after we had been working together for a couple of days on strategic thinking issues. Instead of using my drab terms, level I and level II domains, he quickly coined the concepts in everyday terminology that made sense to him. I borrowed the terms because the imagery works, and it conveys the concept quickly. For these reasons I have decided to pass along the terms, which parallel other terms, such as *single loop* and *double loop* (Schon), *model I* and *model II* (Schein), and *instrumental* and *communicative* (Mezirow), or whatever works for you. As William Shakespeare put it, "A rose by any other name would smell as sweet."

The British investment bank board member likened the *surf* domain to surfing. This kind of learning happens on the surface, is easy to understand, and relatively safe, and we can make sense of things through transacting information and events, a series of responses, and new actions.

On the other hand, the much deeper and more complex level of learning requires us to *dive* beneath the surface in order to make meaning of data, information, and situations. This learning domain is about exploring the unknown and the unfamiliar, has no boundaries, and can be very risky; it is difficult to describe with words and is heavily reliant on experience.

Executives are frequently hammered for not being good strategic thinkers, but rarely do they (or their bosses) know what to do to improve.

I find that once clients have some knowledge about learning domains, it accelerates the strategic thinking development process considerably. Executives are often defined by perpetual activity: doing deals, running meetings, and conducting transactions. If executives are to be successful strategists, they must indeed get things done, but they must also take time to critically reflect. This is not an option or an indulgence but a necessity.

Strategy development can be a sensitive subject. Executives are frequently hammered for not being good strategic thinkers, but rarely do they (or their bosses) know what to do to improve. Therefore, those involved in strategy generally feel vulnerable, defensive, or resistant. By offering a bit of information about the learning domains, executives gain a renewed sense of control over their own learning because it gives them a vocabulary, a process, and a choice. They can choose and be responsible for the level of learning required for various phases of strategy making.

We can choose which learning domain we need to use at any given point within the strategic thinking process. What we call it is not important. What is important is to get on with developing the abilities and skills necessary for each domain in order to support the requirements of our strategic situations. Understanding the learning domains can also help us keep track of where we are in the strategic thinking process and facilitate our own and others' learning.

Table 11.1 shows the learning domains necessary to function when learning to think strategically. The domains of learning and implications for thinking strategically are presented later.

The model on which surf and dive domains of learning is based is what theorist Jack Mezirow calls instrumental, communicative, and transformative domains.[6] While Mezirow draws on Cell's work and the thinking of John Dewey and William James, his work is grounded in the critical social theory of Jurgen Habermas' domains of interests and knowledge.

Mezirow's critical pragmatism defines learning as the process of using a prior interpretation to construe a new or revised interpretation of the meaning of one's experience in order to guide future action.[7] For Mezirow, "Action is an indispensable phase of the process of adult learning. But action

TABLE 11.1   The Surf and Dive Learning Domains

Domains of Learning	Description of Learning	Common Meaning-Making Techniques	Significance to Strategic Thinking
Surf Domain	Linear Sequential Progressive Mechanistic Predictable Transactional Instrumental Routine Instructional Informational Avoid surprises "What" "How to"	Analysis Deductive reasoning Tactical reasoning Logical reasoning Identifying "correct" and "incorrect" answers Exchanging data and information Reporting Feasibility studies Problem solving Decision making Debate Discussion	Convergence oriented Positions formulated and defended Opponents and proponents identified Competitive data collection Analysis Closure
Dive Domain	Nonlinear Intuitive Logical or a-rational Strong affective component Invite surprises "My opinion" "My beliefs" "My values" "My conviction" "My principle" "Why" "What else"	Critical reflection Dialectic thinking Metaphoric speech Analogic thinking Storytelling Collaborative inquiry Critical questioning Imagining Improvising Experimenting Expanding perspectives Testing Challenging Creating Critical dialogue	Divergence oriented Is "messy" Continuously changing Open to exploring new ideas and perspectives Imaginative
Transformative Domain Can occur in surf or dive domains	Triggered by disorientation or catastrophy "Why" "How" "What next" "What else"	Critical reflection Critical dialogue	Transformative Dramatic shift Unpredictable

Based on the model of instrumental, communicative, and transformative domains by Jack Mezirow.[7]

can mean making a decision, being critically reflective or transforming a meaning structure as well as a change in behavior."[8]

The Surf Domain

The surf learning domain is premised on the notion that learning "what" and "how" will accomplish tasks or solve problems because we control our environment by acting on it. It is basically instrumental, mechanical response learning. In organizations, this domain is the one in which meaning is attached to the day-to-day mechanical, transactional kinds of actions. Learning in this domain is primarily about determining cause–effect relationships and learning through task-oriented problem solving. This surf domain uses a kind of learning that "involves predictions about observable events which can be proven correct, determining cause–effect relationships and task-oriented problem solving. The logic of instrumental learning is hypothetical-deductive."[9]

I find that senior executives and those responsible for the development of strategy thinking try their best to simplify and reduce strategic thinking to a "how-to" model. Consultants, trainers, and learning development professionals use the very best instructional design techniques to come up with an approach to teaching or training strategic thinking — but often to no avail. Very often they restrict their learning techniques to the surf domain and teach or train strategic planning.

Most traditional, formal, and behavioral programs directed at strategy performance improvement are based in this domain. For example, surf learning can occur through strategy planning demonstrations, lectures, exercises, analytical model simulations, and visual presentations. Many management programs, technical training, and leadership development programs include these elements of information and skills development, followed by simulations or role-playing. It is an effective learning domain for facilitating the development of strategic planning.

The Dive Domain

The second domain, dive learning, is about making sense — learning to understand what others mean and learning to make our deeper selves understood. This domain draws on Mezirow's communicative domain of learning, which emphasizes the use of communication (language and nonverbal, cognitive and affective) to interact in an attempt to anticipate the actions of others and delve deeper into our own actions and decisions. This domain of learning is essential to developing strategic thinking. Critical reflection (detailed in Part VI) is heavily dependent on critical dialogue, which is central to this domain of learning.

Mezirow describes this learning domain as follows: "It involves understanding values, ideals, feelings, and normative concepts like freedom, autonomy, love, [and] justice. It identifies and clarifies the known through a process whereby each step suggests the next."[10] This is a form of situational learning in which we expand or change our frame of reference. It provides the contextual framing for strategic performance initiatives. For example, in strategic discussions, various opinions are sought, only to be shot down before being explored because someone declares, "We can't do that here because . . ." or "That won't work these days because . . ."

The dive learning domain serves to identify, test, challenge, refine, and possibly alter our frames of reference in order to increase the quality of strategic thinking. The result may be a frame change of varying degree. Minimally, we may change the way we see patterns and specific situations. Maximally, we may experience a total transformation, a true life- or business-altering experience.

Dive learning requires critical dialogue and often integrates experience in order to construct meaning within a social context. It may also consist of discussion and debate. But most importantly, purposeful dialogue is essential to make meaning of information and to frame perspectives and habits of thinking.

Dissention, contrariness, and opposition can be particularly useful triggers to dive learning because they are an invitation to critical reflection and dialogue. We learn tacitly what frames are acceptable and unacceptable for use within our respective organizations, and it is through this critical reflection and dialogue that we decide which frames we will use.

Understanding what frames are used as part of the organizational culture is critical, but it is equally essential to have a process in place to continually challenge, test, revise, and reframe for a winning strategy. A company's frame is a belief schema or an organized cognitive way of perceiving a complex set of behavioral patterns and decisions. A frame is a way of categorizing or compartmentalizing patterns of behaviors and decisions. For example, a particular frame might be regarded as *functional*, and actions and decisions would be judged according to their degree and definition of functionality. Or a frame may be called *economical*, and actions and decisions would be evaluated according to their cost and value within that framework.

In order for strategy to be regarded as a valuable human asset and as a sustainable capacity, it cannot be viewed as a product. Innovative, adaptive, sustainable strategy requires that a strategic thinking process become habitual. This requires key leaders who are able to live with, appreciate, and embrace the tension inherent in dive learning.

False Frame Change

A challenging example of surf learning that I encounter as a very common strategic mistake, particularly in overseas factories and offices, is the false sense of frame change. This occurs when executives believe their team is using the dive learning domain but are actually using surf learning to perpetuate same-frame thinking.

> *Executives will "act" in accordance with compliance requirements by modifying their behavior, yet their beliefs and biases remain unchanged.*

The strategic decisions we make are influenced by strongly held national, ethnic, cultural, gender, religious, and sexual orientation biases. Executives may modify their behavior (i.e., actions and words) after taking courses, practicing role-plays, seeing a video, or receiving feedback in order to conform to the corporate culture norms or to avoid disciplinary actions. Executives will "act" in accordance with compliance requirements by modifying their behavior, yet their beliefs and biases remain unchanged. In other words, response learning will follow the training experience, but the fundamental frames of reference do not change. The underlying beliefs these executives hold are what keep their strategic decisions contained within the same frames. This impedes strategic innovation, adaptability, and sustainability because frames have not been shattered, only temporarily disguised.

Two Traps

I have noticed two very common traps that executives often set for themselves: unintentionally or intentionally restricting the tip of the triangle to a small group and encircling themselves with loyalists and similar-minded thinkers. Both traps result in the exclusion of contrary opinion, ignoring opposing data, avoidance of controversial dialogue, and canceling the very process needed to learn strategic thinking.

The unintentional learning that occurs as the result of these two traps makes us think about strategy in terms of using familiar frames. The incidental learning that often comes from such inclusion and exclusion is that expressing opposition and contrary views, or challenging authority or testing tradition, is punished, whereas conformity is rewarded. Yet challenge and testing are essential for shattering frames and learning to think in an innovative and adaptive way. Foresight, hindsight, or information that may be critical to avoiding a misstep in strategy may be overlooked by excluding these data, opinions, and viewpoints.

I am not suggesting that loyalty should not be rewarded—it should be. But it is not a criterion that supports quality strategic thinking. It can, in fact, have the opposite effect on strategy thinking by reinforcing a habit of maintaining the same frames and ensuring that no new or different patterns are noticed or explored and that no shattering or reframing occurs. I see this particularly in times of urgency and desperation, when strategy is deteriorating and executives are frantically seeking a new strategy. Yet this trap ultimately undermines the strategic intent.

True Frame Change

Frame change can be a result of learning in the dive domain. For simplicity we can say that a frame of reference is a perspective organized by the assumptions and expectations that filter how we perceive the world. Every aspect of our thinking about strategic situations is influenced by our frames of reference; until we become fully aware of them, we limit our capacity to think strategically. Identifying, challenging, testing, refining, or altering frames of reference is a critical characteristic of the dive domain of learning.

Our frames of reference have two dimensions: *habits of mind*, consisting of a set of assumptions and broad, generalized predispositions that guide our interpretations of events and experience; and *points of view*, which consist of clusters of beliefs, feelings, attitudes, and judgments that are specific expressions of our broader habit of mind. These tend to operate outside of our awareness most of the time.

*The ability to change the frame of reference
is a hallmark of successful strategists; in
order to do this, strategists need to be able
to shift perspectives and create new ways of
looking at situations.*

Both the surf and the dive learning domains have their own standards of valid-ity. Surf learning holds to validity tests of facts, measurements, and outcomes; something is true or false, accurate or inaccurate. The validity test is seen in concrete experience — something happens or it doesn't; there's a result or there's not. This kind of testing is typical and familiar in strategy discussions and debates.

Dive learning has more nuanced validity tests, including the assess-ment that others make of our own and each other's authenticity, truthfulness, and qualifications as we test the meanings of experience. It is heavily influenced by, and in turn shapes or transforms, the cultural context in which we act. We can easily draw erroneous conclusions from reflection alone on the content of our experience, leading to a closed cycle of nonlearning learning. Therefore, practices such as reflecting on the foundations of our beliefs (premise reflection) and publicly testing our conclusions with others are effective methods of validity testing within this domain of learning. We can test the validity of the conclusions we draw from reflective observation.

Shattering or "unlearning" existing frames of reference is easy to articulate yet difficult to carry out, as anything worthwhile is. The ability to change the frame of reference is a hallmark of successful strategists; in order to do this, strategists need to be able to shift perspectives and create new ways of looking at situations.

Purposeful dialogue enables reframing of perspectives and adapting to dif-ferent patterns. In the absence of open dialogue, we make judgments about the validity of the message based on the assessment of the trustworthiness of the source. Reflective ability is necessary for deeper-level, dive learning to occur. Playing the devil's advocate and intentionally testing assumptions through direct and open inquiry are two of the surest methods for validity testing.

One of the key objectives to strengthening our ability to use this dive domain of learning is that we can greatly enlarge the scope and depth of our strategic thinking by modifying or dramatically changing our frames of reference. Our frames of reference shape our understanding of both the surf and dive domains of our experience. In other words, even neutral data and information are interpreted by our frames, often unconsciously or instantaneously.

Some learning is basically additive in nature, as when we elaborate or extend an existing frame of reference or add a new frame of reference without changing the beliefs and presuppositions of existing ones. There is nothing wrong with this. But in the strategic thinking process, we need to be aware of the learning domain that is required for the situation so that we can choose the level of questions and responses. In other words, we want to deliberately choose to extend an existing frame, not mistakenly believe we have shattered and reframed it.

SCENARIO

For example, Tyson, an American executive based in Detroit, who fundamentally believed numbers tell the truth and nothing but the truth, was unaware of how his strategic decisions impacted others in the global rollout of several plans. Reflecting on his assumption — numbers are facts and facts equal the truth — he extended an existing meaning frame when he decided to hire an external consulting firm to analyze the data and the findings against additional information to which his company did not have access. His basic frame did not change; he just extended it.

After a move to an office in Paris, Tyson began to have regular, long lunch conversations with colleagues and other business associates that included heated arguments. This was something new for him. They questioned his every action, didn't accept his numbers at face value, and demanded to know the "why" behind every decision he made — they were challenging the very decisions that had successfully opened markets in 21 countries. As much as he found them irritating, he noticed that they seemed to enjoy this lunchtime exchange. After months of seeing no end in sight, he began to treat it as a daily workout. He gradually came to realize the significance and expanded meaning that the story behind the numbers offered in terms of how the decisions he made affected customers, shareholders, and employees around the world. He slowly began to invite challenge about the numbers he once considered sacred.

Developing the Dive Learning Domain

Strategic situations can, according to learning theorist Jack Mezirow, be reinterpreted according to one of the following four ways:

Extend or develop an existing frame of reference.
Learn a new frame of reference and adopt it.
Change viewpoints (create new patterns for certain situations or issues).
Transform frames (construct new belief systems and adopt new values).

In my consulting practice, I am constantly astounded by the number of global CEOs and presidents who have developed or are developing business in emerging markets who do not have even a rudimentary knowledge or interest in historical, cultural, and current political affairs. The potential implications on their long-term business strategy is handwriting on the wall. Not only do they not know, but they don't seek out political, humanitarian, social, educational, or military perspectives in their strategic dialogues, and they often dismiss such perspectives as being irrelevant and superfluous to strategy. Including these diverse data, opinions, and perspectives in a strategic dialogue are essential to having a competitive edge.

SCENARIO

From the very beginning, it seemed like a great business idea: an American automobile company selling Russians a stripped-down, locally assembled version of an American SUV at a premium price. The research confirmed that the demand was there, as well as the purchasing power. With the seemingly low labor costs and the tax breaks negotiated with the authorities, the financials looked very promising.

The problem, which didn't appear on the radar of the American strategic planners, was that most of the Russians in this particular market segment and price range believed that a Russian car is a contradiction in terms. They applied the same attitude to any car assembled by Russian workers at a Russian–American joint venture. (The fact that Russia is one of very few car manufacturing countries where the head of state doesn't use a locally manufactured limo as his official car attests to the prevalence of this attitude. As the saying goes, if you want to buy Russian, stick to vodka!)

As soon as the Russian potential clients realized that several thousand dollars more would get them the same SUV—a slightly used standard

American model, but (and here is the deal breaker) made in the U.S.A. by American workers—the future of the project was doomed. The U.S. corporate strategists and CEO had concentrated only on the economic and financial research, at the expense of cultural, social, and political information and data. Shortly thereafter, they faced the realities of the market and began lobbying the Russian authorities to raise custom duties for importation of used American SUVs to Russia.

This scenario illustrates why developing a capacity to use the deeper domain of learning must be a part of any strategic thinking approach. A competitive strategy does not result from brilliant analysis alone. It is essential to make critical reflection and critical dialogue a part of the entire strategic thinking process. Risk management models and formulas generate excellent analysis, but they are no substitute for critical reflection and critical dialogue. Analysis can be an excellent starting point for dialogue. This is essential to know when we think about facilitating the development of strategic thinking, because reinterpretation of situations is what we want to happen as a result of critical dialogue in order to generate new possibilities about varied and diverse opinions and perspectives.

Transformative Learning

When a fundamentally disconfirming experience or a disorienting dilemma challenges our frame of reference, we are presented with the opportunity to dive to the deepest levels of learning in an effort to make meaning of the catastrophic experience. So powerful is this kind of learning that Mezirow described it as "emancipation from libidinal, linguistic, epistemic, institutional, or environmental forces that limit our options and our rational control over our lives, but have been taken for granted or seen as beyond human control."[11] This experience can lead us to critically reflect on our beliefs and presuppositions, resulting in either a transformed way of pattern recognition or, at the deepest level, a totally transformed framework.

Although this kind of transformative learning can occur in either the surf or the dive domain, it requires critical reflection in order to make new meaning. It can be epochal in nature, such as an abrupt, seeing-the-light kind of instinctual experience; or it can be incremental in nature, as the result of a gradual accumulation of experiences that transforms a person's perspective.

*Fear can be a strong and compelling
impetus for learning.*

While a frame change of this degree is hardly an everyday experience for most strategists, it does occasionally occur. Such kinds of dramatic frame transformations result in major overhauls in the way a company approaches business. This kind of deep transformational learning can and sometimes does lead to a dramatic change in strategic thinking. Everything looks different, so we either no longer recognize or we reject our old patterns and frames.

Truly innovative strategy can emerge from these kinds of experiences. While the experience itself may be frightening and painful and have the potential to destroy us, it is in the critical reflective learning process that transformation occurs. This can yield a remarkable, miraculous, positive outcome. Such profound experiences need not be regarded as being detrimental to learning; rather, they can serve as an impetus for transforming a learning experience from a negative into a positive experience. This degree of transformational learning requires that we experience situations that put us totally outside of our realm of familiarity and control; our world feels upside down —belying the notion that learning is always fun. Fear can be a strong and compelling impetus for learning.

Business clients with whom I work have on occasion experienced this kind of intense, life-redefining frame change as a result of major expected or unexpected loss. Such experiences have included a corporate takeover, death of a partner, spouse or child, or the diagnosis of a critical disease, among others. An intense transformational learning experience can also result from a gain, such as the realization that over the years their income is substantially more than that of their parents, a corporate takeover, the birth of a child, recovery from a critical illness, or adjusting to living in a different country. Executives who have experienced this kind of learning sometimes exclaim they have been "enlightened" or become a "new person."

The CFO of a pharmaceutical company with whom I was working experienced this kind of frame change due to a facility bombing in southern Thailand that killed his best friend and two coworkers. He referred to it as an emotional "earthquake"—one thing happened, and, after the initial shock and ruinous aftermath, it triggered changes in every aspect of his business and personal life. After a year or so of "soul searching," he described these changes as a "total rearrangement of my life."

Although it generally takes a catastrophe or a disorienting dilemma for us to experience learning of this magnitude, it is important to remember that going through a catastrophe is not enough for learning to result in change. It is the capacity to critically reflect that leads to shattering and reframing and eventually to changed frames. Just because we have a profoundly unusual or disorienting experience, either inside or outside of the workplace, does not guarantee that we will have a learning experience. To ensure that learning results from the experience, or at least to facilitate the likelihood of a learning outcome, it is necessary that the experience be reflected on critically and new action tested and incorporated into a new frame. Experience alone does not guarantee learning. Critical reflection is required.

Knowledge of learning domains can facilitate learning from experience. When strategy works well, executives rarely focus on improving their strategy development—it is taken for granted. It is when problems creep up and the company's profit, revenue, market share, or reputation is at risk that the sirens blare. An integration of learning domains, emphasizing extensive use of critical reflection, should be an ongoing aim of strategic development programs. Anything less will not yield sustainable, adaptable, innovative capability. It is not enough to be satisfied with the transactional, instrumental, mechanical surf domain.

Here are several suggestions I have found helpful for fostering frame change.

- Vary the usual composition of groups and teams to increase exposure to new perspectives.
- Invite provocative conversations and presentations with "outsiders," including those outside a functional group, a product group, an industry sector, or a particular level of management. Establish interactions with academics, politicians, consultants, professionals from various fields, children, teenagers, young adults, middle-age and mature adults, religious leaders, people from an extreme range of economic backgrounds, and those of diverse cultural and ethnic backgrounds.
- Volunteer to be part of an action learning team to solve a problem for tasks that are outside of familiar functional or product areas.
- Join conversations, discussions, and meetings where your perspective is an isolated one.
- Participate in high-level strategy-making meetings.

An ability to use both learning domains profoundly differentiates successful strategy thinkers from planners. The capacity to move from one domain to the other is an internal resource available to each of us for everyday access. It sharpens the focus of strategic thinking and deepens and broadens the scope of the resultant strategy.

By developing the dive domain, we can ensure that the organizational and individual strategic capacity is addressed. Innovative, sustainable, and adaptable strategy becomes possible. The dive domain of learning allows for renewal and the re-creation of strategy, not just a reframing of existing habits of action. This is the domain of learning that "involves identifying ideas, values, beliefs, and feelings, critically examining the assumptions upon which they are based, testing their justification through rational discourse, and making decisions predicated upon the resulting opinion."[12]

Successful strategy is always past tense.

The ability to think and be reflective is threatened if we live a life with no moments of solitude and silence. Executives who are incessantly connected to the muddle of other people's voices have difficulty hearing their own voice.

Successful strategy is always past tense. A one-time strategic win is only a historical business event; the continuous ability to re-create wins requires strategic thinking and meticulous execution. In order for this to occur, traditional and conventional methods of strategic development will not suffice. Learning initiatives must first and foremost be guided by strategic aims and integrated with important business initiatives through both formal and informal methods.

V

HOW CAN WE TALK ABOUT ALL OF THIS?

Dialogue: An Essential Part of Learning to Think Strategically

The greatest problem with communication is the illusion that it has been accomplished.

George Bernard Shaw (1856–1950), British playwright

12

The Role of Dialogue in the Strategic Thinking Process

When we think of dialogue within a strategy context, we often have an image of people getting together to talk. But that is far too general and obvious. We tend not to differentiate the various ways of structuring talk to support the strategic thinking, nor do we think about the purpose of the talking that is necessary.

Most of us have forgotten or have never known how beneficial dialogue is to the creative and cognitive learning process that is essential for learning to think strategically. Debate and discussion have fallen into favor during the last century as instrumental learning methods that are compatible with the needs of the technical rational scientific era. As we move away from a strategic planning framework toward a strategic thinking framework, we need to familiarize ourselves with dialogue.

Part V consists of two chapters. Chapter 12 compares, dialogue, discussion, and debate within a strategic thinking process. The three are distinguished for the purpose of learning to think strategically, not to split hairs. Thereafter, the focus is solely on dialogue. A discussion of three factors of a good strategic dialogue is also included in this first chapter. Chapter 13 presents critical inquiry as an integral part of dialogue and also outlines seven strategy dimensions that are beneficial for enriching a strategic dialogue. The final subsection looks at how dialogue is learned and used within the three-stage informal learning process.

There are already many excellent sources for developing and incorporating debate and discussion within most traditional strategy development environments, such as corporate and university courses, but far fewer sources on dialogue exist. Therefore, Part V looks most closely and specifically at the role of dialogue in learning to think strategically. The emphasis here is on dialogue as an essential communication tool for exploration within the deeper, dive domain of learning and as a means of supporting the strategic learning process.

The good news is that dialogue has been around forever, and it can be learned. There is a chunk of dialogue that is skill based and can be taught in a conventional formal learning setting. There is another aspect that is experience based, and this requires critical reflection, which can only be learned informally. The bad news is that dialogue requires time, discipline, and a commitment to practice in order to benefit the strategic thinking mind-set. Dialogue is not about efficiency or brevity in the short term. It is about sustainability and adaptability for long-term strategy development.

> *Most corporate and university executive programs teach strategic thinking as if time were the most important aspect of judgment, rather than investing in developing the habit of critical dialogue, which leads to trusted experience.*

From political leaders to media coverage of international government organization proceedings to corporate meetings, there is a lack of positive role models who demonstrate constructive and collaborative discourse, dialogue, or even good debate. Our commercial business world provides lots of shortcuts to rescue our tuckered-out minds. Bullet points and sound bites have replaced dialogue, discussion, and debate when it comes to strategy presentations. We expect and accept sound bites as the mode for giving and receiving information in meetings, e-mails, phone calls, conference calls; and Power-Point presentations serve as a respite for our satiated gray matter in seminars and courses. "Get to the point" takes precedence over a dialogic thinking process that is generative, adaptive, and innovative. We have sadly convinced ourselves that we need only the facts to think strategically. Brevity represents facts, and facts represent "close enough to truth."

At the opposite end of the spectrum are strategy meetings conducted using so-called "diplomatic" discourse—in which the intent is deliberately diluted and the message is so convoluted that it lacks authenticity or relevance. Both ends of the dialogue spectrum lack any critical inquiry or reflection. Little wonder there is a shortage of strategic thinkers. Abbreviated thinking is mistaken for analysis, and it is taught and rewarded as if it were able to lead to innovative, sustainable strategy.

Quite often, I find that many of my executive clients have no personal memory of dialogue for use as a reference point to strategic thinking. Ironically, companies claim to be desperate for strategic thinkers, but many resist or ignore the inclusion of critical dialogue in the process of learning to think strategically.

Furthermore, most corporate and university executive programs teach strategic thinking as if time were the most important aspect of judgment, rather than investing in developing the habit of critical dialogue, which leads to trusted experience. This outmoded frame—the one that has established time as being paramount to anything else—is begging to be shattered.

Comparison of Dialogue, Discussion, and Debate

Dialogue is a versatile, vital, and trustworthy capability in a global strategy-making environment where many things are uncertain, constantly changing, and beyond control. The terms *dialogue*, *discussion*, and *debate* are often used synonymously when referring to the nature of the talk in strategy meetings. Though *dialogue* is a word that is commonly batted about, it is often used quite generically. Dialogue is the most critical communication technique for use in supporting the strategic learning process, but discussion and debate also have a place—each can and should be used at various places within the strategic thinking process.

Both discussion and debate have limitations in their ability to create and further foster new possibilities in thinking, because neither debate nor discussion challenges or tests underlying assumptions. Discussion and debate are most useful as focused testing techniques for the specific ideas that are generated as a result of the dialogue process. Discussion and debate can serve to highlight and challenge gaps generated by dialogue that need to be addressed. They can be useful means of directing and guiding strategy conversations toward dialogue.

Discussion and debate, when applied to conflicting frames of reference, depend on data. When we hold conflicting frames, we pay attention to different facts and make different meaning of the data we notice. It is not through debate or discussion (which use mechanical, sequential learning for problem solving) that we convert situational discrepancies into well-formed strategic perspectives; rather, it is through shattering our existing frames and reframing through dialogue that strategic problem solving becomes beneficial. Dialogue within the deeper domain of learning is required when there is conflict.

Dialogue

Before proceeding further, we should take a moment to look at what dialogue is and what it is not. Originating from Greek roots, the word *dialogue* consists of two parts, *dia* and *logos*, or "meaning flowing through."[1] It is not between people arguing or chatting, hoping to defend their positions against one another. Rather, it is between and among people. Dialogue is conscious and deliberate and requires discipline and practice.

In differentiating debate and discussion from dialogue, William Isaacs, former director of the Dialogue Project at MIT's Organizational Learning Center, notes:

> *Dialogue seeks to have people learn how to think together — not just in the sense of analyzing a shared problem, but in the sense of surfacing fundamental assumptions and gaining insight into why they arise. Dialogue can thus produce an environment where people are consciously participating in the creation of shared meaning.*[2]

Strategy making is a high-stakes endeavor occurring in a very unpredictable and highly competitive environment. I find it is extremely difficult to get gangbuster executives to slow down long enough to engage in critical dialogue; but, ultimately, it allows them to speed up and get ahead. This paradox is exactly what we need to acknowledge in order to learn to think strategically.

> *Dialogue acknowledges that each person, no matter how brilliant or able, still sees the world from a particular perspective and that there are other credible and legitimate perspectives that can inform that view.*

In an article for The Center for Creative Leadership publication, N. M. Dixon explains the importance of the relationship in a dialogue and the idea that through the interaction, people acknowledge the entirety, not just the utility, of others."[3] Dialogue is a unique kind of communication in which listening and learning take precedence over talking and persuading. It requires the suspension of criticism and opinion and, instead, promotes an exploration of issues and problems. Dialogue promotes collective and collaborative thinking through a balance of inquiry, listening, reflecting, and talking.

An important point to highlight, particularly within an ego-driven high-pressure strategy environment, is that dialogue acknowledges that each person, no matter how brilliant or able, still sees the world from a particular perspective and that there are other credible and legitimate perspectives that can inform that view. As I have mentioned, for most executives, critical dialogue is not part of their experience, so there are skills to develop on a fundamental level. Such practice takes time and commitment. But once executives see it, hear it, do it, and reflect on critical dialogue, the quality of their contribution to the strategy process speaks for itself.

Discussion

The roots of the word *discussion* come from the Latin *discussus*, meaning "to investigate by reasoning or argument."[4] This also implies a linear progression to a sequential end. Discussion, as differentiated from dialogue and debate, focuses on problem solving; like debate, it uses convergent thinking. Discussions generally do not have the intent of exploring or altering underlying patterns of meaning, and they are generally used most effectively for analysis that is primarily quantitative and conclusive. With both discussion and debate, we strive to articulate our position with persuasion and argument.

Debate

By contrast, the word *debate* has Latin origins of *de* and *battuere*, which mean "to beat." It is defined in the dictionary as "a contention by words or arguments; a regulated discussion of a proposition between two matched sides."[5] Debate can constructively be used in the strategic thinking process to move toward a decision. It is a good way to identify weak spots in our thinking and a good way to identify baseline assumptions that need to be challenged about company values and competencies. Prior to or after debate, it is important to use critical dialogue to sift through the data, validate them, and test for inclusive and broad perspectives. By engaging in dialogue prior to debate, the quality of debate can be enhanced. Participating in dialogue after a debate can further challenge and test assumptions highlighted during the debate.

Technique	Definition	Direction	Graphic Representation
Dialogue	To explore and search. Share and grow by listening and learning from different perspectives. Create individual and collective meaning through expression and empathetic listening. Suspend opinions. Inquiry and disclosure. Partner is an equal to be understood.	Divergent Emerging proposition Nonlinear process	
Discussion	To establish or fix. Find a solution to a problem. Investigate and examine. Present and convince in detail a predetermined meaning. Give answers and explanations according to a predetermined agenda or position. Aim is single agreement or conclusion. Partner is an equal to be convinced.	Convergent Push–pull proposition Linear process	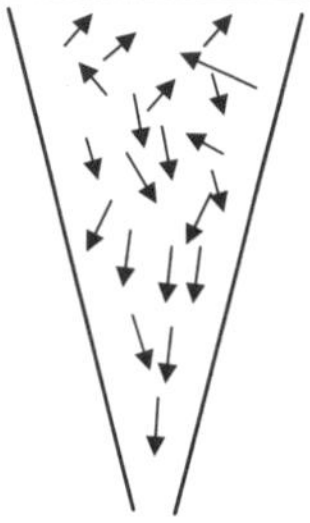
Debate	To defend or argue. Win by persuading opponent. Contention by argument. Convictions already held. Judgmental, competitive, and combative. Partner is a rival to be defeated.	Convergent Win–lose proposition Linear process	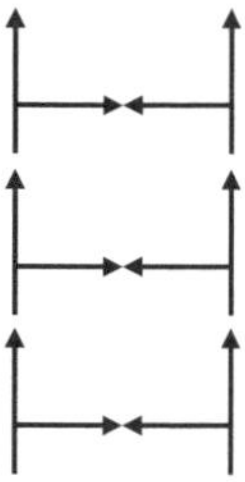

FIGURE 12.1 Dialogue, Discussion, and Debate: Intent of Three Communicative Learning Techniques.

Dialogue, discussion, and debate can each serve as a support and a source for the other within the strategic thinking process (see Figure 12.1). There is no "correct" linear progression or sequence *per se* of when to engage in dialogue, discussion, or debate in the real life of strategic thinking. What is important is to have the skills and versatility to participate in all three (dialogue, discussion, debate) and to know which one is most appropriate and constructive at any point in the strategy process.

The global head of engineering for a medical equipment company offered the metaphor of a water faucet as an image to assess which of these three communication techniques (dialogue, discussion, debate) is needed during the strategic thinking process. He claims the image helps him to keep track of where he and his global team are at any given time. It's a fun image, and it works! Using this metaphor, if we want to expand our thinking and need a rush of ideas or divergent thinking, then we need to "open the faucet" and practice dialogue. On the other hand, if we have thoroughly explored ideas, listened, tested opinions, and invited contrary positions and have a wide range of people involved, then it may be time to gradually converge and "close the faucet" by defining a problem vis à vis discussion. In order eventually to make a decision and draw conclusions, we may want to use debate to "turn off" the faucet and stop the flow.

Dialogue encourages win–win scenarios and does not try to convince or convert others. Rather, the emphasis is on a cycle of asking good questions and focused listening. The role of dialogue in learning to think strategically is to pose questions rather than supply answers and to emphasize the creation of shared meaning rather than imposing or pushing the meaning of any one partner. Dialogue is divergent by its nature; therefore it includes an inherent quality of uncertainty and change. It supports the learning process by enabling us to see things more clearly and truly.

Three Factors of a Good Strategic Thinking Dialogue

I am amused by the reactions of executives with whom I work when they hear the word *dialogue* within the context of strategic thinking: They cringe and roll their eyes, certain that dialogue will be detrimental to the strategic thinking process. They fear an endless spewing of pointless garble, or they are reticent to open a can of worms they may be unable to contain or control. I find that executives are often afraid that the dialogue process may not contribute to the content or enrich the strategic thinking process. A good dialogue is quite different; it is informed, risky and critical. Isaacs notes, "Dialogue is a discipline of collective thinking and inquiry, a process for transforming the quality of conversation and, in particular, the thinking that lies beneath it."[6]

A good strategic thinking dialogue is informed, risky, and critical.

Speaking, listening, and reflecting are three parts of a good strategy dialogue. Each can be the particular focus of skill development, yet the three are inseparable in practicing good dialogue. Some degree of trial and error occurs through the use of dialogue as we react to others' feedback on our recent or past actions and decisions. I find that reflection in action frequently occurs as executives respond to counter questions and criticisms and as they experience the dynamics of a verbal and intellectual joust — a test of opposing wills. They are suddenly taken aback, either by hearing themselves say something or by the unexpected response of a listener.

Among the executives interviewed, dialogue metamorphosed into conscious habit through practice. They developed a routine of testing and validating their assumptions against their prior successful life experiences, which included various forms of dialogue with a wide variety of people. These strategists eagerly anticipated and incorporated a rigorous dialogue and recognized it as an intentional learning method. Their comments indicated that challenge, often encountered through the use of dialogue, was an important facilitator for learning to think strategically.

For example, the Hong Kong executive recommended that aspiring strategists

> talk to many people and read everything, and insist that others ask you questions. We must think about what we don't know. I think that I talk to so many different people and bring our different ideas and opinions together — and that's very good. Sometimes maybe it looks like we spend a lot of time talking about things that are not related to economics or technology, but everything is connected when you're trying to put together a big puzzle — so why not? It's the most helpful thing.

One of the American technology company executives said he thrives on

> smart people to talk to and bounce ideas off of. We have a lot of really smart people here — and egos are in check. And we all are really focused and want to make things work, so it's good. That's a good learning space — where ideas are tossed around and you can try things — and then toss them around some more.

In starting to practice dialogue about strategic issues, I find it useful as a means of testing information that is known or understood to incorporate a six-round habit of asking the following questions: (1) What else? (2) Why else? (3) Who else? (4) Where else? (5) When else? (6) How else? It generally takes at least six rounds of all six questions before executives start to hit on something—that something being beliefs, assumptions, or new creative thoughts and an understanding and appreciation for the possibility of quite different perspectives and assumptions. With practice, this simple drill becomes a thinking habit leading to reflection. Eventually it contributes to generating meaningful strategic dialogue.

> *If we are to learn strategic thinking, we must be able to take part in dialogue, and we must make strategy to some degree in order truly to participate in the dialogue.*

Dialogue is a critical part of the deeper domain of learning, and it requires commitment and practice to master to any extent. For those responsible for facilitating strategic thinking, bear in mind that if we are to learn strategic thinking, we must be able to take part in dialogue, and we must make strategy to some degree in order truly to participate in the dialogue. Regardless of how awkwardly or mechanically we carry out these initial dialogues, we must begin doing so in order to learn what it feels like and to experience the changes they bring to strategic decision making. We learn the meaning of the actions by performing them, just as we practice riding a bicycle, skiing, or driving a car. Dialogue is the same.

In order for strategists to begin to see the collective patterns of their dialogues, it is important to take some time after meetings to pay attention and reflect on the dialogue or the discussion or the debate. This is where reviewing records or notes can provide data to identify emerging or entrenched patterns of exclusion, limited breadth, or premature decisions.

Good Strategy Dialogue Is Informed

Good dialogue is informed, in the sense that the partners have substantive knowledge and engage from a position of curiosity about wanting to understand the other person(s). Starting with intent, an informed strategy dialogue's purpose is to stretch the parameters of current thinking, deepen our knowledge base, introduce new data, expand information and ideas, and allow us to listen in different ways. Engaging in this kind of dialogue can lead us to new possibilities if practiced with regularity and in a disciplined and trusting manner.

The human ability to convert data into information should drive the data-gathering effort in the strategic dialogue process, not the reverse.

Prior to having a meaningful dialogue we need to have some degree of substantial instrumental learning. In other words, we need to know what we are talking about. The surface, or surf, domain of learning is generally how we get a broad range of data and information. We analyze according to various models in order to have valid information as part of an informed dialogue. This is what allows us to enter a dialogue with something other than our untested feelings; it gives us data and information to bring something to the table to transform into shared knowledge and new meaning. As we see in Figure 12.2, data are used to inform good dialogue and dialogue interprets the data.

The unparalled ability that exists to gather data today is extremely seductive. Unfortunately, the focus is all too often on more data rather than on good data. The task of filtering, filing, cross-referencing, and categorizing data can easily take on a life of its own. Converting all of these data into information requires reasoning, interpretation, and judgment—all human mental functions that are slower processes than those used by technology. Therefore, our ability to generate vast amounts of data has far surpassed our ability to convert it into meaningful information. The human ability to convert data into information should drive the data-gathering effort in the strategic dialogue process, not the reverse.

Dialogue partners must agree that a dialogue will emerge and go places that a discussion or debate would not, because dialogue is divergent. There is always an element of surprise and uncertainty in a good dialogue.

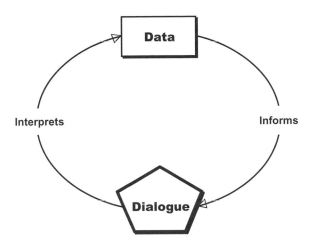

FIGURE 12.2   The Data–Dialogue Cycle.

An informed dialogue is not about data dumping. An informed dialogue revolves around three issues. First of all, we must deal with the substantive problems of the task. We must describe in whatever way is available to us — questioning or explaining — the problem as we see it. Second, we must keep our descriptions and examples particular. Descriptions must be linked to the immediate questions, confusions, difficulties, or potentials. And third, dialogue partners must agree that a dialogue will emerge and go places that a discussion or debate would not, because dialogue is divergent. There is always an element of surprise and uncertainty in a good dialogue. For some this is exciting and fascinating; for others it is intimidating and dreadful.

Good Strategy Dialogue Is Risky

A good strategy dialogue is also risky, because it requires challenging and testing the underlying assumptions and beliefs of our information and thinking. In strategy, such a dialogue exposes our flaws in thinking and can touch raw nerves that are deeply embedded in our thinking process. It requires us to be vulnerable about what we tout and test as our various "truths" of matters. The questions are difficult to ask and equally difficult to answer.

Without this testing of data and information, we run the danger of having not a constructive dialogue, but meaningless talk that simply perpetuates our current frames of reference. We end up using our communication efforts to defend untested information and possibly to sever relationships. This does little to further strategic thinking. It keeps us locked in the same frameworks and only allows us to persuade, convince, pressure, or coerce others to accept our frameworks—a trap that defeats the very aim of learning to think strategically.

The affective dimension of cognition rears its head when we take the risk of engaging in dialogue. I find that apprehension and frustration are two common responses of executives who engage in strategy dialogue early on. The dialogue process includes a large learning component, which creates a state of imbalance. This causes a natural feeling of uncertainty, a lack of control and vulnerability. In contrast, discussion and debate are convergent by nature, and there is some comfort in knowing that an endpoint exists. But dialogue is divergent and requires creating a shared meaning. This requires figuring out a rhythm with our dialogue partner(s), who may have a different pace of reflecting and a different style of expressing and responding. The endpoint is unpredictable.

*Meaningful strategy dialogue requires
honesty and authenticity.*

In an effort to reduce the risk and enhance our ability to speak, listen, and reflect optimally, we need to have confidence to speak, which can be greatly enhanced by experience and practice. We also need to have something specific and valid to say, and we need to trust the immediate and greater environment. Retribution, ridicule, interruptions, and having ideas nipped or robbed can all be inhibitors to meaningful dialogue, as can an environment that does not reward collaboration. Furthermore, we need to trust the intention and skills of the partners with whom we are in dialogue. Meaningful strategy dialogue requires honesty and authenticity. Language and articulation sometimes interfere, but these are minor issues if the intent of the dialogue is genuine and true.

A Polish executive explained:

It's necessary to have other people, especially people who are younger or from a different industry, to talk to and get their ideas and opinions. And we must talk to each other often—but I don't mean in an organized way necessarily—you know, I think it makes most people uncomfortable and they cannot think in a good way if it is too

organized. That's why coffee shops will never be out of fashion (laughter)
— they are necessary for good business! It is the only place people really
think! (more laughter)

Actively seeking out critical dialogue with colleagues, other professionals, and strangers is risky but essential to broadening our perspective, stimulating our imagination, identifying factors we can and cannot control, and increasing the level and quality of thinking—in order to create a winning strategy.

Good Strategy Dialogue Is Critical

The purpose of critical dialogue is to bring the strategy partners to a juncture in thinking and acting. A critical dialogue is not intended for the purpose of attacking or beating the opponent, as in debate, or for the purpose of convincing, as with discussion. Nor is it to criticize or belittle. The element of listening is closely tied to thinking and speaking and is held to a higher level than talking or persuading. Inquiry is used to probe and explore assumptions and beliefs.

A critical dialogue involves an honest exchange of probes as a means to reflection, and it involves variant perspectives on the dialogue topic at hand. Reflecting and responding to questions enables dialogue partners to become aware of inconsistencies as well as consistencies in their ideas and opinions. The process of critical dialogue causes us to think aloud, thereby creating clarity and insights not possible when our thoughts and feelings are contained internally.

A critical dialogue includes reflecting from time to time on our own decisions and actions. During strategy dialogues, executives routinely ask themselves, "What are my solutions and evaluations right now?" and "What do I habitually and spontaneously do in this situation?" and "Why?" I encourage executives to jot down their responses, which allows them to pause, suspend their judgments, and more accurately describe the actions they offer to others. Writing—even quick notes—can be a useful readiness exercise for reflecting because it allows us to acknowledge thoughts and feelings that free us to listen openly, suspend judgment, and explore. Writing down original thoughts and judgments makes them accessible and easy to retain or retrieve, but only after exploration. A purposeful critical dialogue requires some affective and cognitive readiness on the part of both parties, including an attitude of curiosity.

13

The Role of Inquiry in Critical Dialogue

Inquiry serves many purposes in supporting a good dialogue and in learning to think strategically. It forces us to think and enables us to clarify, to understand, and to seek answers. Questions also provide a springboard for generating new possibilities, ideas, and insights for strategic decisions. Additionally, inquiry acts as a basis for individual and organizational learning.

According to communications researcher William Isaacs, "The central purpose [of dialogue] is to establish a field of genuine meeting and inquiry —a setting in which people can allow a free flow of meaning and vigorous exploration of the collective background of their thought, their personal predispositions, the nature of their shared attention, and the rigid features of their individual and collective assumptions."[7]

Inquiry Supports Good Strategy Dialogue

Within a strategic thinking context, questions are an effective means of gathering information. Asking and responding to questions helps us to analyze a situation, broaden our perspective, and challenge our assumptions in order to strengthen strategic thinking. A Japanese financial executive forthrightly commented: (smiles) "You know very well, that I like to ask many questions! (laughter) So I have always tried to do my best, and for me that is to try many new things and watch other people and ask questions, many questions. Then I read and talk to people—especially people who are different from me, and then I ask new questions! (laughter)"

Interestingly, it is nearly impossible for any one person to dominate within a good dialogue, when everyone is expected to focus on questioning.

Inquiry is a particularly appropriate form of communication for learning to think strategically because there is no need for any dialogue partner to defer to another based on hierarchy or expertise. Everyone must be able to inquire of everyone else in order fully to benefit from the dialogue process. Interestingly, it is nearly impossible for any one person to dominate within a good dialogue when everyone is expected to focus on questioning. When inquiry is paired with reflection, the mind is encouraged to work. Questions require us to listen attentively, which in turn generates a need to reflect. This leads to subsequent questioning that requires more careful listening and reflection, and so a cycle is set into motion.

Critical inquiry is essential for probing deeper in an effort to understand patterns and predict strategic opportunities. In fact, inquiry is probably the easiest way to predict patterns and trends. When we become comfortable with a pattern, we often become complacent in assuming that it will remain static, so we fail to look at its potential for variation or innovation. Inquiry can help us project where a pattern or trend is headed.

It is essential to encourage inquiry if meaningful thinking is to occur. Reflection does not come easily for most. There must be space and time to step back and examine questions and responses that have challenged our basic assumptions and beliefs. Reflection involves more than recalling and dissecting. It involves thinking about and paying attention to feelings, making sense of and attempting to understand what supports an opinion, an idea, or a belief. Good questions are often the impetus to meaningful reflection.

In my practice I find that no two executives are the same with regard to time and space needed for reflection. Some require periods of several weeks or months away from the place, people, and the topic at hand in order to reflect. Others need to pull away mentally and retreat to a quiet shade tree or different room for only a short while and then reengage intermittently in dialogue.

Executives often comment that when they are responsible for asking good questions, it reduces the pressure of solving the strategy problem because they trust the process and know it ultimately produces better solutions. They feel less defensive and are able to think more openly because the search for answers becomes an exploration of ideas and generation of alternatives that is shared by all the dialogue partners. This is one of the amazing things about inquiry.

Inquiry builds on the knowledge that partners bring into a dialogue group; at the same time it constructs new knowledge, fosters learning, and develops shared meaning. By beginning with questioning rather than using past knowledge as the starting point, partners can assess whether the current available information and knowledge is sufficient and relevant to the situation. Questions enable us to remove the layers around the problem and uncover the core issues necessary to discover the solution.

Isaacs points out:

> *Unlike most forms of inquiry, the inquiry in dialogue is one that places primacy on the whole. Dialogue's aim is to take into account the impact one speaker has on the overall system, giving consideration to the timing of comments, their relative strength, their sequence, and their meaning to others. Dialogue seeks to unveil the ways in which collective patterns of thinking unfold — both as conditioned, mechanistic reflexes, and potentially as fluid, dynamically creative exchanges.*[8]

An American technology executive explained his appreciation of strategy dialogue:

> *We kind of realized that we'd never have all the answers to all our questions. You know how it is — once you find one answer, you suddenly have a thousand more questions. (talks faster, raises voice, gestures with hands on tabletop) At some point you just realize its part of the process.*
>
> *And it's kind of a gamble. You never know exactly which questions you need to pay attention to at that moment. I don't want to say it's hit or miss, but you do the best you can. You read everything, you look at what other people are doing all over the world — and you plug in every imaginable number. (leans forward, moves toward researcher) You spot trends across all kinds of industries — and then I think there's an element of luck. I don't know, it's probably just me, but at some point you just have to put it [strategy] into orbit.*

Good Dialogue Questions

As any strategist knows, asking the right questions is not easy, especially when grappling with a serious or complex problem. The ability to ask good questions in a strategy environment of risk, constant change, confusion, and uncertainty is, however, a competitive advantage. In these circumstances a "right" answer very often does not exist, only an answer that is "good enough until the next change." Experience, confidence, and an ability to ask good questions is conducive to and supportive of adaptive and competitive strategy.

A quick reminder that the beginning of an answer most often lies in the questions we ask. A focus on the best kind of questions rather than on the right answers is important. But for some this requires a leap of faith. Asking good questions eventually leads us to the best answer. The better the questions, the better the solutions will be, as well as the learning. Likewise, the deeper the reflection, the greater the individual learning. Attentive listening followed by open questions will constructively move dialogue partners to deeper thinking and eventually to problem solving and decision making.

Questions are more powerful than statements when attempting to solve difficult strategy problems.

So what makes a good question? There is no single answer to this question. Yet there are several key characteristics of good questions. Good questions take courage to ask and cause us to:

Stretch
Squirm
Unveil a true perspective or belief
Challenge assumptions that prevent us from taking a new/different action
Reflect deeply
Become more insightful
Take action

Furthermore, good questions are:

Offered with a caring and sharing intent
Presented as selfless and not asked to "show off" the knowledge or wit of
    the questioner
Asked with courage and are difficult to answer

Supported with good listening
Followed through with time for reflection and responses

Often, the most obvious way to start a good question is to build on a previous question. Another way is to ask a question based on the response that was just given. Selecting from the who-what-when-where-why-how is also good for starters. Another option is to ask a question from an opposing point of view or ask "Why not?" or "How else?" Draw questions from both the surf and dive domains of learning. But remember that dive-level questions, those that test why, are bound to cause stretching, squirming, and deeper reflection and are more likely to uncover a true belief. It is worth remembering that questions are more powerful than statements when attempting to solve difficult strategy problems.

Analogies

Analogies are another useful and very common way that successful strategists talk about how they learn to think strategically. An analogy begins as just a simple story or situation. It becomes an analogy only when it is compared to something else. Analogies do not have to be long or complicated; a simple action may suffice. In order for an analogy to be of any use it must be familiar, there must be something happening or a particular process occurring, or there must be a special kind of relationship to the observer.

Analogies are vehicles for relationships and processes. These relationships and processes are embodied in actual objects, but the relationship and processes can be generalized to other situations. This can be expressed directly in terms of the actual objects involved, or it can be expressed in terms of the process involved.

Analogies are useful to provide thought movement. The problem under consideration is related to the analogy, and then the analogy is developed along its own lines. We can translate the problem into an analogy and then further develop the analogy. At the end we translate back and see what might have happened to the original problem. Convoluted as this may sound in writing, it is interesting that all of the executives I interviewed made extensive use of analogies to describe how they learned to think strategically. I continue to be fascinated as I listen to the animated analogies that passionate strategists from various countries share with delight—storytelling in all its grandeur. I find it a pity that that so few executives and managers allow themselves to play with the language and imagery of analogies, an ability that is undeniably relevant and constructive for learning to think strategically.

Seven Strategy Dimensions for Critical Dialogue

There are seven dimensions of strategy that I consider necessary for successful strategic thinking. If we genuinely consider "human capital" as a valuable asset, then these dimensions are imperative to strategic thinking. Most often, we limit our strategy thinking to discussions and debate of data, analysis, and metrics drawn primarily from the finance dimension, with other dimensions randomly appearing as time allows. I suggest bringing data and diverse perspectives from all seven dimensions to the table initially to engage in dialogue and postponing the discussion and debate of the dimensions until somewhat later in the strategic thinking process.

The current and potential influence and consequences of all of these dimensions should be included at every stage of the strategic dialogue because they are critically important to strategy success and offer yet another way of thinking about strategy. Figure 13.1 illustrates the dimensions.

Outer Ring:

- Finance (economics, budget, profit/loss, investment)
- Risk assessment (financial security, physical security, intellectual property)
- Technology (hardware, software, integration)
- Integrity (authenticity, truth, honesty)

Inner Ring:

- Business value (stakeholder, customers, products, services, expansion, improvement)
- Individual development (learning as investment, "asset development," satisfaction, knowledge/thinking/creativity capability)
- Social contribution (environment, human rights, arts, health, politics, community development)

The four dimensions in the outer ring of Figure 13.1 (finance, technology, integrity, risk assessment) influence what, how, and why we think and believe as we do about the three dimensions on the inner ring (individual development, business value, social contribution). Critical questions from inside and

FIGURE 13.1 Seven Strategic Thinking Dimensions.

outside the organization should essentially center around: How will this decision help or hinder the strategic intent and the corporate values? What impact will this (financial/technology/risk assessment/integrity) decision have on individual development? business value? social contribution? Who might see this very differently? Why? Who gains and who loses from this decision? By how much and for how long? Who cares? and Why?

The underlying assumptions and beliefs about these dimensions, and their impact and relation to one another, need to be challenged on an individual and corporate level. When we include and rigorously test all of them at every stage, the resulting strategy will support human capital development, long-term thinking, and a broader perspective and also align strategy with espoused values and intent.

> *If we genuinely consider "human capital"*
> *as a valuable asset, these dimensions are*
> *imperative to strategic thinking.*

By inviting contrarian opinions and provocative ideas on each of the seven dimensions, executives can be encouraged to critically reflect, to challenge, and to refine their strategy decisions so that they can move toward becoming more adaptive, innovative, and competitive.

Structuring strategy dialogue according to these seven dimensions highlights potential risks, offers new perspectives, and invites new data immediately. As a result, I find that strategic priorities are often shuffled, new connections are forged, and impact and consequences can be disclosed in the initial thinking stage rather than in the implementation stage of strategy.

Nothing fundamentally unique is required to use these dimensions in constructing a strategy dialogue. Framing the conventional strategy categories (shareholders, products, services, customers, employees, and industry sector) within these seven dimensions simply, but not easily, expands the dialogue by bringing in new players, posing additional questions, and connecting the data differently. Various analytical models and metrics can be brought in to support and challenge each dimension, which further enriches the dialogue.

The interplay and infinite connections between and among these dimensions serve to test, check, balance, build, refine, and strengthen the overall strategy thinking process. Among the executives with whom I work, I find that when including these seven dimensions as part of the strategy thinking process, issues of integrity, ethics, core competencies, values, and hidden agendas tend to enter the conversations much earlier and more candidly. Incongruency, inconsistency, and misalignment also become more visible. It makes sense that exposing discrepancies through initial dialogue brings a sense of ethics and sustainability into the strategy thinking process. Aside from Selznick in 1957, most design school theorists do not focus a great deal of attention on values and ethics, at least not explicitly. Values and ethics were most often offered as an afterthought.

Strategy dialogue that is structured around these seven dimensions allows for nonlinear, a-rational, affective, and innovative thinking in addition to linear, logical, rational, and cognitive thinking to be brought into the strategy process. Organizations need to think broadly and authentically when creating an innovative, renewable, and sustainable strategy.

Learning to Dialogue

The dialogue process lends itself well to informal learning. Dialogue can happen constructively anywhere and at any time. A young technology executive said, "I just draw on my own experience, and I've also tried to learn from others' [experience]. I guess I'm just curious, for better or worse (laughter), and it's so important to talk to a lot of people — learn from them this way. People are happy to tell you their experiences. Nobody taught me, I just learned things, you know . . . my life experiences were all I ever had."

More structured and formal approaches to facilitating dialogue can also be useful. In terms of structuring a strategic dialogue, there are several small details that I find helpful to ensuring that the critical dialogue process takes root. Care needs to be given to keeping a record of strategic dialogues that identify and track who has and has not been included on what issues on what date. This can take many forms. The important thing is to record and collect this information in a simple way that makes sense to everyone involved. Time needs to be allocated to reflect collectively on the dialogues themselves. What insights did the dialogue generate? In which areas should the partners seek more knowledge, and where is further fact finding necessary? Why were certain ideas abandoned for others? Was participation sufficiently broad?

An excellent process to incorporate in strategy meetings as a means to keeping track of dialogue and uncovering surprise is the *after-action review* (AAR),[9] a process developed by the U.S. Army to identify lessons learned. This technique can be useful after a major decision has been taken, after a surprise outcome has been caused by our action, or as a routine meeting process. While the AAR is based primarily on the surface domain of learning, it offers room to move into the deeper learning domain.

An AAR is conducted immediately after a decision or a major action is taken and generally includes at least three leadership levels and others who were involved in the action. A trained facilitator monitors the dialogue process to ensure that the review is honest and candid and that members are mutually respected monitors. It is not an open-ended brainstorming session, but a straightforward process of experiential learning structured around five questions:

1. What was the intent?
   What was the strategy at the time the action began? What was the desired outcome? How was the strategy expected to be achieved?
2. What actually happened?
   What were the actual events as they occurred within a specific timeframe? Who did what? Where? How? When? Reactions? Blame is not ascribed, but rather a factual chronology is collaboratively pieced together.
3. Why did it happen?
   This is the diagnostic portion. Commentary is offered about possible reasons that the specific outcome was not the intended strategic intent or about reasons for success.

4. How can we do better? What was learned?
5. What do we do now?

Lessons learned from the events of each action are identified to enable others in similar situations to carry out actions that will more closely achieve the strategic intent. I find AAR is an effective, structured way to get strategists to capture the learning from their experiences.

Dialogues often start between two people, though they can be and often are expanded to incorporate other partners, including experts and outsiders. Prior to a strategy meeting and again at the beginning of the meeting, all partners need to be explicitly informed as to the talk mode that will be used. A quick e-mail or mention such as "We'll be using dialogue for part A and debate for part B" should suffice. It is equally important that all partners consciously develop skills and confidence to participate in dialogue, discussion, and debate. Strategy meetings are like preparing for a triathlon. Explicitly stating expectations and systematically preparing allows participants to do their best. Triathletes need to know that the first part requires running, the second part requires swimming, the third part is cycling, and so on. Otherwise, a well-intentioned strategy meeting can end up feeling like a sumo wrestling match or a free-for-all.

Good dialogue requires that all partners take responsibility for ensuring that the other(s) have what they need to fully express their perceptions, perspectives, ideas, feelings, and thoughts. More than anything, this requires an attitude of sincere interest and curiosity and disciplined restraint to suspend judgment in order to listen. Being curious and open to learning something new can guide our listening, our questioning, and our speaking. Also, the successful strategists I interviewed reported that having an expectation to learn is critical, for this becomes a self-fulfilling prophecy. When we enter a strategy dialogue expecting to learn, we most likely will learn something.

Most often we need to expand our understanding or our definition of learning to benefit from critical dialogue. We may learn new information or information from a different perspective. Or we may learn from having our long-held belief attacked or shattered; or we may be jolted into questioning the intensity of an idea we hold simply by hearing ourselves talk and by saying it aloud. The very act of speaking an incomplete thought aloud can be a new learning. Another learning may be the sheer exhilaration of being questioned —and listened to. Dialogue can be an excellent technique for clarifying thoughts, testing convictions, and building confidence.

Surrounding ourselves with people who can and will challenge, test, and engage in meaningful critical dialogue is easier said than done. We tend to like people who reinforce our perspectives and echo our opinions. I cannot count the number of "monkey-say-monkey-do" strategy meetings I have observed. The bearers of bad news are thrown in the den with those who persistently question the way things are done. Anyone who attempts to challenge an existing frame is blackballed. The strategic result is anything but innovative, adaptive, or competitive. When we learn to challenge and test underlying strategy assumptions and basic beliefs, the value of dialogue can be tremendous to strengthening strategic decisions. Coaches can be beneficial to facilitating the introduction of dialogue into meetings until the practice becomes a habit.

In order to develop strategic thinkers, good dialogues initiated and modeled by senior leaders are required. Connections must be made with diverse knowledge sources both inside and outside the company, and a vast range of professional relationships must be made and rewarded. These relationships must then be given adequate attention to support meaningful dialogue and challenge. Creating a culture where learning is valued and knowledge is shared and dialogue is practiced is among the most challenging issues facing conscientious executives and those responsible for supporting strategic thinking.

Dialogue in the Three-Stage Informal Learning Process of Strategic Thinking

Dialogue is important in all three informal learning stages: preparation, experience, and reevaluation. As mentioned in Part III, the three stages of the informal learning process are not distinct from one another, but, rather, iterative in nature. This makes it challenging to discern one stage from the next, for we tend to vacillate between the preparation, experience, and reevaluation stages, continuously gathering information and engaging in dialogue, discussion, and debate as a means of testing our thinking. We also bounce between the domains of learning (surf and dive) by varying the kinds of questions we ask from one domain to another.

Preparation Stage

Dialogue within the preparation stage guarantees that the data and information are substantiated and validated. In the preparation stage of learning, dialogue serves as a means of information gathering as we seem to consciously seek out different opinions, different data, ideas, and new interpretations of regulations, procedures, and information. Dialogue in this stage of strategic thinking can also greatly enrich the quality of analysis by testing the intent of the source and relevance of data and information.

Experience Stage

We tend to vacillate between the preparation and experience stages and use dialogue in both stages. In the experience stage, dialogue serves as a means of testing and challenging. This is regarded as a critical part of learning from experience and was commonly described in the executive interviews with words such as *exciting, intellectually stimulating,* and *invigorating.* Dialogue with total strangers from diverse age, industry, cultural, and education backgrounds can test our ideas and thinking and reveal underlying assumptions. In the experience stage, dialogue also serves to explore different perspectives, test assumptions and underlying opinions, and challenge ideas. It also serves to stimulate our imagination.

As one of the financial executives indicated:

> *I'd say I'm heavily influenced and dependent on listening to many different people. I look to economists, forecasters, politicians, journalists, experts in many fields, let's see — associates sometimes (laughter), friends, books, even neighbors, my children, and strangers — and lots of other people I talk to. I'm constantly talking to people in all kinds of fields to see what they know and what they're thinking — this is so important. You can't just rely on the experts. Everybody sees something different, and it all needs to be considered.*

A Chinese executive explained, "We spend a lot of time hanging out, talking about things. We just spend a lot of time talking about different possibilities, we draw pictures, tell 'what if' stories. This probably doesn't sound too organized (laughter); it isn't! But it's fun, a good time. You just keep repeating it."

Dialogue in the experience stage is a critical part of learning in action and learning on action, both of which are essential for learning to think strategically. The difference between learning in action and learning on action is largely related to tense: In action is present tense, and on action is past tense. We learn in action and on action through critical dialogue with our experiences, colleagues, professional associates, casual acquaintances, and strangers in both work and nonwork places.

The German manufacturing executive described what happens when she was involved in thinking strategically:

Every few months we seem to have some debates—you might even call them arguments about what's happening in the industry or with economy trends. And then we discuss different scenarios about what it may mean for us. Do we need to change something? Do we need to stop doing something? And I always calculate from a financial perspective— it's my job, and he [CEO] usually disagrees. (laughter) He [the CEO] likes to disagree, and so do I, because it makes you think of other questions . . . and in a different way And then he [CEO] talks to other people. I do the same thing. And then we sit down and talk again. And this is how it happens, over and over.

When asked what the advantage of this kind of dialogue and disagreement pattern was, she replied:

Oh, I think it's the most important reason our company is so successful! And he [CEO] is very successful and well respected in the industry. It's just his ways are a little different from the ordinary, usual theory. I've learned so much from him—he thinks that he needs to ask questions to get clear in his own mind—so he talks to everybody he can, not just in textiles or manufacturing. He likes to debate because he never believes anything anybody tells him; so he always says that debate is a way to test and purify ideas. (laughter)

*   So you can imagine, it's a very good way to make high-level thinking—which I think is important to making good strategy. I suppose this doesn't make sense as the way I explain it, but it's much better than a model with some artificial, detailed rationale and charts. (laughter)*

Elements of dialogue, critical reflection, inquiry, and challenge are a constant learning theme within the experience stage.

Reevaluation Stage
In the reevaluation stage of learning, dialogue serves as a means of critical reflection and assessment. The very nature of recalling an experience that is no longer current and verbally articulating the experience to another moves us into the stage of reevaluation. In this stage of informal learning we use dialogue to test and to challenge comprehensive frameworks and to retest and refine belief systems and assumptions. Dialogue is used deliberately to escalate thinking and refine ideas in order to continue to move the decision-

making process forward. Strategic thinking is dependent on dialogue to uncover assumptions and is directed away from producing results and toward a sustainable process of critical questioning and reflection.

Dialogue is a versatile, dynamic, and trustworthy process that can be enormously beneficial in a global strategy-making environment where many things are uncertain, constantly changing, and beyond control. Serious strategists know they must take the time and discipline to develop the habit of engaging in critical dialogue in order to create competitive and new possibilities from situational discrepancies into well-formed strategic perspectives. Critical dialogue is fundamental to the cognitive and creative process that is essential for learning to think strategically.

VI

WHY DO WE LEARN STRATEGIC THINKING THIS WAY?

We Just "Know": Intuition as an Outgrowth of Experience

The intuitive mind is a sacred gift and the rational mind is a faithful servant. We have created a society that honors the servant and has forgotten the gift.

Albert Einstein (1879–1955), scientist and Nobel prize winner

14

Intuition as a Must-Have for Learning to Think Strategically

Anton is a hedge fund whiz. At just 25 years of age he has such a feel for numbers that big names from all over the financial world want to run their ideas by him. If they have Anton's nod, they move forward with a plan. In spite of enormous amounts of data, he knows what to focus on. He can sift and filter volumes of information and figure out what is relevant, highlight key points, and prioritize in minutes. Although he dropped out of graduate school, he had lots of experience analyzing numbers while helping his dad and uncle run a small investment business and as a trader for two years. He has learned to trust his gut to such a high degree that he can listen to analytic reports and in fifteen to thirty minutes "know" his decision. No need for detailed explanations. His experience allows him to see what he needs, interpret, and decide in a flash. This makes Anton seem almost supernatural to his colleagues. He relies on his judgment, and everyone else envies it. His bets are on and he rarely loses.

With strategy, everything hinges on decision making. Since we are often neither fully aware of how our experience influences our ability to learn to think strategically nor fully aware of how we learn informally, a discussion of the role intuition plays in strategic decision making is a necessary means of making the connection.

Part VI is divided into four chapters. Chapter 14 focuses on tacit knowledge and how intuition is an imperative for strategic decision making. Chapter 15 looks at the strong influence of intuition on pattern recognition and framing and the effect it has on strategic decision making. Chapter 16 considers the role of critical reflective processes in shattering frames of reference. And Chapter 17 discusses reframing.

There are two premises underlying this part on intuition. The first is that intuition guides strategic thinking, though this runs counter to what traditional strategy development approaches teach. And second, intuition and analysis are complementary to the strategic thinking process, which is similar to the more expansive notion of strategy making offered by the ancient Greeks.

In my practice I often notice that merely uttering the word *intuition* can make strategic planners grimace and unseasoned strategists squirm, for the term seems to conjure images of a loosey-goosey chase or some kind of navel gazing. But among successful strategic thinkers, intuition is a very familiar and comfortable concept, though sometimes an experienced concept without a name. Bringing intuition into the strategic thinking process is simply about paying attention to another way of knowing that can facilitate learning to think strategically. In my experience, it is actually much less intriguing and far less frightening than it sounds.

Intuition is a natural outgrowth of experience and a vital component for learning to think strategically. Intuition researcher Gary Klein notes, in *The Power of Intuition*, "The evidence is growing that those who do not or cannot trust their intuitions are less effective decision makers, and that as long as they reject their intuitions, they are destined to remain less effective."[1]

There are several areas of strategic thinking that are particularly relevant to intuition. I am advocating the type of *deliberative rationality* that Bert and Stuart Dreyfus described in their book *Mind Over Machine*: "The . . . split between the mystical and the analytic will not do . . . for neither pole of that often misleading dualism names the ordinary, nonmystical intuition that we believe is the core of human intelligence and skill. . . . Analysis and intuition work together in the human mind."[2]

Among the executives with whom I work on strategic thinking, I have found that although intuition is the driver, analytic thinking is necessary for beginners learning a new skill, any new skill. The Dreyfuses contend that, analytic thinking is good for scrutinizing data and information for validity, reliability, etc. "It is also useful at the highest levels of expertise, where it can sharpen and clarify intuitive insight. . . . Detached deliberation and intuition need not be viewed as [opposite] alternatives, as is all too often [the case] in simplistic treatments."[3] In the strategic thinking process, they are very much complementary parts of the whole. This is just as the ancient Greeks defined strategy, not as competing parts, but as a whole.

I find corporate strategists are most often overwhelmed with strategic decision making, which involves constantly changing information, uncertainty, incomplete data, and things they cannot control. Most are constrained by some of their strategic actions or perspectives and need to be challenged in order to revise them. These strategic decision makers notice and think while they are in the process of managing complex and high-stakes situations — they notice subtle cues without realizing it. Decisions are made subconsciously before they even start to perform the analysis. What explains this, and how can this process be used to facilitate strategic thinking?

> *Our intuition is based on accumulated and*
> *compiled experiences, not on magic.*

Strategic thinking includes continuous decision making; therefore, learning to think strategically can be enhanced by understanding how our intuition effects our ability to make choices. Our intuition is based on accumulated and compiled experiences, not on magic. Solid intuition is like solid data — it is neutral and free of interpretation or evaluation.

In learning to think strategically, we should not blindly follow our intuition, because intuition can be unreliable and requires monitoring. Yet we should not suppress our intuition either, because it is essential to our decision making and cannot be replaced by analysis or procedures. We rely on intuition to make all kinds of judgments related to strategy. Thus, a real competitive option is to strengthen intuition so that it becomes more accurate and provides us with better insights.

A Japanese finance executive I interviewed insisted:

> *Thinking about strategy is not a "task" — it is about what you think and*
> *feel and believe and how you react . . . and don't try to separate your*
> *feelings from your thinking — I don't understand how that helps anyone*
> *because it is not possible to do. But many people try only to think*
> *[without feeling] when they make strategy. It's a mistake.*

As any strategist knows, there is a difference between an informed and uninformed gut feeling, or intuition. We want to avoid impulsive actions and make decisions based on informed intuition. Luckily, skillful intuitive decision making can be learned. Intuition skills can be acquired and expanded by building a richer experience base and putting the skills to better use. We are not born with good judgment skills, just as we are not born good skiers, skaters, or swimmers. Similarly, the kinds of know-how and judgments that successful seasoned strategists make also require tremendous energy and work. They have to build up an experience base that lets them accurately size up situations and know how to respond. The better we understand situations and the more expansive our experience base, the higher the level of our intuitive skills.

Know-How: Our Tacit Knowledge

The term *tacit knowledge* connotes knowing in action, or what is commonly called *know-how*. The tacit knowledge of a prima ballerina, for example, is embedded in and revealed by the way she glides imperceptibly across the stage — her knowing is in the action. A pro tennis player's tacit knowledge is in his serving to an opponent's weakness or automatically changing his pace.

Tacit knowledge is not about the know-how in the rules or detailed plans of the action that we entertain in the mind prior to action; it is a kind of knowing in the action. Tacit knowledge is not to be confused with either luck or some "gift." It comes from accumulated and acquired success experience, disciplined skills, knowledge, and extraordinary amounts of focused practice. The fact that tacit knowledge becomes spontaneous, like a sixth sense, deceptively makes it appear to happen easily. It seems simple, but it is anything but easy.

Although we sometimes think before acting or deciding, in much of the spontaneous decision making of skillful strategic thinking, we reveal a kind of knowing that does not stem from a prior intellectual operation. It comes from a tacit knowledge that we accumulate through successful repetition. Tacit knowing is partly intuitive and is triggered by our feelings and affective responses; it also draws from exceptional mastery of disciplined techniques that have become automated. Once we set aside the mental model of technical rationality — the linear scientific framework Western societies adopted in the late nineteenth century — there is nothing strange about the idea that a different and a very particular kind of knowing is inherent in intelligent action.

When a tennis pro has a "feel for the ball," it lets her repeat the exact same thing she did previously that proved successful. She is noticing, at the very least, that she has been doing something right, and her "feeling" allows her to do that something again. She uses a kind of reflection on her patterns of action and on the situations in which she is performing. She is reflecting on action and, in some cases, reflecting in action. Numerous theorists point out the limitations of technical rationality and explain how we think on our feet or just know what to do, based on our tacit knowledge and habits of acting.

Learning theorist Donald Schon notes:

We learn to execute such complex performances as walking, skipping, riding a bicycle, skiing without being able to give a verbal description even roughly adequate to our actual performance. Indeed, if we are asked to say how we do such things, we tend to give wrong answers, which, if we were to act according to them, would get us into trouble.[4]

When we go about the spontaneous, intuitive thinking of strategy in every-day life, we demonstrate our knowledge in a particular way. But when we try to describe it, we find ourselves at a loss. Our knowing is often tacit, implicit in our patterns of action and in our feel for the stuff with which we are dealing. Our knowing is in our action.

The role tacit knowledge plays in strategic thinking is often underestimated and ignored. In their book *Enabling Knowledge Creation*, Georg Von Krogh, Kazuo Ichijo, and Ikujiro Nonaka state, "In a business context, knowledge can be separated into two broad categories: unique knowledge, held exclusively by the firm, and public knowledge, held by several competitors."[5] What they refer to as *unique knowledge* is what this book calls *tacit knowledge*. *Public knowledge* is typically what is shared in strategy models, conference publications, research reports, textbooks, consulting manuals, and strategic training programs. Public knowledge is predominantly explicit social knowledge. It often represents general technical solutions that are readily available on the market.[6]

> *Every competent strategist can recognize groups of "normal" patterns associated with a specific market, peculiarities of a certain kind of organizational structure, or irregular patterns of data—for which he cannot give a reasonably accurate or complete description.*

Strategic thinking depends on tacit knowledge. Every competent strategist can recognize groups of "normal" patterns associated with a specific market, peculiarities of a certain kind of organizational structure, or irregular patterns of data—for which he cannot give a reasonably accurate or complete description. In the day-to-day operations, a strategist makes innumerable decisions but cannot state specific criteria, and a seasoned successful strategist demonstrates skills for which he cannot state the rules and procedures. Even when making conscious use of research-based theories and techniques, strategists are dependent on tacit recognitions, judgments, and skillful past experiences. In other words, a seasoned strategist operates automatically much of the time because of trusted intuition due to a vast repertoire of successful experience; but she also has the capacity to pause and critically reflect. Critical reflection is a part of a successful strategist's autopilot setting.

We need to become comfortable knowing that learning is sometimes elusive and complex and that it is only in retrospect and through critical reflection that we may recognize it as having occurred. Nevertheless, through experience, strategists can learn to trust the informal learning process. For tacit knowledge to be a strategic source of sustainable competitive advantage, it has to be valuable, difficult for competitors to imitate, and difficult to substitute.[7] While it is possible to learn from others' experiences, successful strategy cannot be imitated. As T. S. Elliot noted, "Talent imitates, genius steals."

15

Framing

So what role does intuition play in how we make strategic thinking decisions? It is what allows us to recognize patterns and frames that we use as part of strategic decision making. As noted in Chapter 11, a frame is a belief schema or an organized cognitive way of perceiving a complex set of behavioral patterns and decisions.

For example, take the problem of obesity among children in the most economically developed countries. A business executive may frame the issue as one of market potential for new lines of food and clothing. But an educator may frame it as a problem of learning deficits, behavioral disorders, and long-term development issues. A scientist may see the obesity problem and frame it as a population growth rate that has outstripped agricultural activity. A sociologist might well frame it as inadequate family and social structures. An economist may frame the problem in terms of insufficient purchasing power or the inequitable distribution of agricultural commodities. We frame problems according to our experience, or what we "know," and we proceed accordingly with decision making.

From a strategic thinking point of view, the most beneficial and straightforward thing to do is to invite and include as many people with diverse experiences as possible in the early stages of dialogue. Without coaxing, we bring our frames with us. Offer some key questions, provide data (we tend to gather data that fit our frame), and then listen attentively, inquire further, and dialogue. The challenge is to get everyone to try to see the others' perspectives as a means of generating more alternatives, rearranging patterns, and possibly constructing a new frame, not to debate right or wrong.

Our frames of reference outline the categories of patterns. For example, *honesty* is a frame of reference commonly used to define patterns. When we encounter certain circumstances and observe specific behaviors, we then place them within the framework we call *honesty*. If a supplier is supposed to deliver a product according to specs at a certain cost on a certain date but pockets a healthy 3% off the records, I might frame that behavior as dishonest. Someone with different cultural insight may frame the same action as a "face" or shame frame.

A word of caution about same-frame thinking is necessary, however. The influence of corporate culture can supercede that of a national culture, particularly in companies that have invested heavily in teaching and creating a distinct corporate culture. If the strategic learning process is not monitored, this can lead to a "corp-think" mentality—or perhaps, more appropriately, a "corps"-think—when collective critical inquiry ability is allowed to atrophy and executives from everywhere in the world begin to think the corporate way.

While this can be a very efficient environment in which to manage, it can be equally detrimental to strategic thinking because everybody shares the same frame. Employees, managers, and executives at all levels and in all locations often do not realize that their individual frames have a strategic value. They are eager to be rewarded as a good corporate player. As companies approach globalization in a variety of ways, corporate culture assimilation and acculturation are becoming influential forms of incidental learning, and companies need to keep tabs on their approaches to testing for same-frame thinking so that the corporate culture doesn't become an impediment to learning to think strategically.

Pattern Recognition

Interestingly, we recognize patterns primarily through a process based on intuition. A *pattern* is a set of cues that usually appear together, so when we see a few of the cues we automatically expect to find the others. In other words, a pattern is any repeatable concept, thought, or image whose repetitions together make up an approach to a problem, a way of looking at things, or a perspective. It is a repeatable sequence of neural activity.

A particular viewpoint may also have developed gradually over time. An idea that was beneficial at one time may not be useful today, and yet the current idea will have developed directly from the outdated idea. A pattern may develop in a specific way because it was derived from the combination of other patterns. However, because we tend to form patterns based on partial, inaccurate, or incomplete information, if all the information had been available at one time, the pattern would probably have been quite different. A pattern may persist because it is useful and sufficient; yet, if we allow ourselves to pause and step back from the situation, a restructuring of the pattern could create something even better.

Once experienced intuitive strategists see a pattern, any decision they have to make is usually obvious. This can be enormously useful when we are dealing with day-to-day decisions that occur in rapid succession, when we are under pressure or dealing with scenarios that include a lot of inconclusive, uncertain, and incomplete information that makes it difficult to find patterns. We need to be able to filter and sift rapidly. Intuitive pattern recognition is how we do this.

Pattern recognition can take place in a split second and without conscious thought. Therefore, we are not aware of how we arrived at an intuitive judgment, which is precisely why it seems mysterious to us. Even if the situation is not identical to what we have seen before, we can recognize similarities with past events and so we automatically "know" what to do, without deliberately having to think through the options. When we recognize a pattern, we gain a sense of a situation. We have a "feel" for what will work and what won't. Basically, it is at this point that our decision making becomes intuitive.

> *Formal analysis can be valuable to supplement intuition, but it cannot substitute for intuition when it comes to complex strategic decisions.*

Very large repertoires of patterns that have been acquired over years of practice enable successful strategists to make good decisions using intuition. Without these patterns, without this experience base, strategists would be paralyzed as strategic decision makers. The formal methods of analysis are not enough, even when applying advanced strategies and using the fastest computers to crunch all the numbers. Strategic analysis serves to generate testing, challenging, reflecting, and acting on the intuitive hunch. Formal analysis can be valuable to supplement intuition, but it cannot substitute for intuition when it comes to complex strategic decisions.

What we need to be mindful of in strategic thinking is to understand that pattern recognition is an automatic process of making sense. Problems emerge when we expect to see a certain pattern and are blinded from seeing anything else. It is up to us to judiciously monitor ourselves by making sure we can and do switch off our autopilot from time to time and deliberately set forth to test and challenge the patterns we notice and the meanings we attribute to them. That is our strategic thinking advantage. An inability to recognize our patterns can get us locked into constructing strategy based on false or irrelevant assumptions.

We intuitively know what cues are going to be important and need to be monitored. We "know" what types of results we "should" be able to accomplish. We have a sense of what to expect next because of our patterns and frames of reference. So detailed and habitual are our patterns that they include routines for responding and *action scripts*. If we see a situation as typical, we can recognize the typical ways to react. That is how we have hunches about what is really going on and how we know what we should do about it.

Figure 15.1 illustrates the process of intuitive pattern recognition and framing that we typically and automatically use in strategic thinking.

Just as we see a new problem as a variation on patterns from the old one, so our new problem-solving actions and decisions are a variation on the old. Just as we are unable at first to articulate the relevant similarities and differences of the situations, so are we unable at first to articulate the similarities

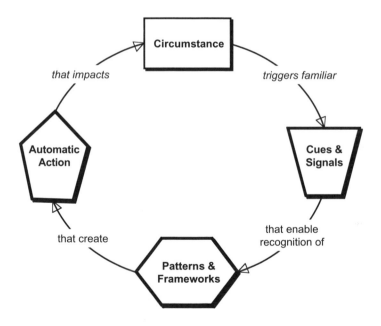

FIGURE 15.1 Intuitive Pattern Recognition and Framing Process That Occurs in Strategic Thinking.

and differences of our problem-solving procedures. Indeed, the whole process of seeing as before and doing as before may continue without conscious verbal articulation.

It is our capacity to see unfamiliar situations as familiar ones and to decide and act in unfamiliar situations as we have done in the familiar situations that enables us to bring our past experience to bear on a unique situation.

It is our capacity to see unfamiliar situations as familiar ones and to decide and act in unfamiliar situations as we have done in the familiar situations that enables us to bring our past experience to bear on a unique situation. It is our capacity to see as and do as that allows us to have a "feel" for problems that do not fit existing rules. The ability to do this rests on the range and variety of the repertoire we bring to unfamiliar situations. Because we are able to see these new and unfamiliar situations as elements of our repertoire, we are able to make sense of the uniqueness and need not reduce them to instances of standard categories.

Intuition is the way we translate our experiences into judgments and decisions. It is our ability to make decisions by using patterns to recognize what is going on in a situation and to recognize the typical way to react. We use our experience to recognize and determine what to do and how to respond.

When strategists fail to recognize or respond to patterns of value conflicts, violate their own ethical standards, fall short of self-created expectations, or ignore public problems they have helped to create, they are increasingly subject to expressions of disapproval, failure, and ineffectiveness. These most important areas of strategic thinking stretch beyond the conventional boundaries of analysis. Our a-rational processing becomes eminently important. These are the skillful judgments, decisions, and actions we make tacitly and intuitively, without being able to state the procedures or rules we follow. The successful executives I interviewed vacillated back and forth between rational and a-rational thinking with ease and had a well-developed intuitive sense of the situational appropriateness required for using rational and a-rational thinking. This is a characteristic that comes from successful intuitive experience.

Noticing Red Flags

What makes us recognize the red flags waving in front of our faces? It is our intuition, built up through repeated experiences that we have unconsciously linked together to form a pattern. When we notice a pattern, we instantly have a sense of familiarity—"Yes, I've seen that before!" Pattern recognition explains how we can make effective decisions without conducting a deliberate analysis. Regardless of the business or functional area in which we make strategy, we accumulate experiences and build up a repertoire of recognized patterns. The more patterns we learn, the easier it is to match a new situation to one of the patterns in our repertoire. When a new situation occurs, we recognize the situation as familiar by matching it to a pattern we have encountered in the past.

> *Pattern recognition explains how we can make effective decisions without conducting a deliberate analysis.*

For example, in a quarterly meeting in Jakarta, Tobo, a lifetime Indonesian, hears the global strategy team suggest trucking the product across the country. He automatically sees a red flag waving as a cue that there will be a potential problem with security, and, without thinking, he grimaces and abruptly shifts the topic to alternative transport options because he "knows" the danger sign.

SCENARIO

As he is scouting for a new, economical plant facility, Nicholas quickly reviews the demographic data of a fairly desolate area of Romania, zooming in on a 70% unemployment rate in the group of 18- to 50-year-olds in eight surrounding villages. He also notes that the average education level is fourth grade. A warning light flashes in his mind, and within minutes he outright dismisses this as a potential site for a new commercial container assembly plant because he can read the handwriting on the wall—disaster!

As the global chief operating officer of a commercial container manufacturing company, his gut feeling is that operating costs will be sky high. Expats will have to be cajoled to join his team as supervisors and as top management, local staff training will nibble chunks out of the budget, and equipment replacement costs will be exorbitant because everything will "grow legs" and walk away. He knows that a bribe cache will need to be constantly replenished to appease the local government officials, not to mention drugs, crime, theft, lack of loyalty, and a deplorable work ethic. Nicholas "knows" the rest of the story because he grew up in Romania and witnessed four similar assembly plant mistakes (against his advice) as chief operating officer of his previous company. He sees the data, recognizes a familiar pattern, and makes a negative judgment in a matter of minutes.

Across the table from Nicholas sits Chiho, who can't believe what she is hearing. These same data make her salivate! She had championed the company in their business development initiatives with tremendous success in Vietnam. She has scrutinized these data, not just zoomed in on a couple of points. It looks like a dream to her—no competitors, a captive recruitment ground, eager and appreciative employees, no distractions from work, no labor unions, rock-bottom operating costs, and an opportunity to contribute to the future of the region.

As it turned out, the company heeded the gut feeling Nicholas had and decided to postpone a decision while they studied other options. Within months, a competitor set up shop, only to find themselves involved in a nightmare of expenses and crime. They closed shop after a year.

Executives from different countries see very different patterns—pattern recognition comes from our experience, culture, education, and life—all contributing to our repertoire of experiences. Needless to say, this can complicate strategy making because it is possible that we see the same data in different patterns, or we see different patterns from the same data, or we may see the same patterns from different data. Although a certain pattern may be a red flag to me, the pattern itself may not even register with my colleague. Knowing this requires us to identify and explicitly articulate the patterns we see, as well as the assumptions we make about them, through critical reflection and dialogue. Bringing people from other socio-national, functional, and corporate cultures into strategy making ensures we get some degree of variation of the interpretation of data, because all unconsciously bring along their patterns and frames.

Experienced executives often make the mistake of assuming that their colleagues can see the patterns that seem so obvious to them. The ability to detect patterns is simple and easy to take for granted but difficult to learn because it is largely tacit. It is critical that we challenge ourselves and others to carefully describe, see, and listen to patterns. The differences in pattern recognition can be as important as the similarities when creating winning strategies.

16

Shattering Frames

This chapter consists of five sections. This first section looks at shattering frames of reference, while the second discusses critical reflection as a tool for shattering frames. The third section examines reflection in action and reflection on action in terms of learning to think strategically. The fourth section presents the element of surprise in the critical reflection process, and the fifth section looks at three specific kinds of critical reflection.

Once we have collected patterns and put them into frames, our patterns and frames become compatible and help us make meaning immediately. But when our intention is to create an innovative, sustainable, winning strategy, it is vital that we be able to slow down and turn off this autopilot pattern recognition and deliberately challenge the very process that has served us in the past. The rearrangement and innovative arrangement of patterns created by escaping from the fixed patterns that have been established by experience provides the basis of what I call *shattering*.

Truly innovative strategic thinking is not about playing out new patterns in existing frameworks, but, rather, about creating new frameworks and different patterns within these new frameworks.

We want to be able to switch off our old habits of mind and to experiment with forming new habits of mind. In order to do this we must consciously seek out, explore, and create totally new combinations of patterns and frames, test existing frames, and experiment with reframing. Having an understanding of pattern and frame construction in relation to strategy and an appreciation of how we make decisions is essential to being able to think strategically.

Research studies show that executives use intuitive pattern recognition to create mental simulations in order to imagine how a scenario might play out when they think strategically.[8] In order to recognize in which framework we are playing our scenarios, we need to learn to stop the automatic process. Truly innovative strategic thinking is not about playing out new patterns in existing frameworks, but, rather, about creating new frameworks and different patterns within these new frameworks.

Rational linear thinking is selection by exclusion. We work within a frame of reference and toss out what is not relevant. With a-rational lateral thinking we realize that a pattern cannot be rearranged from within itself, but only as a result of some external influence. Part of the shattering process is to invite and embrace outside influences for their provocation.

I find many of the techniques developed by the originator of the concept of lateral thinking, Edward DeBono, to be helpful for expanding perspectives as well as for identifying dominant ideas and giving vague ideas definition. Without bringing dominant themes into focus, good strategic ideas remain stuck, tangled, or oblivious within patterns secured in old frames. Goodwill itself cannot generate possibilities and options. We need to develop ways of generating alternatives. The technique of lateral thinking can increase the chances for rearranging a pattern, which may in turn generate a strategic insight or innovative idea. DeBono reminds us: "The more irrelevant such influences are, the more chance there is of altering the established pattern. To look only for things that are relevant means perpetuating the current pattern."[9]

The differences between rational linear thinking and a-rational lateral thinking are fundamental. The processes are quite distinct. It is not that one process is more effective than the other for the purpose of learning to think strategically, but that both are necessary. It is a matter of realizing the differences in order to be able to use both effectively. Developmentally, there may be situations that require an emphasis on strengthening the rational linear thinking process, while other situations may call for a focused approach to learning a-rational lateral thinking. Strategists need to be aware of and adept at shattering and recreating patterns and frames in order to be generative and innovative.

Critical Reflection as a Tool for Shattering

In my practice, I find that seasoned strategists are often disturbed to discover that they cannot account for processes they have come to see as central to strategic thinking. It is difficult for them to describe and teach what actually happens when they make sense of uncertainty or make difficult high-risk choices. Their real processes seem mysterious in light of the prevailing strategic knowledge.

Less experienced strategists often recognize that what they are doing is not creating a winning strategy. But they are frustrated by not having a vocabulary or a learning process they can use to improve and develop their strategic thinking. They do not want yet another model—they want something they can do on their own and use wherever they may be that will help them in a vast array of unpredictable circumstances. Contrived as it may sound, critical reflection is one of the best-kept strategic secrets. In fact, an executive committee with whom I work claims it is all a wonderful conspiracy theory—they want to keep it under wraps as a strategic advantage!

Critical reflection is the central process for learning to think strategically and requires a high degree of both the affective and cognitive dimensions of learning. Critical reflection is what we use to challenge assumptions, test beliefs, broaden perspective, and imagine possibilities—the very things that allow us to make strategy that is generative, innovative, adaptive, sustainable, and ultimately winning. Critical reflection is not synonymous with retrospective thinking or hindsight. A relatively awkward thing to describe, it is perhaps the most difficult yet most important process to enact and to develop for strategic thinking.

Critical reflection is a broad process. "The form of inquiry in critical self-reflection is appraisive rather than prescriptive or designative,"[10] writes learning theorist Jack Mezirow. The components of critical reflection are identifying and challenging assumptions, imagining and exploring alternatives and possibilities, analysis, and ultimately taking action. Critical reflection consists of two interrelated processes: learning to question and then replacing or reframing an assumption that is accepted by majority opinion as representing common sense.[11] It is the primary tool for shattering frames of reference—an essential for every serious strategist to master.

Figure 16.1 shows the process of *shattering* which is a deliberate interruption of our intuitive pattern recognition process. The *pauses* may be momentary or take weeks or months. It is during the pause periods that it is essential to engage in critical dialogue and exercise critical reflection.

Critical reflection needs to be understood as being essential to the strategic thinking process, and it involves more than cognitive skills such as logical reasoning or deconstructing arguments for assertions that are unsupported by empirical evidence. Critical reflection involves our recognizing the assumptions underlying our beliefs and behaviors.

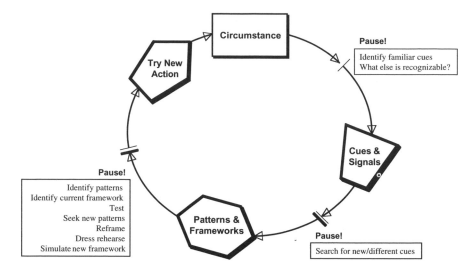

FIGURE 16.1   Shattering and Reframing That Can Occur in Strategic Thinking.

Challenging Through Reflection in Action and Reflection on Action

What distinguishes reflection in action from other kinds of reflection is its immediate impact on action. When we define the scope and breadth of strategy, we choose what we pay attention to and we name the things we will notice. What we generally do when we examine strategic situations is to repeat the familiar patterns and frames we have acquired through our experience. Reflection in action requires that through naming and framing, we select things for attention and organize them in the moment; this can alter the meaning and suggest a new direction.

Reflection in action, based on Donald Schon's work on reflective practice, is a process consisting of "on-the-spot surfacing, criticizing, restructuring, and testing of intuitive understandings of experienced phenomena."[12] Learning takes place when action is informed by reflection. Action and reflection are considered not as separate concepts, but parts of a single process by which we become aware of our underlying assumptions, reflect on their initial understanding of the problem, and develop new ways of defining problems. Reflection in action implies that we learn as we define and implement new strategic decisions and action.

As Schon sees it,

When someone reflects-in-action . . . [h]e does not keep means and ends separate, but defines them interactively as he frames a problematic situation. . . . [H]is experimenting is a kind of action, implementation is built into inquiry. [Therefore] reflection in action can proceed, even in situations of uncertainty or uniqueness, because it is not bound by the dichotomies of technical rationality.[13]

> *If we can place technical, analytical traditional problem solving within a broader context of reflective inquiry, strategic development will be greatly enriched.*

Reflection in action has a critical function in questioning and identifying the assumptions underlying our tacit knowledge or knowing in action. In other words, we think critically about the thinking that got us into a predicament or an opportunity. In the process, we may restructure a sequence of action, re-create the meaning, or devise a new way of framing problems. We begin to ask, "What else could I do?" or "How else could I see this?"

Through reflection in action we can slow down and suspend the process and actively diverge and expand our patterns and frames. We can widen and deepen our lens and intentionally distort the familiar in order to explore and create, because we frame strategic problems in different ways according to various perspectives.

For these reasons, the process of reflection in action is critically important when facilitating the learning of strategic thinkers. Questions about the legitimacy and relevance of reflective capacity to strategy may dissipate when we understand how reflective capacity balances the analytical dimension of learning. If we can place technical, analytical traditional problem solving within a broader context of reflective inquiry, strategic thinking will be greatly enriched.

Strategic problems are interconnected in very complex ways. Indeterminate factors, such as uncertainty, uniqueness, contradictions, and value conflict, defy the basic tenets of technical rationality. What is necessary when making strategic decisions involving these factors is not only the analytic techniques that have been traditional in strategic development, but the reflective action abilities. Reflection in action and reflection on action involve the natural process of learning decision making and problem solving in a way that fuses the cognitive and the affective dimensions of learning. As we can clearly see, reflection in action and reflection on action require extensive use of the deeper, dive domain of learning.

It is this process of reflection in action that is essential to dealing well with situations of uncertainty, instability, uniqueness, and value conflict. Western historical and cultural bias toward rational thinking blinds us to the a-rational process that is omnipresent in developing critical reflective capability. Our ability to learn to think strategically is therefore thwarted, because we simply have not learned to pay attention to the affective dimension of learning and to appreciate how it impacts strategic thinking.

Phrases like "thinking on your feet," "keeping your wits about you," and "learning by doing" suggest that, believe it or not, we are capable of, and sometimes actually do, think about what we are doing in the midst of it—when we reflect in action.

The Element of Surprise

Much reflection in action hinges on the experience of surprise. When intuitive, spontaneous performance yields nothing more than the results we expect, we tend not to think about it. But when an intuitive decision leads to surprises, whether promising or unwanted, we may respond by reflecting in action. Until this moment of surprise, we have been deciding and acting via autopilot. After the moment of surprise, we focus on what we have unintentionally created. In such processes, reflection tends to focus on the outcomes of action, the action itself, and the intuitive knowing implicit in the action. Very often it is due to a surprise that we reflect on the understandings that have been implicit in our decision. Due to the surprise, we are able to uncover assumptions, criticize, restructure, and reframe for further critical action.

Strategists often do think consciously about what they are doing—sometimes even while doing it. Particularly when struck by surprise, they reflect back on action and on the knowing that is implicit in their decisions. They may ask themselves, for example, "What features do I notice when I recognize this incident as being familiar or dubious?" "What are the criteria by which I make this judgment?" and "How am I framing the problem that I am trying to solve?" The aftermath of a surprise is generally when we look reflectively and introspectively on these opportune moments—in an attempt to describe the tacit knowing implicit in our knowing in action. Our descriptions of the surprise may vary, depending on our purpose and the language of descriptions available to us. We may refer, for example, to the sequence of operations and procedures we execute or to the clues we observe and the rules we follow, the values, hunches, and assumptions that underlie our reasons for action.

The sequence involved in the process of reflection in action looks something like the breakdown outlined by learning theorist Donald Schon. Initially, we are involved in a situation where we take action spontaneously and routinely — using our autopilot response. This reveals our tacit knowledge and is our way of framing a problem appropriate to the situation. This knowing in action is spontaneously delivered without conscious deliberation. This sequence of pattern recognition works, providing intended outcomes, so long as the situation falls within the boundaries of what we have learned to treat as normal.[14]

Second, a routine response produces a surprise — an unexpected outcome, pleasant or unpleasant, that does not fit the categories of our tacit knowledge. Inherent in a surprise is the fact that it gets our attention. Our autopilot is jolted. What we pay attention to has significant implications on our ability to choose what to critically reflect on in strategic decision making.

Third, the surprise leads to reflection in or on the present action. Reflection is to some degree conscious, although it need not be conveyed with words. We ask ourselves, "What is this?" "What's happening?" and at the same time "How have I been thinking about it?" Our thought turns back to the surprising incident and, at the same time, includes our present thinking and feeling.

Developing a well-honed reflective capacity is essential to a strategist because it serves as a corrective tool to overlearning, averting complacency, and to overreliance on our autopilot. Through critical reflection, a strategist can recognize and greet surprises as an opportunity to reveal and critique the tacit understandings that have developed around the repetitive experiences of a specialized area of expertise and habits of mind. This can create a chance to make new sense of the situation and to look differently at uncertainty or uniqueness that is an inevitable part of a global strategy environment.

Pseudo Frame Change

An increasingly common global strategy problem is what I call a *pseudo frame change*. This originates from the best of intentions, but it can result in companies' pounding a nail through their own shoes. What senior leadership often says it wants from their global "high potentials" is a "pipeline" of strategic thinkers capable of generating winning strategies; but what senior leadership often does is lock them within existing corporate frames. Two things need to be addressed: (1) Senior leadership needs to understand the learning process required for strategic thinking; (2) senior leadership needs to support that process as they develop high-potential candidates.

A typical scenario tends to play out in the following manner: High-potential candidates from various countries are selected to develop their strategic thinking. These are the brightest and the best from around the world who are being groomed through succession plans to eventually step up to executive positions. Frequently they are shipped to headquarters for a stint in which they are doused in the corporate ways or given a development assignment in a challenging market to hone their leadership skills and knowledge. Both approaches can be very beneficial. Once in their development assignments, they typically attend a lot of strategy meetings, congregate with key strategists of the company, and are grilled on the various methods of analysis. The expectation is that these bright minds will generate the next winning strategy—or so the message goes. But the course of action often undermines this intent.

In order for either of these leadership development scenarios to advance strategic thinking, these high-potential candidates need to acquire and become adept at critical reflective processing, not just analytic skills, in order to convert their multitude of experiences into creating and recreating successful strategy.

Most often, these high-potential candidates are essentially placed firmly inside the corporate frame to learn its construction (i.e., the corporate way). This is important for building a knowledge base and reinforcing the organizational culture. But frequently this is where the strategy development process ends—and where the strategic thinking problem begins. These high-potential individuals learn the existing corporate frames and all of the subtle messages about changing or not changing those frames.

What does not happen is that they don't gain an understanding of the learning process of strategic thinking (so they confuse strategic planning with thinking), and they fail to adopt a habit of challenging these existing frames. They are unclear about their strategic role. Is it to maintain existing frames, or is it to shatter and reframe? Nor do these high-potential candidates typically familiarize themselves with and challenge their greatest strategic asset—their own frames, which are built on their own unique experiences. Without this critical reflective ability, they cannot challenge and test their own frames, nor can they test the existing corporate frames on which strategy is currently made.

Unless frame testing occurs, the personal beliefs and assumptions of the high-potential individuals and those of the company are never made apparent. Granted, this sometimes happens by chance, but luck is not the aim or a process. In order truly to create an innovative, adaptive, and sustainable strategy, the ultimate intent is to shatter (deconstruct the existing frame) and reframe (reconstruct it). High-potential individuals must understand and articulate what their own existing frames are and those of the company (they tacitly know both).

Without a habit of challenge and testing, the multitude of diverse frames that each high-potential candidate brings to the problem cannot be optimally leveraged as a point of collective strategic advantage for the company. A knowledge base of making strategy within existing corporate frames is often thoroughly learned, but the critical step of learning the process of shattering and reframing is omitted from the typical strategic development program. This is, after all, the whole aim of a strategic thinking initiative, and it is the only way a company can grow talent capable of creating innovative and adaptive strategy.

Senior leadership must explicitly state and model this expectation of critical reflective processes as part of learning to think strategically. If this is not explicitly demonstrated by senior leadership, their best strategic efforts amount to little more than making extensions to the existing frames — pseudo frame change.

At the end of such a development assignment, high-potential candidates should be confident and experienced in their ability to challenge, test, revise, and refine strategic ideas and propositions. It is through this critical reflective process that authentic frame shattering and reframing enables the creation and re-creation of winning strategy and a pipeline of strategic thinkers.

Content Reflection, Process Reflection, and Premise Reflection

A useful way to start practicing critical reflection is to distinguish three specific kinds of critical reflection: content reflection, process reflection, and premise reflection.[15] This is a useful distinction both in clarifying the definition of reflection and in understanding the deeper, dive domain of learning.

Content Reflection

The focus is on the content or description of a strategic problem. Content questions aim to tell us "what." What aspect of the problem are we paying attention to? Content questions enable us to get more specific information and details about a topic. For example, if the problem seems to be one of diminishing global market share of a particular automobile, the strategist might look for indicators of trends and attempt to associate those behaviors with development initiatives. What is the problem? What are the factors to examine? Also, the strategist might ask transactional kinds of questions such as "How much will it cost?" and "How much time will it take?"

Process Reflection

Process reflection involves thinking about the approaches used to implement the strategic solution rather than the content of the problem itself. Process questions push us to examine how we make strategic decisions. How did the problem come about? What did we do? What did others do? Process questions enable us to trace the steps and to challenge the quality of the rationale that underlies our strategic decision by describing the process we used to make the decision. The strategist interested in diminishing global market share of a particular automobile might ask whether or not the effort to find indicators of weakening oil supply was adequate. What was the progression or sequence of events? Were the indicators relevant? Are the data reliable, accurate, and comprehensive? How were the data collected? If the same problem came up in another country, business unit, or product, would the same procedure solve the problem? It is a rational and linear kind of reflection and does not always include an affective or an intuitive component; it requires critical thinking. Process questions draw on the deeper, dive level of thinking.

Premise Reflection

Premise reflection leads us to question the relevance of the problem itself. Why is this issue relevant to the strategy? A strategist might ask, "Is market share my real concern? How else could this be framed? What other alternatives did I consider? Is market share the only or primary indicator of success? Success as defined by what timeline? Can I control market share? Is market share dominance a valid concept?" In premise reflection, the assumptions, beliefs, or

TABLE 16.1   Content Reflection, Process Reflection, and Premise Reflection

	Type of Critical Reflection		
	Content Reflection	**Process Reflection**	**Premise Reflection**
Description	Focuses on *what*	Focuses on *how*	Focuses on *why*

Approaches	Restate problem
	Identify key issues
	Summarize major points
	State indicators of
	    trends and patterns
	Identify factors
	Confirm data
	Validate data
	Verify sources
		Map actions and
		    reactions of steps and
		    approaches used to
		    implement strategy
		Explore how the
		    problem emerged/
		    grew/shifted
		Map and discuss step-
		    by-step actions,
		    reactions, and
		    responses
		Discuss progression
		    and sequence
		Discuss scope,
		    impact, and influence
		Discuss relevance
		    and reliability of
		    indicators
			Inquire about relevance
			    of problem: "Why is
			    this issue relevant to
			    strategy?"
			"Is this my concern?"
			"How else could this
			    be framed?"
			"Is the key concept a
			    valid concept?"
			Challenge assumptions,
			    beliefs, and values
			    underlying key problem

Relevance	Surf learning
	Cognitive and
	    instrumental
		Dive learning
		Cognitive and
		    instrumental
		Critical thinking
			Dive learning
			Cognitive and affective
			Critical reflection
			Critical dialogue

values underlying the problem are questioned. Premise reflection consists of an unmistakable affective dimension—we feel a "twitch" that sometimes makes us resistant. Distinct from problem solving, premise reflection can lead to a deeper domain of learning.

Part of a meaningful strategic dialogue is the ability to ask and respond, to critically reflect. For developing process and premise questions, I find it beneficial to have executives get comfortable using strategic situations that are unfamiliar to them, consisting of functional or technical details with which they are not knowledgeable. This can be done informally or through various action learning teams. In such situations executives are not tempted to get stuck in content questions because they lack expertise. Instead, they tend to focus and persist with excellent process and premise questions. Also, these process and premise questions allow the executives to determine the degree of confidence they have in their conclusion, based on the soundness of their strategic thinking process and the clarity and authenticity of their underlying premise. Table 16.1 outlines content reflection, process reflection, and premise reflection.

Content, process, and premise questions are essential for learning to think strategically. In my work with executives, I have found that in strategic situations the questions most commonly asked are content questions. Process and premise questions require focused and guided attention and practice. If companies are to develop an innovative and sustainable strategy pipeline within an organization, then critical reflection must be central to the learning. This is not to say that surface, or the surf domain of learning, does not have a part in a strategic thinking. Rather, that development of strategic thinking requires moving beyond the acquisition of new knowledge and understanding and into a process of questioning existing assumptions, values, and perspectives in order to be able to begin to imagine alternative patterns and frames for strategy.

17

Reframing

The need to reframe becomes increasingly important when thinking strategically. We ordinarily frame situations very quickly using our experience to make meaning of issues. Through the process of critical questioning and testing, we sometimes refine or change frames. The reframing of a problem reveals the mistakes we made precisely because of our familiarity or our expertise or because we have cemented our perception of the world and cannot see it in any other way.

Reframing becomes even more complicated when the context in which the information is learned and the context in which it may be used are different. When dealing with uncertainty, contradictions, and conflict in strategic thinking, we informally learn to conduct *frame experiments*. These frames impose a kind of coherence on messy situations, and we discover consequences and implications of our selected frames through testing.

From time to time, our efforts to give order to a situation provoke unexpected outcomes that give the situation a new meaning. We pay attention to the feedback and reactions, and we reframe the problem or situation. It is this combination of problem framing, on-the-spot experimenting, identifying consequences and implications, feedback, and responding to feedback that constitutes a reflective dialogue with the situation. This process is learnable and coachable but not teachable. It is primarily learned through experience and critical reflection—they are internal occurrences that happen informally and mostly outside of the workplace.

Expertise and Experience: The Double-Edged Sword of Intuition

Expertise is both a charm and a curse. It lets us quickly categorize a situation as typical. It lets us know where to focus our attention and what to ignore. But sometimes we can become so complacent about what we think we know that we are caught off guard when the unexpected happens. This is the flip side of expertise; it can blind us and give us a false sense of knowing. Expertise enables us to ignore cues and options we don't think are worth attending to.[16]

Yet when we are tasked with making strategy, this same mind-set can lead us to miss relevant but novel cues, to ignore potentially useful ideas, and to fail to notice important opportunities. Reframing is a very common strategic thinking challenge for senior strategists whom I coach, primarily due to their expertise and experience. An important part of learning to think strategically is that nonexperts need to be able to challenge the experts in a group. I hear successful strategists repeatedly mention that expertise in confronting problems is much more valuable than expertise in answering the problem.

When we look at or listen to data, we need to question whether anything is unusual with the picture. We need to imagine new patterns even when the old patterns are very vivid. The reframing problem shows that our intuition is fallible. Even when intuition is based on expertise, it is no guarantee that we haven't overlooked something important. Too often, experienced strategists can fall into a routine that blinds them to new possibilities. The habit of critical reflection is essential for breaking through this barrier.

Many novice strategists get locked into a view of themselves as technical experts, and they find nothing in the process that warrants reflection. They have become too skillful at techniques of selective inattention, fake frames, situational control—techniques that they use to preserve the constancy of their habit of mind. For them, uncertainty is a threat; its admission is a sign of weakness. Others, more adept at reflection in action or on action, may also feel profoundly uneasy because they cannot verbalize their know-how and cannot justify its quality or rigor, but they regard the imbalance and tension as an opportunity for deeper critical inquiry and reflection.

In order to facilitate the shattering and reframing process, it is important for strategists to have both an understanding of the informal learning process involved in strategic thinking and a basic vocabulary they can use. These two things can facilitate and enhance the strategic thinking process enormously. Our expertise is what often allows us to be tapped for entry into the elite chambers of strategy courses and the tip of the triangle, yet it too often

TABLE 17.1 Example of Knowledge Tracker for Strategic Thinking

Category: Technology

What I Must Know	What I Know	What I Don't Know	What I Think I Know	Somebody Else Knows	Keeps Changing	Can't Trust

becomes the trap that trips because we don't understand how to develop our strategic thinking capability.

One simple exercise is to explicitly identify and test what you know you know and what you know you do not know. While this may sound obvious, it can lead to excellent follow-up dialogue. A simple table, something like Table 17.1, can get things started. Select a single strategy dimension shown on Figure 13.1 for a given issue, for example, technology or finance, and just start filling in the table that follows. After some time, you will want to compare and begin to clarify your thinking through dialogue with a colleague or coach. The expectation is that you will seek out those whom you are certain will have different perspectives, knowledge, and experiences.

Just because intuition is fallible doesn't mean we can't make good use of it. Our eyes are not perfect — they blur and have blind spots, they often require lenses to correct for distortions. Yet we don't reject the information we receive from our eyes. So, too, with our intuition. We need to pay attention to it and cultivate it with the same degree of seriousness we give to analysis.

VII

WHAT ABOUT THE NUMBERS?

Strange Bedfellows: Intuition and Analysis as Partners in the Strategic Learning Process

You cannot feed the hungry on statistics.

David Lloyd George (1863–1945), British statesman and prime minister

Reporting facts is the refuge of those who have no imagination.

Luc de Clapiers Marquis de Vauvenargues (1715–1747), French soldier

161

18

The Roles of Analysis and Intuition in Strategic Decision Making

Her opening words to her executive committee were: "No more marketing research. No more focus groups. No more promotions, commercials, and television jingles—we've been sinking money in this black hole for a couple of years. No more. I should've trusted my gut feeling long ago!" That was the decision made by Louisa Perez, the country manager of an American soft drink corporation operating in Venezuela.

For the first time in her life she could not get answers to a problem from the research and analysis. For the longest time she had had an uncomfortable feeling that something wasn't right, but she ignored it in favor of persisting with more analysis. Louisa is known within the company as a meticulous analyst; her decisions are always based on well-researched data. She has been annoyed at the song the locally hired managers sing every day, "My gut feeling tells me this, my gut feeling tells me that." It's not that she didn't have guts— she just never felt like basing her strategy on it.

She continued, "It's amazing—we're beaten to pulp in the orange soda drinks segment of the Venezuelan market by a newcomer, which doesn't invest any money in marketing its own product. It just dumps the drink concentrates, at the feet of local bottlers and waits for more orders—which come like clockwork."

Later, at a dinner with the sales team of the local distributor, Louisa couldn't help but share her frustration with a young sales manager seated beside her. He awkwardly smiled and said:

I'm sorry, Mrs. Perez, that nobody told you about it earlier. But I believe the reason your product's sales are going down has nothing to do with your marketing efforts. Some dishonest soda fountain operators have figured out a way to open sealed concentrate containers and dilute the beverage with tap water. The competitor's containers are much easier to tamper with than yours—that is why they keep buying them; it's not the quality of the soda. Your company's technological prowess and the growing numbers of dishonest operators have driven you out of the market.

Louisa's gut feeling has turned out to be right. The problem wasn't about jingles and research. She faces another dilemma now—to start researching the new phenomenon, or to skip the research and deal with it by relying on her newfound strategy tool: intuition.

Part VII consists of three chapters. This chapter looks at the complementary roles of analysis and intuition and considers how intuition is a balance for analysis and how analysis provides a check for intuition in strategic thinking. Chapter 19 discusses the traditional strategic decision-making process and then offers an integrated strategic decision-making alternative. Chapter 20 discusses coordinating intuition and analysis to strengthen strategic thinking.

Rational analysis can never substitute for intuition within the process of strategic thinking.

Intuition within the context of strategic thinking has to be balanced with deliberate, rational analysis. But rational analysis can never substitute for intuition within the process of strategic thinking. Cognitive knowledge must be integrated with having "a feel" for the situation, which is otherwise known as tacit knowledge. While analysis has its function and intuition is not perfect, trying to replace intuition with analysis is a huge mistake, if the intention is to think strategically.

Analysis has a proper role as a supporting tool for making intuitive decisions. The concept of rational, logical thinking is one of selection based on the process of rejection. Information and ideas are put in order and tested according to linear criteria; and they are then discredited and discarded if they do not fit. When time and the necessary information are available, analysis can help uncover cues and patterns as well as provide new points of focus for the creation of different patterns and reframing. Analysis can also help evaluate a decision. But analysis cannot replace the intuition that is at the center of the strategic decision-making process.

Therefore, we need to explore the connection between them. Ultimately, we need to learn how to conduct analyses that improves intuitive thinking — and to distinguish what types of decisions are most appropriate for analytical thinking and for intuitive thinking. Intuition expert Gary Klein notes:

> *Our intuitions function like our peripheral vision to keep us oriented and aware of our surroundings. Our analytical abilities, on the other hand, enable us to think precisely. We may believe that everything we think and decide comes from our analytical thinking, the conscious and deliberate arguments we construct in our heads, but that's because we're not aware of how our intuitions direct our conscious thought processes.*[1]

In situations that require strategic thinking, sometimes we need to rely more on intuition and other times we need to draw more on analysis. According to intuition experts and research, when the situation keeps changing or when the time pressure is high or when the goals are vague, we cannot use just analysis. We have to go with what we "know." These situations require risk taking, yet they can also yield strategic rewards if we invest in building a repertoire of successful intuitive experiences. By contrast, when our strategic decision involves a lot of computational complexity, such as determining whether there is a cost advantage, we are doomed or duped if we do not do the analysis.

> *Numbers are not always any more*
> *trustworthy than intuition.*

Because our intuition can mislead us, we often opt to track events using objective measures — which are quick and easy things to share. Relevant or not, this feels safe. To do this, we develop metrics that will record what we need to know, a rater of change, a degree of progress, or some other feature that will help us make decisions. For example, the metrics of market share tell us the extent to which a company dominates its industry.

On the other hand, intuition comes to us through emotional reactions and perceptions, not through numbers, so hunches just pop into our minds without leaving any trail about how they were formed. In contrast, metrics provide firm documentation for our decisions. If someone questions us, we can point to the numbers to explain our decisions. Intuition cannot really help us figure out overhead rates or make budget projections.

Unfortunately, numbers are not always any more trustworthy than intuition. Too often, accurate, reliable numbers are difficult to obtain, subject to multiple interpretations, and difficult to apply. Quantifying the elements of a situation doesn't guarantee that we will make a good decision. Metrics can even interfere with intuition. For example, the hard numbers of a particular niche market don't necessarily add up to a story that explains the sequence of events as to why we feel a strategic decision is just plain wrong. There is considerably more to a strategic decision than a chain of numbers.

Nevertheless, we cannot dispense with numbers. They force us to align our intuition with reality. For example, numbers keep us from continuing a strategy whose image masks the reality of reduced capacity, changed circumstances, overextended budgets, or disappointing rates of return. Therefore, numbers cannot be discounted or discredited totally.

Intuition as a Check on Analysis

How does intuition keep analysis in check? Intuition can help us monitor our attention by signaling us to be more alert in high-stakes situations. For example, we "smell a rat" or get that gut feeling that something is not quite right. Intuition can help us spot problems earlier and warn us that our decisions and actions based on those decisions are insufficient to reach our goal. It is our intuition that enables us to pick up on subtle inconsistencies in patterns, which triggers a feeling, which then leads to a certain decision or action. Because of this, we draw confident and incredible conclusions from very little information. Intuition is what we use when we try to see patterns when we look at data and facts. The patterns are not linear, so they are not always obvious. That is when intuition becomes our best friend—we look over a set of data or variables and suddenly a pattern pops into our mind. The ability to recognize patterns is intuitive. Our experience is what arranges things into patterns.

One strength of metrics is that we get a snapshot without the cumbersome details of the process by which that snapshot was acquired. This absence of history and context accelerates communication in strategic meetings, however, because details of the method for obtaining data are not usually shared. This means that we have to judge the numbers on face value—the risk is in not knowing if we can trust the numbers.

I am not suggesting we reject or be shielded from data; rather, we need to use critical dialogue and inquiry to scrutinize the data. We need to ask, "Whose data?" "Where did they come from?" "Why were they collected?" "Whose interest are they intended to serve?" "Whose interest do they serve?" "Why were they compiled in a particular way?" and "Who paid for the data collection and analysis?" in order to get the story and the context behind the numbers. The trouble is that seeing numbers out of context can cause us to misinterpret information and lead to regrettable strategic decisions and conclusions. In this strategic environment of ambiguity and paradox, analysis will take us only so far.

Analysis as a Check on Intuition

While it is important to emphasize the role of intuition in strategic decision making, it is equally important to note that intuition alone does not generate or constitute strategic thinking. What are some of the limitations to intuition? Why does intuition sometimes prove unreliable? Several important limitations to the use of intuition come from the types of decisions we face, the opportunities we have had to develop our intuition, and the inherent nature of expertise. Intuition researcher Gary Klein suggests four reasons our intuition may not serve us.[2]

First, while complex and uncertain decisions make intuition difficult to apply, these are the very kinds of situations in which we need to use highly skilled intuition more than ever. Since much of strategic thinking includes dealing with very complex, incomplete, and uncertain information that is constantly changing, it is absolutely critical that we develop our intuition to a degree that we can trust it as a tool. Analysis alone does not suffice. Intuition must be tested against analysis, and analysis must be tested against our intuition in these highly complex and constantly changing circumstances.

It is hard to develop intuition based on pattern matching when the strategic situation we are trying to resolve is complicated. Even if we think that we recognize a pattern, we may be fooling ourselves. This is why we must be adept at using critical reflective processes (i.e., dialogue, reflection, challenge, testing, reevaluating) in order to challenge our perceptions, perspectives, and assumptions. Testing and reflecting have no substitutes.

Second, the strategist may not have had a chance to acquire expertise. We may not have a chance to build a strong experience base because we cannot get feedback about our judgments. A lack of a strong experience base results in a lack of confidence and trust in using intuition.

Third, the experience base of our intuition may be distorted. Even if we know how to acquire and evaluate our intuition, we still have to worry about the validity of the feedback we receive. Therefore, it is important to habitually test validity through dialogue and critical inquiry.

Rational and intuitive thinking are not mutually exclusive. When both are well developed, the combination is extremely useful in learning to think strategically. We need to be skeptical of intuitive decisions when we do not have experience or trust our experience with a situation because our intuition represents our composite knowledge.

19

Decision-Making Approaches to Strategic Thinking

Decision making is central to making strategy, and it is therefore an important reason for developing strategic thinking—as a means of refining the decision-making process. The familiar and traditional Western approach to strategic decision making is first discussed, followed by an approach that integrates intuition and rationality.

Traditional Strategic Decision Making

Traditional strategic planning approaches, steeped in the customs of the technical rational scientific school of thought, emphasize some variation of the familiar classic six-step model of decision making:

Analyze the problem
⇓
List alternatives
⇓
Evaluate alternatives against a set of criteria
⇓
Weight each criterion
⇓
Rate each option on each criterion
⇓
Sum it up—Compare—Voila!

This model of decision making in some sense is very comforting and appealing. It is straightforward, based on solid analysis and logic, not gut feelings; and it is linear, systematic, rational, and methodical. Leaving nothing to chance, a good decision is guaranteed if we just follow the process. This model allows us to intelligibly justify our decision to others — there is something reassuringly "scientific" about it.

The catch is that it provides a false sense of assurance. It is a sanitized sequence that omits the untidy parts of the problem-solving process. The messy, nonlinear parts are critically important to distinguishing strategic thinking from strategic planning.

Critical reflection is essential for the reframing that is necessary for strategic innovation, adaptability, and sustainability. Strategists may reflect on their tacit action or in their tacit action. Sometimes, in the relative tranquility of a post-mortem, they think back on a decision they have made or a situation they have survived, and they mull around the meanings they have brought to their handling of the situation. They may do this in a mood of idle speculation or in a deliberate effort to prepare themselves for future strategy. They may reflect on the action, or they may also reflect in action while they are in the midst of it.

Reflection in action may not be very rapid. When a strategist reflects in and on his action, the possible targets of his reflection are as varied as the kinds of factors, variables, and patterns before him and the multitude of underlying frames, assumptions, and belief systems he brings to them. Reflection may be on the tacit norms and reasons that underlie a particular judgment or on the theories implicit in a pattern of events or decisions or reactions. Reflection may also be on the feeling about a situation that has guided a particular course of action or decision. It is also possible that the reflection could be about the way in which he has framed the problem encountered or on the role he has constructed for himself within a larger organizational or business context.

Although reflection in action is an extraordinary process, it is not an unusual occurrence among successful strategists. Indeed, for many strategists it is the defining trait of their success. Nevertheless, because strategy making is still mainly identified with technical expertise, reflection in action is not generally accepted, even by those who "know" it as being central to learning to think strategically.

We must be willing to enter into new kinds
of confusion and uncertainties when we
engage in critical reflection on action.

Our attitude toward inquiry greatly influences our attitude toward the reality with which we deal, and therefore it affects the strategy we create. We probe the information and stories of the directors of the key business units and systematically pursue the implications of our familiar and chosen frames. At the same time that we try to shape the situation to our frame, we must hold our self open to any "playback" from or of the situation. While judgments must be grounded in relevant data, conclusions should remain open to reevaluation. This can be stressful and requires dialogue and deeper-level learning in order to impact our strategic thinking positively. We must be willing to enter into new kinds of confusion and uncertainties when we engage in critical reflection on action.

In order to do this we must adopt a split-vision approach. As the risk of uncertainty increases, so does the temptation to retain or retreat to our existing frame. Nevertheless, if we maintain a split vision, even while strengthening our commitment to a particular frame, we increase our chances of developing a deeper and broader perspective on information and concepts, and we ultimately make better decisions.

According to learning theorists Chris Arygris and Donald Schon, in order for reflection in and on action to be applied to strategic thinking, the following tenets of learning must be followed:[3]

1. Give and get valid information. Valid information is essential for informed decisions.
2. Seek out and provide others with directly observable data and correct reports so that valid attributions can be made.
3. Create the conditions for free and informed choice.
4. Try to create, for ourselves and for others, awareness of the values we embrace in making the decision, awareness of the limits of our capacities, and awareness of the areas of experience free of defense mechanisms beyond our control.
5. Increase our internal commitment to decisions made. Try to create conditions, for ourselves and for others, in which we are committed to an action because it is intrinsically satisfying, not because it is accompanied by external rewards or punishments.

Integrated Strategic Decision Making

In an effort to strengthen the strategic decision-making process, it is useful to be mindful of and adept at integrating the roles of intuition and rationality. Critical reflection is an approach that can effectively help to integrate intui-

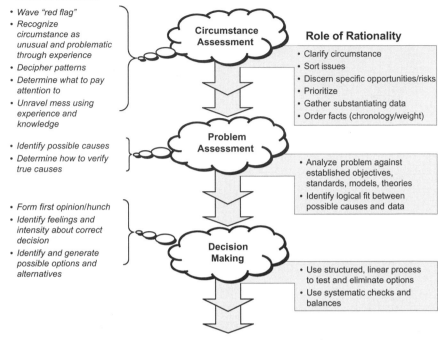

Role of Intuition

- *Wave "red flag"*
- *Recognize circumstance as unusual and problematic through experience*
- *Decipher patterns*
- *Determine what to pay attention to*
- *Unravel mess using experience and knowledge*

Circumstance Assessment

Role of Rationality

- Clarify circumstance
- Sort issues
- Discern specific opportunities/risks
- Prioritize
- Gather substantiating data
- Order facts (chronology/weight)

- *Identify possible causes*
- *Determine how to verify true causes*

Problem Assessment

- Analyze problem against established objectives, standards, models, theories
- Identify logical fit between possible causes and data

- *Form first opinion/hunch*
- *Identify feelings and intensity about correct decision*
- *Identify and generate possible options and alternatives*

Decision Making

- Use structured, linear process to test and eliminate options
- Use systematic checks and balances

FIGURE 19.1   Integrated Roles of Intuition and Rationality in Strategic Decision Making.

tion and rationality in strategic decision making. Figure 19.1 illustrates the complementary roles of intuition and rationality in the overall strategic decision-making process. Although in reality, intuition and rationality coexist, they tend to alternate in taking a predominate function within the strategic decision-making process.

Upon encountering a circumstance, intuition is what waves the red flag or kicks us under the table. It gets our attention and helps us to recognize a circumstance as problematic through the use of experience and knowledge in a nonanalytical manner. Intuition helps us determine what to pay attention to and helps us to sort issues. Then the role of rationality kicks in by clarifying and systematically discerning issues and opportunities that warrant further consideration. Rationality is essential for ordering facts in a linear and logical way. Meticulous prioritization, data collection, and analysis are essential in order to move the circumstance assessment forward.

As the problem assessment takes form, our intuition is essential to identify possible causes and to verify true causes. Without a well-honed intuitive sense, problem analysis can remain sanitized, clinical, and ineffectual. Problems are only superficially exposed and analyzed without the "truthfulness" of the cause exposed or explored. Rationality plays the critical role, then, of identifying relevant information and analyzing facts. It serves to evaluate a logical fit between possible causes and data by analyzing the problem against established objectives, standards, formulas, and models.

The final decision-making step is where the tension between intuition and rationality is most apparent. The consequences of making a strategic decision today can be daunting—huge stakes within an unpredictable future makes the risk factor enormous. Executives I interviewed consistently noted that intuition most often leads their strategic decision making; and if it is not countered by rationality, runaway intuition can be as detrimental and destructive to strategic decision making as it can be beneficial and crucial. Intuition offers our first judgment or gut reaction to a decision. The role of rationality is essential and imperative, then, as a "testing" method, to verify the hunches and preferences we intuitively made. We need to work through the rigors of a disciplined rational process while noting and suspending our initial claims.

The focused and skillful use of both intuition and rationality offers a structured process of checks and balances to strategic decision making. Developing and reinforcing critical reflection as part of the strategic thinking learning process can ensure that intuition and rationality are aligned, for each is insurance on the other.

20

Coordinating Intuition and Analysis to Facilitate Strategic Thinking

Neither analysis nor intuition alone is sufficient for effective strategic decision making. The challenge is to find a way to balance intuition and numbers. We do not want to abandon metrics, but we do not want to be fooled by them either. We need to find ways to use numbers effectively to support and correct our intuition so that we can benefit from two different ways of interpreting events.

The synthesis of intuition and analysis that seems most effective for strategic thinking is when we allow intuition to direct our analysis of the circumstances to guide the strategic thinking process. This way, intuition helps us recognize situations and decide how to react, and analysis verifies our intuitions to make sure they are not misleading us. Table 20.1 highlights the optimal use of intuition and numbers in strategic decision making.

There are several other things we can do that combine intuition and analysis, including (1) mapping the strengths and weakness of strategic options without attaching metrics and (2) not replacing intuition with procedures as a means of taking control over gray areas, which is a very common mistake. Another integrated approach is to fuse numbers and intuition by using stories —a narrative describes how the metrics came to be. These stories can describe how a few primary influences caused the outcome we are trying to grasp. Stories add context and support the making of meaning of metrics—and the metrics help us to impose discipline in our stories.

TABLE 20.1 Constructive Uses of Intuition and Numbers for Strategic Decision Making

Use Intuition to Support Strategic Decisions by	Use Numbers to Support Strategic Decisions by
Initiating strategic concept and framework ("gut sense")	Testing intuitive framework
Formulating frameworks	Establishing strategic targets and goals
Identifying patterns ("hunches") that are negative and positive	Making comparisons
Making sense of incomplete, partial, inaccurate information	Ensuring compliance
Making sense of rapidly changing data	Spotting trends and patterns
Mentally simulating scenarios ("dress rehearsing")	Evaluating strategic performance
Exploring new possibilities and alternatives with stories/expand and enrich context of data	Testing stories and creating and re-creating new stories
Constructing new frameworks	Constructing new frameworks

Just because someone has run the numbers does not mean that we have to believe the conclusion. Numbers are not necessarily more credible than intuition based on experience. Once we know what the metric is, we can usually find a way to play with it or play around it—to show that we are doing well according to the official yardstick even though we are not making progress toward the larger objectives.

Regrettably, traditional strategy development approaches tend to focus almost exclusively on analysis. Learning methods that involve only the cognitive domain tend to emphasize linear thinking. Logical, rational, and methodical thinking is taught and rewarded at the expense of an awareness, appreciation, or skill practice involving the affective domain. The strategic role of the affective domain, including intuition, tacit knowledge, a-rational thinking, and feelings, are not only ignored, but often mocked or discredited. Essential capabilities, such as critical reflection, confidence, well-developed intuition, awareness, the ability to fuse feelings, critical inquiry, and dialogue, are absent from most strategy curricula, nomenclature, and knowledge bases.

It is little wonder then that we are struggling to develop strategic thinkers. These affective dimensions require a considerable amount of time, tolerance for ambiguity, heightened sensitivity, and discipline to develop. Yet they are an essential requirement for learning to think strategically. In attempting to combine intuition and analysis, we need to accept a degree of ambivalence—it is part of strategic reality.

Strange as it may sound to those who have not experienced it, I encourage and sometimes coax the strategists with whom I work to participate in one of the performing or visual arts if they are serious about developing their strategic thinking. Engagement in the arts provides an experience in broadening perspective, macro–micro thinking, dealing with paradox, inconsistency, and unpredictability, using imagination, and honing reflective capacity—things the ancient Greeks considered essential to making strategy according to their concepts. These critical abilities can be strengthened through committed engagement in photography, painting, acting, singing, dancing, sculpting, or any other art.

An action-learning approach can be very beneficial for making implicit intuitive judgments explicit. This can help with strategic thinking because the more we are aware of why and how we are successful, the more likely we are to repeat those learning patterns.

Regardless of its limitations, we depend on intuition to think strategically; therefore, it is critical that we develop it into a reliable instrument. There are no magic formulas or shortcuts that improve judgment. We can develop our intuition for making decisions by making it a priority. This means continually challenging ourselves to make tough judgments, honestly appraising those decisions in order to learn from the consequences, actively building up an experience base, and learning to balance and blend intuition with analysis.

Key strategists and those responsible for developing a cadre of strategic thinkers must include intuition in their learning approach because it is precisely the reason why others trust their opinions and decisions. They are known to be right on the mark. Key strategists are the ones who spot the early signs of problems and recognize opportunities without having to gather all the relevant data and perform all the required analysis—they just "know." Through years of experience, they have developed and translated that experience into a level of confidence necessary to make important judgments. If key strategists understand where their intuition is coming from, if they can discern when their intuition may be misleading, and if they can convince others to take their intuition seriously, then they are able to justify their authority.

VIII

WHAT DOES CULTURE HAVE TO DO WITH STRATEGIC THINKING?

You'd Be Surprised: Culture as a Factor of Irrelevance for Learning to Think Strategically

"What kind of bird are you, if you can't fly?" chirped the bird.
"What kind of bird are you, if you can't swim?" retorted the duck.

From Peter and the Wolf *by Sergey Prokofiev (1891–1953), Russian composer*

The Role of Culture in Strategic Thinking

Why address strategic thinking in relation to socio-national culture? Because it is a topic that is either forefront in the minds of or buried deep into oblivion within the minds of those responsible for the strategic success of companies and other organizations. As this part will point out, we need to understand the learning process involved in strategic thinking in order to constructively position the role that culture plays in strategic thinking.

This part consists of two chapters. This chapter looks at the need to think about strategy in relation to culture, the role of culture, what typically goes wrong, and the cultural dimension of hierarchy as it impacts frame formation. Chapter 22 discusses the challenge of introducing strategic thinking across cultures. It consists of a section on shattering and reframing across cultures and common factors to consider when dealing with other cultures in developing strategic thinking.

Intricate webs of executives, managers, professionals, entrepreneurs, customers, suppliers, shareholders, governments, and competitors of various cultural backgrounds in vastly different locales around the globe are all influential to making strategy. Expatriates, repatriates, and nationals are involved in developing the in-house capacity to create and re-create innovative, sustainable and adaptable strategy.

As mentioned in previous chapters, successful strategic thinking does not occur in a vacuum. Innovative, sustainable, adaptive, and winning strategy can only occur when those involved are able to shatter and reframe their own basic assumptions and those of the organization. This means supporting the frame-change process by endorsing the use of critical reflective processes (critical inquiry, critical reflection, and critical dialogue) to constructively challenge anyone involved in the strategy process. It also means everyone is invited to question the business, political, social, and economic environments and to test the company capabilities on a continuous basis.

I am constantly bombarded with this question: "Why can't I find any good strategic thinkers in such and such a country?" In fact, this is often the springboard to many of my client relationships. In working with strategic development issues all around the world, I have found executives in every country, every industry sector, and private and public organizations who persist with the second part of the question: "What can I do to make 'these people' think strategically?" What clients want to hear, of course, is a simple diagnosis indicating that their strategic thinking problem is due to "cultural differences," followed, of course, by a three-step solution, accompanied by a tomorrow time line, training course proposals, and a correlated metrics table. (These dreamers are in for a surprise!)

Unfortunately, the remedy is not quite that simple or clear. Usually, it is more a matter of not understanding or misunderstanding the strategic thinking process, not differentiating between strategic thinking and strategic planning, not understanding the learning process involved in either, and being unaware of the role that culture plays. Typically, I find that senior executives and corporate boards use a strategic planning framework as a basis for complaints about the absence of strategic thinkers. This is like saying you want to grow and harvest strawberries, yet you continue to plant onions.

Most often I find that clients lack a process or criterion by which to identify and develop strategic thinkers, because they lack knowledge about the informal learning process or an awareness of attributes by which to proceed. Furthermore, they rarely have foundational information about the cultures with which they are working. Once these pieces are clear, culture becomes just another variable to identify and work with in facilitating learning to think strategically.

Culture's Impact on Pattern Recognition

What role does socio-national culture play in learning to think strategically? It plays a significant role in shaping our frames of reference, because culture teaches us what to pay attention to, it carefully outlines the patterns we must recognize, and it rewards us for learning these. The specific patterns teach us what to be afraid of or skeptical of, what we can and cannot trust, where to attach values, and what values to assign to certain patterns and frames.

Culture *per se*, however, is not a differentiating factor in the learning process of strategic thinking. Culture is but one factor that influences our experience. The strategic thinking process is identical regardless of culture, because strategic thinking is driven by the informal learning process, not by culture.

If we are unaware of the informal learning process that underlies strategic thinking, it is easy to mistakenly blame culture as the culprit for not having strategic thinkers in certain sites across the globe. The informal learning process required for strategic thinking exists at a level that supercedes culture — socio-national culture, organizational culture, or functional culture.

> *Culture* per se *is not a differentiating factor in the learning process of strategic thinking. Culture is but one factor that influences our experience. The strategic thinking process is identical regardless of culture, because strategic thinking is driven by the informal learning process, not by culture.*

Management researcher Kahlid Alaya's studies on Middle Eastern senior managers support this notion that at some point, national culture becomes irrelevant to thinking and learning. His extensive research on management cultures of the Middle East concurs with other findings, which claim to a certain extent that "people act and . . . organizations operate the same way regardless of where they are located, . . . regardless of the culture or historic experience of a society. Democratic practices such as empowerment, decentralization, and participation that prove to be successful and effective in one setting are transferable to other national settings."[1] What is most important for global organizations is for their managers and executives to model and establish an expectation for critical reflection and to reframe experience. This reflective capacity enables us to learn from our experiences and fosters learning to think strategically.

Too often, I find that *culture* is a convenient veil with which to cover our odds and ends, frustrations, and unanswered questions about the strategic thinking process — particularly when we are working with executives from outside our primary culture. Things become more complicated because, as I have already mentioned, strategic thinking is an overused and underdefined term. Furthermore, the informal learning process of strategic thinking is generally not well understood, so we attribute the whole mess to culture and absolve ourselves of development responsibility.

> *All cultures have customs and deeply*
> *embedded values that help us determine*
> *what we know, how we know it, and how*
> *we know the degree to which it is safe or*
> *unsafe for us to use challenge, dialogue, and*
> *critical reflection within our respective*
> *organizational context.*

Although culture *per se* is not a primary factor of learning to think strategically (the learning process is), culture has a very visible impact on the patterns we learn to recognize and the frames we use to outline and assess strategic data, information, and decisions. For example, culture determines the way we assess creditworthiness for mergers, it influences why we predict political stability for investment, it affects how we judge a provincial governor's or deputy minister's trustworthiness for a joint venture, and it determines how we plan our market entry strategy.

All cultures have customs and deeply embedded values that help us determine what we know, how we know it, and how we know the degree to which it is safe or unsafe for us to use challenge, dialogue, and critical reflection within our respective organizational context.

Typical Faux Pas

What kinds of cultural things typically go wrong in global strategy-making meetings? I find that very often we think we know more than we actually do about foreign markets, about the capabilities of our local businesses with regard to implementation, and about local agendas and priorities.

Furthermore, we generally have inconsistent understandings about the way that global operations are positioned relative to the organization's core strengths. One strategic learning imperative is that we take the time to critically reflect and critically dialogue with others to determine the limits of what we know and what others know at the beginning of and throughout the strategy-making process.

I find it rare for companies to have any consistent understanding or expectation of a strategic thinking process in place where those involved engage in critical reflective processes, regardless of geographic location. Mind you, this is different from having an official, formal strategy-making routine in place. The kind of mechanical strategic planning process that is well known and logistically clean basically consists of people showing up at a certain time and place with requested information and analysis, conducting a surf-level discussion within existing corporate frames of reference.

Very often when making strategy outside our primary culture, critical information is missed or misinterpreted because it is not available through the usual market research processes. Essential perspectives may be omitted from strategy discussions because the relevance of the perspectives is not visible in the same way as back home. Furthermore, key people are frequently overlooked due to language or geography, time zones, or technology issues; and we falsely believe that getting their partial insight or fragmented bits of their information is good enough.

Cross-Cultural Dimensions That Impact Frame Formation

We carry our existing frames with us across continents and time zones without realizing they may be juxtaposed on a pile of other existing frames that are very different from our own. This can be destructive if left uncovered and unchallenged, or it can become a constructive source of innovation if the frames are identified, tested, shattered, and reframed. In order for this to happen we need to engage in the deeper, dive domain of learning to examine the role culture may play on our attitudes and beliefs, particularly with regard to the notion of challenging others and being challenged ourselves.

Cross-cultural theorist Geert Hofstede, in his 1980 seminal work, *Culture's Consequences: Power Distance, Individualism, Masculinity, Uncertainty Avoidance, and Long-term Orientation,*[2] identified five dimensions that exist to varying degrees in every culture. These dimensions exist within every culture to varying degrees and certainly impact our frames of reference. While his studies have been criticized in a number of ways, his cultural dimensions provide us with a convenient way of classifying the differences among cultures and have continued to be a subject of revision and debate for subsequent cross-cultural theorists.

Alfons Trompenaars and Charles Hampden-Turner modified these dimensions in their 1993 book *The Seven Cultures of Capitalism* to include seven dimensions: universalism vs. particularism, analyzing vs. integrating, individualism vs. communitariansim, inner-directed vs. outer-directed orientation, time as sequence vs. time as synchronization, achieved status vs. ascribed status, and equality vs. hierarchy.[3] Many excellent sources are available on cross-cultural dimensions, and an understanding of the dimensions can serve as a basis for inquiring and challenging assumptions underlying strategic decision making.

Regardless of the specific terminology, all of the cultural dimensions play a role in shaping frames of reference that need to be tested in order to learn to think strategically. When working with clients around the world, I am frequently asked to pare down the cultural dimensions to the single most influential aspect related to learning to think strategically. It is, of course, the complex combination of cultural dimensions and individual personal traits that impact our capacity to learn to think strategically, rather than any single dimension.

For the purpose of demonstrating the impact of the combination of cultural dimensions on strategic thinking, I reluctantly and cautiously stick my neck out and mention *hierarchy* as but one manifestation of the combined dimensions — only by way of exemplifying the impact culture has on learning to think strategically. Hierarchy leaves its sticky fingerprints on every aspect of strategy making, and I find it to be particularly important to address early on in working with executives because of its pervasive influence. Hierarchy is evident in a multitude of ways, making it convenient as a starting point for challenging beliefs and starting a critical dialogue about content, process, and premise assumptions.

Hierarchy as a Factor to Be Reckoned With

How a culture perceives hierarchy within a business environment can determine the experience that managers and executives typically have with challenging information and expressing divergent opinions. We learn from our respective cultures very specific things about hierarchy, for example: Who is it okay to question? Under what circumstances? What is a question versus a threat or an insult? How do we structure a question? What is the right way to respond to questions? Why? When do we attempt to save face or to display status through questions and responses?

In some cultures it is considered disrespectful to challenge a colleague, a superior, or a visitor because this is interpreted as an attack, an interrogation, or humiliation; such a challenger is labeled as disloyal or untrustworthy. This can make it difficult to incorporate a rigorous routine using critical inquiry that is necessary for learning to think strategically. It can also make it difficult to develop trust required for making and implementing strategic decisions.

And most importantly, the quality of strategy can be substantially weakened if the deeper, dive domain of learning is not embraced and practiced by everyone involved with strategic issues in every geographic location.

To remain within the surface, or surf, domain of learning is considered in some cultures to be polite business and interpersonal interaction, because nobody is challenged except in accordance with hierarchical rules — there is no loss of face. In these cultures, it can be more difficult to use critical dialogue and inquiry openly for testing. At the same time, a particular individual within that culture may have strong critical reflective capacity, but public and open challenge and testing may be culturally difficult to do. The dilemma becomes one of relative consequence.

SCENARIO

Junichiro had recently been promoted to be the Asia president of a German international investment bank. A big part of the position was obviously strategy, and the stakes were high. He had a stellar strategic planning and execution track record. In fact, that is why he was promoted into the position. But his rope began to fray when his strategic thinking ability was put to the test. His role within the bank had changed overnight: from being a brilliant strategic planner to becoming a successful strategic thinker. Without the capacity to create and re-create strategy, there would be nothing to implement.

He was caught between a rock and a hard place. He knew that within Japanese business society, he would quickly lose the respect of the very people he needed if he questioned them overtly or publicly. At the same time, his own neck and the bottom line of the bank depended on him to routinely scrutinize every particle of data and analysis. He realized that he needed to think differently in order to do this. Panicked, he sought help.

During our initial meetings, Junichiro mentioned that he had never learned to "think"; what he had learned was to be very adept at rapid pattern recognition and correcting imprecisions. In fact, that is how he had made a name for himself because in minutes he could automatically and accurately solve complex problems with mounds of data. He quickly discovered that this was not enough for strategic thinking.

In order for Junichiro to commit to taking the risk of learning the critical reflective processes that he understood were essential for learning to think strategically, he had to resolve the polite, on-the-surface Japanese cultural requirement that clashed with the particular practices required in critical reflective processing. This first step was a confidence builder. He identified several key strategic thinking strengths he already possessed (confident and experienced with his intuition, experience using reflection in nonwork contexts, access to positive role models, fierce desire to win). He also established strategic thinking as distinct from strategic planning within the executive and management vocabulary. And as the new company president, he set an expectation within the corporate culture of practicing critical inquiry— challenging, testing, and refining strategic ideas.

Furthermore, Junichiro retained his personal and cultural preference of dealing with people one-on-one, and he somewhat modified his indirect style so that he didn't feel as though he was "attacking" his Asian colleagues. This was important in terms of remaining authentic. Junichiro took great care to preface his critical inquiry with an explanation of the mutual and collective benefits of such a process. He invited them to reciprocate and demonstrated appropriate language of questions—making a game of the process. He also took care to thank each person before and after each critical dialogue encounter for supporting the long-term strategic capacity building of the bank. Once Junichiro had drawn up this list of conditions he felt were culturally necessary, he was satisfied he could commit himself to the learning process. The very process of drawing up the list engaged him in identifying and testing his own assumptions and beliefs about the learning process involved in strategic thinking.

It is important to remember that just because we "don't" doesn't mean we "can't" learn to recognize different patterns and develop different frames of reference. Pattern recognition and shattering is learnable! Culture is not an excuse to hide behind. Culture certainly has a very strong influence on the patterns we learn to recognize and also on the frames we learn to use; but reflective capacity is a human ability. Therefore, we can learn to shatter and reframe through critical reflection if we seek to and commit to it.

Regarding the influence of hierarchy: Some cultures consider it disrespectful and disloyal for junior executives or those from a certain group (e.g., women, newcomers, functional groups, nationalities) to express alternatives, to imagine beyond their prescribed status in society or outside the bounds of the hierarchy of a specific team or job description.

I find it quite common for executives from these cultures (organizational cultures as well as socio-national cultures) to lack an ability to even notice pattern variations, because they lack the experience base. Their culture has

taught them to follow a tightly defined, prescriptive approach to pattern identification. The idea of imagining new ways of seeing things is not even a
concept that registers because they have no experience in doing so. Their forte
is in paying attention to and quickly noticing a set of "correct" or "incorrect"
patterns in a given circumstance. While this has advantages, it is a habit of
mind that needs to be tested in order to learn to think strategically.

After several months of working on strategic thinking with a newly promoted ambitious Chinese global head of manufacturing for a multinational
paper company, this executive described the difference he noticed in his own
decision making after concentrating on critical reflective processes:

> *It used to be impossible for me to make decisions that were not given to
> me because I didn't even know what "think more strategically" meant.
> But there is a lot of pressure on me in my new job. I couldn't "see"
> anything except [for] what had been pointed out to me. I didn't know
> how to notice things. I was afraid to look for other things. The only
> things I "saw" were the things I was permitted to look at; everything else
> was blackened out in my mind.*
>
> *In my case, it was always important to notice what other people
> expect you to see—the aim in my culture is to avoid seeing anything
> that you are not supposed to see. It was like everything else was in the
> dark, and, naturally, I was afraid of the dark. I was supposed to be
> afraid of the dark. [Anything that is] new or different hides in the dark
> [for protection]—and now, that is what you are telling me and helping
> me to practice! I feel a little bit afraid, but I am amazed already at what
> I can see now that I am looking. I think I only needed permission
> and a guide. It is only now that I realize all the other things that are
> happening at the same time. I am already making better and bigger
> decisions and it's surprising to me, but I have a wonderful feeling of
> freedom and control in this way of thinking.*

22

The Challenge of Introducing Strategic Thinking Across Cultures

Having lived and worked abroad for more than two decades myself, I feel very strongly about the strategic need to transcend culture and to focus as quickly as possible instead on the informal learning process of strategic thinking. This does not mean ignoring culture; it means acknowledging and appreciating it within the larger learning context. The intent of strategic development is to increase the capacity for learning to think strategically, and culture is just one, albeit a significant, piece.

Yet the influence of culture on shaping collective and individual frames can have an impact on nearly every aspect of strategic decision making. Therefore, it is important to understand some common frames that need to be shattered and re-created across cultures. One of these common strategic challenges is getting information — credible, valid, verifiable, relevant, timely information that is necessary for making decisions. Cross-cultural expert Ernest Gundling notes in his book *Working GlobeSmart* that, while there may be numerous reasons that information is not shared readily, "In general, concerns about sharing information directly are more pronounced in hierarchical, group-oriented cultures where enduring personal relationships are a key personal asset. To place in jeopardy your relationship with a senior member of the hierarchy or a key network member could have dire long-term consequences."[4]

> *In many countries, who gives information is
> given greater significance than what the
> information is.*

Business information that is standard in some countries, such as annual reports, auditing and accounting reports and data, marketing data, and economic reports, may not be available, for a variety of reasons. Furthermore, the quality and the objectivity of information can be problematic. In many countries, who gives information is given greater significance than what the information is. Neither the information itself nor the person who provided the information dare be questioned because it would threaten the hierarchy that sustains the culture. There is no line that distinguishes fact from fiction; rather, the quality of the distinction is based on the status of the information provider.

The political background can also influence information gathering and complicate strategic decision making. When working in a country or with people from countries with a history of politically oppressive regimes, the legacy of fear and suspicion remains alive long after changes have been made on the political landscape. The ghosts of experience continue to haunt even the most progressive and bold. Providing relevant and truthful information to anyone outside a tight circle of family and a few friends is considered foolish and risky. Furthermore, the shadow of a thriving Mafia can guide the information flow of local and international businesses, and managers are likely to be guarded and hesitant about sharing information about anything —revenues, plans, or client relations—for fear of how it may be used against them.

As a means of introducing a strategic thinking imperative into a non-Western or culturally diverse environment, I find it helpful to position strategic thinking as a *directive* by having an authority figure from headquarters officially sanction the critical reflective process as being an integral part of making strategy competitive. State it as a corporate culture expectation, followed with modeling by senior management and guided coaching that is respectful of the need for individual practice. This approach bows to the dimension of hierarchy and legitimizes the unfamiliar new practice. It also gives permission to executives and managers to commit to practicing such things as critical inquiry and testing regardless of socio-national culture.

In other words, with this kind of positioning, the expectation of using a critical reflective process for the development of strategic thinking is explicitly stated as an imperative or directive from the top. This places the corporate culture above any socio-national culture for eight hours of each day within a specific context. The emphasis is not on a behavioral change, but, rather, on a fundamental process change that includes behavioral practices that undoubtedly counter existing belief systems on many levels. It will be disruptive, but dealing with disruption is part of adaptation, an essential part of competitive strategic capacity.

Shattering and Reframing Across Cultures

Culture can be influential on our ability to shatter and reframe. As mentioned, cultural values tend to direct what we learn to pay attention to — culture highlights the patterns we're "supposed to see." Culture also creates a context in which we practice and experience the right and wrong ways of identifying, interpreting, and evaluating these patterns. Culture is how we learn our first frames of good and bad. We learn to look at this situation in a particular way and make decisions according to prescribed frames. We also learn the degree of value given to both analysis and intuition. Culture rehearses us in our first tacit ways of knowing.

Shattering requires that we are able to challenge and test ourselves, others, and the habits, beliefs, and underlying assumptions that support the traditions of the organization. Therefore, we must be willing to risk comfort and familiarity in favor of the uncomfortable and uncertain. We need to be able to live with all the what-ifs that will haunt us as a result of shattering: What if my questions are laughed at? What if my data/information/hunch contradicts the commonly accepted way? What if I don't know the answer to my own question? What if I slaughter a "sacred cow"?

Time and again clients from around the world confide and comment that it is actually very liberating and freeing to use the deeper, dive domain of learning because they do not have to give up their authentic self. Instead, they are able to select, discard, borrow, and adapt at will. In my experience, this tedious and emotionally strenuous process of shattering cannot be taught in a traditional manner, but it can be coached. I have found that when clients reach the stage of shattering, the strategic thinking process is identical regardless of culture, because the strategic thinking process is driven by informal learning, not by culture.

Sometimes clients are anxious about the strategic thinking learning process, fearful that they might find themselves reclining on a couch, hanging from tree limbs, or positioned on a yoga mat. Trust me, it is an intensive and exhaustive process but one that is generally lackluster in terms of drama. Knowledge about the three-stage process of informal learning (preparation, experience, and reevaluation) discussed in Part III and the five attributes (imagination, broad perspective, juggle, no control, and desire to win) presented in Part IX are essential for executives in any culture to understand if they are expected to think strategically.

> *Personal and organizational determination*
> *and commitment levels are much more*
> *important for strategic thinking than any*
> *one particular culture's frames.*

Once the informal learning process and the five attributes are understood and attended to, culture becomes irrelevant to the strategic thinking process. The validity of data is greatly enhanced, integrity issues are made apparent, and better strategy making and implementation are a result. Learning to think strategically is well worth the investment if a company truly wants to grow a global pipeline of strategic thinkers. The road can be quite long and full of bumps, but it is certainly worth it. Personal and organizational determination and commitment levels are much more important for strategic thinking than any one particular culture's frames.

Anyone Can Learn to Think Strategically

Although it is a surprisingly pervasive belief in corporate corner offices, ivory towers, and management development circles, it is a myth to believe that someone (or you) may be unable to think strategically just because they (or you) come from a certain culture. Once again, I emphasize that culture is simply one factor that influences our experience. There is beauty to experience—it can be broadened, deepened, acquired, and transferred over the course of our entire life!

SCENARIO

Abo was a fiercely determined, strategically successful African tribal leader who was, unfortunately, illiterate due to sustained and dire economic, political, and social circumstances. His country had the good fortune of his being appointed to a government ministerial post as part of a nation-building process that was being instituted. I had the great pleasure of being invited to work on strategy development with the various government ministers and was told it would probably be easier for me if I just politely ignored Abo, because it would be impossible for him to fathom strategic thinking. But I found his contributions to be original, his questions to be insightful, and his wit to be irresistible — he was an experienced (and perhaps a natural) strategist. Culture, gender, class, intelligence, and education are only individual and collective factors that bear on the frames we shape, but the informal learning process drives strategic thinking.

In spite of my modest expectations, this man tested my beliefs about learning strategic thinking — heretofore, illiteracy had not been part of my strategic development experience. Abo, it turned out, was very adept at using the informal learning process in the same way as literate corporate executives. He methodically gathered and analyzed massive amounts of information from diverse sources, acknowledging that much of it was incomplete and inaccurate; and he asked focused questions that exposed underlying complexity and contradictions.

It quickly became apparent that he had a thinking habit that was admirable and inspiring to other government ministers: He asked critical questions to test the motives and beliefs of himself and anybody else in attendance. His probes were insightful and provocative, and they tested for implications and consequences that were broad based. He dutifully tested and retested his own and others' viewpoints, and he claimed his feisty nature was a result of being doubtful, curious, and eternally hopeful — not dissimilar to those descriptors put forth by the ancient Greeks that included dealing with seeming polarities. This combination compelled him "to fight for what I know in my heart is right." He was an incredible problem solver with an ability to make connections of seemingly unrelated matters in hopes of sowing the seeds of new possibilities.

This was a highly experienced strategic thinker who simply didn't read or write. He was thinking at very deep levels and had extraordinary critical reflection capability. He spoke articulately and profoundly. And Abo had developed an incredible ability to transfer his learning across various contexts. With ease and pleasure he used his learning experiences in the wartime and peacetime villages and mountains to draw analogies and metaphors for the new government challenges — his storytelling was riveting. It was as if he had had years of experience in dealing with members of the new parliament and international agencies because they were like his prior experiences. He was very wise to the ways of politics; none of these strategic policy problems were new to him, only the context had changed.

In addition to further developing his strategic thinking strengths, he chose to focus development on the flip side of the strategy-making coin—building his linear, logical cognitive abilities such as sequencing information and understanding the logic of cause and effect—necessary skills for strategic planning. He also jumped at the chance to enroll in a literacy program to make up for lost time.

Admittedly, this is an extreme example, but only because I point it out as exceptional. Cases similar to this abound in companies and organizations and in communities around the globe (e.g., illiteracy, dyslexia, speech, hearing, and physical disabilities). My point is twofold: We can all learn to further develop the reflective processes that are essential to strategic thinking. The second point is that we need to be aware that our own cultural frames can limit our ability to see strategic thinking talent, because talent may not fit the pattern of what we believe it should look like. Understanding the five attributes (see Part IX) and the informal learning process (see Parts II and III) inherent to strategic thinking is critical if we aspire to develop others and ourselves.

Simply bringing together a group of highly intelligent or well-educated people is insufficient for strategic learning to occur. It requires a mutual understanding among these people about the strategic intent and an awareness of the process involved to achieve that intent. This learning process is dependent on a high capacity for critical reflection, trusted intuition, and skillful critical dialogue that is balanced with meticulous analytic skills among the people involved. Part of strategic capacity building is for this process to become embedded within the organization's culture.

Following are seven suggestions for introducing strategic thinking across socio-national culture.

1. Clarify intent. Is the aim to develop strategic thinking or strategic planning? We need both, and they need to be complementary functions in order to achieve a winning strategy; yet learning is easier if a clear focus is articulated.
2. Pick and choose and self-select. Not everybody in an organization needs to be a strategic thinker. While reflective processes can be developed to varying degrees, we also need strategic planners if an excellent strategy has a prayer of being successfully implemented. Offer information

about developing strategic thinking to everyone with strategic responsibility, but allow people to self-select initially, to create role models and momentum. We need to understand and develop both strategic thinking and planning in order to leverage individual and organizational strengths—forcing one or the other will only create a learning barrier, while supporting self-selection will foster the learning.

3. Give permission to use a deeper, dive level of learning that includes critical reflective processes of inquiry, challenge, reflection, and testing.

4. Provide an abundance of information about the strategic thinking learning process up front. This creates a foundation for trusting the process and encourages self-directed learning.

5. Use an informal development process, such as coaching or mentoring, and be patient with the time frame that may be needed. Don't pressure people to see results. This only stalls the learning process. Focus instead on including and practicing critical inquiry in daily business tasks and increasing the critical dialogue on day-to-day issues. Much of the learning process may be invisible at first, and much of the early learning may be incidental (i.e., trusting senior leadership, trusting the critical reflective process, trusting changed relationships, and so on).

6. Don't assume. Clarify what you know and what others know and what you don't know and what others don't know.

7. Avoid using "culture" as an excuse for not developing strategic thinkers in every area of the world. The informal learning process and attributes required are of a human, not cultural nature.

In summary, we need to understand what influences the way we frame our experiences as well as the assumptions and beliefs we hold. It is imperative that we understand the learning framework into which culture fits. Learning to shatter and reframe beliefs that are culturally influenced must occur in order to learn to think strategically. Admittedly, this can be more or less challenging from one culture to the next, but it is part of human adaptation, and it can be learned. It is inclusive of all cultures.

IS ANYBODY BORN WITH THIS KNOW-HOW?

The Myth of the Chosen Few: Five Critical Attributes for Learning to Think Strategically

A man, though wise, should never be ashamed of learning more, and must unbend his mind.

From Antigone, by Sophocles (442–42 B.C.), Greek philosopher

The Five Critical Attributes

Luckily, and in spite of all the implied messages that are dispersed about strategic thinking as a reserve of the chosen few, strategic thinking is indeed learnable. Is it teachable? Perhaps not directly. But it certainly is learnable.

The temptation to accept a myth about who can learn to think strategically is understandable in a strategic environment that is overloaded with complexities, contradictions, and confusion. A myth, after all, controls the possibility of conflicting evidence — myths help us make meaning of conflict and ambivalence. There are four reasons that propagate the myth of the *chosen few* — those who think strategically.

First, overuse of the term *strategy*, without clear definition about strategic thinking or planning, creates confusion about when we're making it. Because we are unsure when and if we are making it, we assume we really are not making it, and therefore others must be making it.

Second, strategy is generally talked about as something we get to make when we are important; its absence is a well-known, sacrosanct ritual used to prevent people from promotion. And since we tend to know very few people who are truly important, those who make strategy must be among the chosen few.

Third, we recall the capstone strategy courses in most business school curricula and the tip of the triangle in corporate strategy structure. Both imply elitism and illusions of grandeur. Criteria are kept unspoken and mostly vague, so we are left with the impression that whatever it is that is required, we do not have it, which reinforces the myth of the chosen few. In truth, most of what occurs in the strategy meetings of these elite pockets of organizational power is not about strategic thinking — it is about strategic planning. So it's a bottle that hasn't been uncorked, a party that hasn't happened!

Fourth, successful strategy is deceptively simple to see: It either works or it doesn't. This deludes us into believing that making strategy is about the luck or magic of those clever chosen few. The underlying thinking process is mostly ambiguous, invisible, and not understood, so we just chalk it up to the mystical moments of a few. But strategic thinking is an emotionally draining and intellectually challenging process; it is difficult, risky, complex—and learnable.

To dispel this deeply held and widely believed myth of the chosen few is not easy. If, however, we understand the attributes that support the learning process involved in strategic thinking, we can begin to imagine ways to develop our capacity to think strategically.

Part IX comprises three chapters. Chapter 23 discusses five attributes identified by seasoned and successful strategists as being critical to learning to think strategically.

- Having an *Imagination*
- A *Broad Perspective*
- The ability to *Juggle*, or attend to competing, incomplete and inaccurate information all at once
- The ability to deal with things over which you have *No Control*
- An adamant *Desire to Win*

Each of these attributes will be discussed in turn throughout Chapter 23. Chapter 24 describes the interplay among the five attributes. Chapter 25 discusses the notion of adaptation as a strategic expectation.

Something I have noticed across culture, industry, and age is that conceptual, intuitive thinkers often tend to have a natural inclination toward strategic thinking. As with any highly complex and high-stakes endeavor, there are those who have a natural inclination for strategic thinking and those who may be challenged in various ways. It is important, however, to remember that a challenge can be overcome, and a natural inclination is only a "booster shot." By the same token, concrete, linear, analytic thinkers tend to have a natural edge in strategic planning.

Strategic thinking is a highly complex synthesis of the affective and cognitive learning domains that requires extensive use of the deeper, dive level of learning and a high degree of reflective capacity. Personal style preferences need to be respected, and differences must be perceived as complementary to and compatible with the strategic thinking process. In other words, concrete, linear, analytic thinkers can most certainly learn to become more critically reflective, intuitive, and a-rational (though they may squeal from time to time). Conceptual, intuitive thinkers likewise can learn to become more linear, logical, and rational (though they, too, may squawk at times).

Not everyone within an organization needs to be a strategic thinker. The organizational aim is to create a pipeline that is drawn from all levels, locales, and functions within an organization to contribute strategic sustainability. Everyone, however, can improve and informally develop to varying degrees the five essential attributes and critical reflective processes.

It is important to ensure that everyone within an organization has access to resources that support the learning process used for strategic thinking:

- Information about the strategic thinking process
- Opportunities to observe critical dialogue among senior management
- Practice and participation in critical dialogue regarding strategic issues
- Encouragement to engage in artistic and creative endeavors

With such exposure and a learning expectation, some natural strategic thinkers will emerge from the shadows. Skillful planners who wish to strengthen their strategic thinking capacity will also come forth, creating a first link to the pipeline. From here, interest will be generated and others will be attracted and drawn into the pipeline.

Having worked with both accomplished and aspiring strategists, I contend that genuine strategic thinking growth is largely about making sure that they understand what is required for learning to think strategically and allowing them to take the lead in their own learning. This process differs dramatically from one person to another. One strategist may be very confident and adept at linear, analytical, and logical processes and at the same time be lacking in nonlinear, a-rational, and integrative learning, whereas someone else may require emphasizing the reverse.

Once strategists understand how learning to think strategically occurs, I find that executives can and do come up with their own best ideas and approaches to support the development of the five attributes and critical reflective processes. When aspiring strategists lead the learning process, their commitment to breaking old habits, practicing new habits, and taking the risk to trust some informal learning increases considerably.

> *The aim is not to create a worldwide*
> *strategic thinking campaign but, rather, to*
> *create a pipeline of strategic thinkers across*
> *functions and at all levels within an*
> *organization, for competitive purposes.*

It is also important to keep in mind that not every person within an organization needs to be a strategic thinker. The aim is not to create a worldwide strategic thinking campaign but, rather, to create a pipeline of strategic thinkers across functions and at all levels within an organization, for competitive purposes. If we want to further our strategic thinking or if our position requires it now or in the future, then there is no need to panic. Rest assured that each of the following attributes can be developed to some degree of mastery with discipline, determination, and practice.

The executives I interviewed for the study underlying this book were asked to describe what they paid attention to when making good strategy and what was the most essential requirement for thinking strategically. Five attributes emerged as critical requisites for successful strategic thinking: imagination, broad perspective, juggle, no control over, and a desire to win.[1] I had expected that the executives' different backgrounds might generate different attributes they considered essential to learning to think strategically. But a surprising finding of the study was that the five attributes were consistently and emphatically mentioned by executives across the various industries, ages, and nationalities of the professionals represented. The five attributes are not arranged in order of importance; they are *all* identified as being equally essential to learning to think strategically.

Imagination

> *The real voyage of discovery consists not in making new landscapes, but in*
> *having new eyes.*
>
> *Marcel Proust (1871–1922), French novelist*

The ability to use our imagination is a critical factor for the learning of strategy thinking. Simply dealing with information or linear matter is insufficient. One of the Japanese financial executives in the study stated:

To start, I have an idea or a problem. As I become aware, I usually start to ask questions, and, of course, then my imagination begins to act. (leans forward, talks very quickly and gradually louder) And depending on what I do about it, I can get into trouble (laughter) or have some fun! You know, imagination is, I will say to you, a very, very important part of good strategy making. This is probably the best part, and it is necessary to enjoy it—to spend time with your imagination! (smiles, sits back) I think it's a big mistake not to include imagination [in making strategy]. It is something that happens inside—and can happen anywhere. You know, other people tend to ruin this part, so I do it privately and don't tell anybody it's happening! (laughter)

A Polish senior manufacturing executive, explained the importance of imagination in making strategy: "You must always try to imagine what else or how else things could be. Imagination! This is something nobody talks about in strategy sessions; maybe they think it's not so serious or sophisticated. Or maybe it is that you cannot buy it. (laughter) But it's the jewel nobody expects in the pauper's attic."

An American executive commented, "A really important part of making good strategy is being able to imagine things. You can't just work with facts and data. Your mind and imagination have to kick in if you're going to be any good."

The CFO of the technology company concurred with other successful strategists in the study: "Your imagination kicks into high gear, you read everything and talk with everybody—no stone goes unturned; you keep rolling them around." Strategic thinking requires the cognitive duo of convergent and divergent thinking. Divergent thinking is required when we break habits, see new patterns, and imagine possible connections. Reframing is a divergent exercise that simply summarizes novel connections and new possibilities.

Divergent thinking can also be accelerated through travel as we look at information, trends, and data in new ways or see and configure different patterns through the lens of a different culture. Divergent thinking can also be used to create alternative conclusions to the analysis and synthesis of data. It involves having continuous and meaningful internal conversations that are reflective and having external conversations that are informative and testing —conversations with others that focus on data and insight drawn from both outside and inside the familiar sources available within the company and industry. Critical inquiry and critical dialogue are useful divergent communication techniques.

This is very different from convergent thinking, which is used for decision making and concluding. Convergent thinking is essential much further along the strategy thinking process, and it can actually interfere with the process of thinking strategically if applied too early on. Convergent thinking is used to reframe the possibilities that exist for the organization based on objective criteria and eventually for selecting an approach. Convergent conversations can be internal and external and are used to test strategic ideas against the core competencies and values of the organization and to assess feasibility—playing out probable and improbable scenarios. Discussion and debate are excellent convergent communication techniques.

Occasionally some of my business clients tend to lump creativity and intuition together. These aspiring strategists mistakenly assume that if they focus on developing creativity, they will magically improve their intuitive judgment. Unfortunately, the two don't always function well together. It is interesting to note that creativity, by definition, is not tied to our past experiences. Yet intuition is a product of the patterns we experienced in the past as we developed pattern recognition and framing. Therefore, an intuitive approach to creativity relies on previous experience yet also transcends that experience.[2]

Creativity comes from combining different, seemingly unrelated, dimensions of experience.

By any measure, management and strategy are typically not regarded as particularly creative fields. It is easy to understand why: Management generally implies belonging to a compliance squad, and strategy is typically understood as planning—exceedingly beige and bland. Creativity, on the other hand, comes from combining different, seemingly unrelated dimensions of experience.

But these limits are only contemporary myths we have come to accept. Organizational myths such as these need to be identified and shattered if strategists have any hope of making innovative, adaptable, and winning strategy. I believe that one way to shatter the myth is to learn from people who are not locked into the frames of traditional management and strategy patterns and practices. We know that successful strategists delight in using their imagination when thinking strategically and that we all have the capability of transferring learning from one context to another.[3] This transfer is an essential part of the informal learning process that is so vital to strategic thinking; we need to know it and trust it in order to leverage it for strategic advantage.

> *Ironically, at a time when innovative*
> *strategic thinking is among the most*
> *pressing concerns, business schools are*
> *upping the ante on analysis, with the*
> *serious intent of churning out people who*
> *will make innovative strategy.*

One of the biggest problems in this regard is that we treat business and creativity as if they don't belong together, though they do. They seem to be strange partners only because we take the frame of polarity and position them as opposites. Within this framework, we have to pick one or the other because we take an either–or mind-set. For businesses to thrive in a competitive global economy, sustainable strategic capability is an imperative. This requires innovative strategic thinking, which draws deep from the wells of creativity. For serious strategists, I suggest looking to the arts as a rich source for developing imagination, a critical attribute to successful strategic thinking.

Ironically, at a time when innovative strategic thinking is among the most pressing concerns, business schools are upping the ante on analysis, with the serious intent of churning out people who will make innovative strategy. In terms of my earlier metaphor, this is like hoping to pluck strawberries from onion plants! I recommend instead that these MBAs be sent to the strawberry patch. If strategic innovation is what business schools wish to cultivate, students would be much better off engaging in photography, painting, design, or perhaps guitar or piano lessons in order to "know" creativity. This will contribute substantially more to their long-term ability to create an innovative strategy simply because they will have firsthand creative experience on which to draw.

At a time when companies say they are desperate to be more creative, what they do through their daily decisions prevents them from moving in that direction. Truly creative people often do not feel they connect to business. Furthermore, within most businesses there is an aversion to the very word *creative* (*innovative* is the preferred term).

Creativity is about combining the original and the new. The resultant tension is what drives many aspiring strategists to cork the creative process and return to their prior habits of mind and same-frame thinking. Our formal education teaches us that when we feel this sort of tension, we frame the situation as a problem and decide we must choose one way or another. By remaining in this traditional frame of problem solving, we stop short of ever moving forward with the creative process. The tension that is provoked is merely a signal inviting us to move through the situation by using both, rather than either–or thinking.

I find it amusing that although the core business of any company is dependent on the ability to re-create innovative strategy, the creative people in almost every company I know are very rarely part of strategic meetings. They are excluded from a strategic thinking process that requires their greatest corporate asset, creativity, because they are assumed not to know the business side. What would happen if we excluded financial experts from the strategy process because they may not know the creative side of the thinking process?

But how is the business known? It is learned (just as the creative comes to be known). Most business strategies are fragile precisely because successful strategy is always past tense and because senior leadership has no process in place to generate sustainable, adaptive, innovative strategy. This requires including those individuals with very different perspectives and experiences to challenge, test, and refine the underlying frames that support current business strategy; it also requires understanding that shattering and reconfiguring are part of the creative process needed for strategic success.

The challenge for strategists is to analyze and assess creative processes as well as contexts in which creativity might be fostered. Innovative strategy can only come about through the combination of different perspectives and ideas in particular situations and for specific decisions. In order for that to happen, imagination must be acknowledged and appreciated as part of the strategic thinking process.

Broad Perspective

If the doors of perception were cleansed, everything would appear as it truly is, infinite.

William Blake (1757–1827), English poet and artist

The second attribute identified as being critical to learning strategic thinking is the ability to see a situation from a broad perspective. Executives I interviewed maintained that the ability to see things from a wide perspective is an imperative because it allows them to see many things at the same time and to begin to imagine seeing things differently — both as they are and as they might be. In describing how he broadens his perspective, an American technology executive said:

I just talk to people, trying to hear about their experiences . . . all kinds of people. That's what you realize about strategy and why I like making strategy. If you want to develop a big picture or see a big picture, you need to talk to people. I mean everywhere you go, in the market line, at the beach, at the movies—even at my parent's house, flying, you name it. Wherever there are people, somebody's willing to talk. If you listen to all of them and pull back, way back, you start to see things more broadly. You have to look at the picture differently though; when you look at the whole picture, you can figure out how strange things actually fit in—and your options explode.

Interestingly, developing a broad perspective and dialogue were often referred to by the executives in the same thought. They claimed that talking to a vast and diverse range of people helps develop the ability for broad perspective. They also implied that dialogue leads to improved thinking, which leads to a broader perspective, which is necessary for making good strategy.

One of the Japanese executives exclaimed, "You must find a way to be in the highest balloon, because it gives you the very best view. You must talk to everybody all the time, not just a few people during one time of the year. You have to be a big or good listener in order to see the wide perspective."

A Chinese executive said, "I like to look broadly at things and imagine what they might look like in different arrangements—and this is really important, I believe, for making strategy." After reflecting on the question about the most essential requirement for thinking strategically, an American financial executive responded, "You know, another thing I guess I'd say is perspective. That's why you've got to get out and talk to people—it broadens your perspective. And that's what strategy, or good strategy, is all about. (pause) The best vantage point is from the highest point—that birds-eye view."

The technology CFO from Hong Kong explained, "I like to see the big picture—that's why I like making strategy. Even though it is difficult to do, you must make it a habit to talk to many people, about every issue. This is how you get the broad perspective that you need to make successful strategy."

The CEO of a financial company commented that one of the most important reasons to broaden perspective is "to improve your way of thinking. So get to the highest point, to get the best broad view. That's the best way to improve thinking because you see things differently, and then you have more possibilities for thinking."

The most important way these successful strategists broadened their perspective was by diversifying and expanding their interactions and contacts with people because it forced them to challenge their frameworks and to see other patterns. All of the executives interviewed attributed their experience of living and working outside their home country to broadening their perspective in ways that nothing else could.

Social scientists S. Weil and I. McGill maintain that "a person or organisation which knows only their own village will not understand it. It is through dialogue across villages that we are enabled to consider what we intend and what we do from new perspectives."[4] This suggests an experiential link to an expanded perspective, the attribute of broad perspective successful strategists claimed as essential to learning to make strategy. While not everyone tasked with making strategy can or will choose to live/work in another country, it is enormously beneficial to live outside one's comfort zone and to break with the familiar as a means to broadening one's perspective.

The attribute of broad perspective also helps to maintain a rational thinking base for thinking strategically while simultaneously allowing us to be nonlinear and a-rational in the overall process. Rational and a-rational thinking function well together. Although 100% of the executives in the study had advanced educational degrees in science or business (disciplines requiring highly linear and rational thinking), they all seemed to use a broad, nonlinear, a-rational approach to thinking when they made good strategy.

These executives had an extensive capacity to shift between rational thinking and a-rational thinking and an uncanny ability to see connections and create synergies among seemingly unrelated things. This is the essence of creativity and is necessary for taking a broad perspective. Successful strategists also described their thinking in metaphorical terms, relating events and situations to something else; past experiences provided metaphors for new experiences, and the entire strategy thinking process appeared to be connected to life experiences on which they drew.

Juggle

It isn't what we don't know that gives us trouble, it's what we know that ain't so.

Will Rogers (1879–1935), American actor and humorist

The third essential attribute mentioned was the importance of having the ability to pay attention to many things all at once, specifically being able to deal with incomplete and inconsistent information, inaccurate data, and constantly changing information. This is no doubt one of the biggest challenges for global strategists.

The ability to see and to work with
opposing relations and paradoxes is indeed
an attribute identified by effective
strategists as a requirement for strategic
thinking—as opposed to planning, where
the ability to eliminate paradoxes and
ambivalence is required.

A technology executive in the study responded to the question about what he pays attention to and what is essential for learning to think strategically by exclaiming, "Learn to juggle! [You're] bombarded with tons of information, especially about economics and political processes . . . and it changes all the time. [You] need to start thinking about how everything effects everything else. You juggle in your mind—that's how you're able to deal with so many unknowns and unpredictable things."

The ability to see and to work with opposing relations and paradoxes is indeed an attribute identified by effective strategists as a requirement for learning to think strategically—as opposed to planning, where the ability to eliminate paradoxes and ambivalence is required.

The Polish manufacturing CEO quipped, "You cannot just think about the obvious. It is very easy to gather information. Most of it is of no use—or it is not true—it is incomplete always! (pause) You must know this and treat it [information] like you carry hot potatoes!"

A technology company executive emphatically stated:

The importance of filtering and figuring out ways to use tons and tons of information, most of it incomplete and inconsistent, is a must. If you can't work with a lot of incomplete or contradictory information, you'll never be a good strategist. If you can and you enjoy it, and you're driven, then you have a chance.

In describing what he pays particular attention to when making strategy, one of the Japanese financial executives said:

I pay attention to everything all at once. (laughter) It's not good to separate or categorize things when you make strategy—everything must be included and you must figure out a way to think like this if you want to win. If you practice, at first it will look [like] a blur. Then you must keep step[ping] back until you either see something you recognize, or maybe you will see the whole as a new idea. (pause followed by a big breath) That is how to make sense of too much information! And you must never trust it.

A country manager of a pharmaceutical division covering a remote area of southeast Asia smiled as he read his job description aloud: "responsible for corporate compliance and making strategy." Laughing, he described it as "inhaling and exhaling at the same time!" And he's right. On the one hand he is responsible for enforcing compliance with myriad corporate, industry, and country regulations, rules, and meticulous procedures—tasks requiring extreme convergent thinking. On the other hand he is expected to come up with a successful, sustainable, adaptable, and innovative strategy in an unbelievably competitive market—a charge requiring divergent and intuitive thinking is necessary. An ability to juggle the competing strategic demands is a reality of thinking in a global business strategy environment.

It is an everyday strategic challenge to be responsible for compliance (where the role is to ensure that others remain within the existing framework) and also to be responsible for strategic thinking (where the role is to move beyond the current framework). This is one of the great juggling challenges for global executives because they require very different mind-sets and ability sets.

No Control Over

Anyone can hold the helm when the sea is calm.

Maxim 358, by Publicius Syrus (first century B.C.)

The fourth attribute that executives identified as being critical to making good strategy was the ability to deal with things over which we have no control. A Japanese financial executive explained:

I'd say always prepare for the unexpected—you never know. But you'd better plan for a lot of them—things you never expected—they'll be there! (moves forward, talks faster) And I'd say to pay attention to what you can't control. (sits back in chair, talks louder, and gestures with hands) This is backwards from what they teach you in all these courses and books, but it's what I think from my own experience.

The American financial company executive reminded us of the following:

> *The world is full of the unpredictable, and these are the things that make or break business strategy. You need to be on top of these unpredictable things, get comfortable thinking about them. (moves forward, puts both hands on tabletop) When you're talking about developing a good strategy in this kind of a merger-and-acquisition environment, you can't waste your time on things you can control—you'd better spend it thinking about what you can't control.*

One of the Polish executives put it another way: "We must think about what we don't know and expect the worst always. And it's no use having a party about what you now control, because you don't know tomorrow. Control is only in our imagination. If you think in this way, you will ask good questions."

This was supported by a German manufacturing company executive, who explained, "We need to think about everything, especially the things we don't have any power over. These are the things we must include in good strategy thinking."

A Japanese executive commented, "Thinking about strategy is not so predictable—and it is pain[ful]. I must work mostly with unknown information, many missing pieces . . . but always think about the big picture."

To underscore the importance of being able to deal with things you can't control when making strategy, an American executive declared, "You're driven to find ways to overcome the unpredictable and changing obstacles and disasters, things you're totally dependent on yet have absolutely no control over."

Contrary to what is taught in many formal strategy-planning courses, the executives in this study overwhelmingly indicated that it was critical to pay attention to what they could not control, rather than to what they could control, in order to make a winning strategy. This appears to have been a result of their personal experience.

Interestingly, the executives used the attribute of no control as a kind of risk-leverage tool. The elements of risk and fear were referred to throughout the interviews by all of the executives as an emotional motivator for learning to make strategy. Risk and fear also contributed to their incidental learning, particularly about not trusting sources of data, which conversely led them to trust themselves. They learned to reframe situations to enable them to see new opportunities and to think and trust a-rational and intuitive thinking in situations over which they had no control.

I believe this helps explain why these successful strategists thrive on a high level of challenge and why they identified the ability to deal with things over which they have no control as being one of the five essential attributes for making strategy. The ability to deal with things over which they had no control appealed to and tested their competitive drive and strengthened their desire to win. Things over which they had no control offered challenge, which in turn offered meaningful learning, which eventually led to successful strategy thinking. The factor of fear was a motivator, and they incidentally learned to value negative experiences as being important to the learning process. This experience allowed them to take risks with decisions over which they had no control. Through their experience, they learned that negative factors were really just challenges for them to overcome in order to win.

In tough situations, successful strategists act as if they have already won, because they do not believe they can lose—akin to what poet Rainer Maria Rilke penned: "Follow your fear." These strategists experienced the great power that comes in releasing themselves of the very thing that shamed them, and they made the old fear their source of pride.

This attribute of no control appeared to be closely related to the last attribute, desire to win. Fear of losing requires taking risks, and dealing with things over which they have no control creates risk, which means they could lose. These successful strategists have an uncompromising desire to win.

The element of risk appeared to be an enticement to these executives, for it apparently played on their competitive nature. Learning to deal with things over which they have no control seemed to give them a competitive advantage: If everyone has access to the same data, paying attention to what they can't control requires that the executives use imagination to devise a winning outcome. It seemed to appeal to their need for a game, which fed into their intense desire to win.

Desire to Win

What counts is not necessarily the size of the dog in the fight—it's the size of the fight in the dog.

Dwight D. Eisenhower (1890–1969), American general and thirty-fourth president of the United States

The fifth and final critical attribute mentioned by all of the executives interviewed was a strong desire to win. The passion and conviction necessary for driving strategic thinking is connected to this attribute. The element of competition was a critical factor influencing their ability to learn to think strategically. In response to the question "What has allowed you to be successful in making strategy when others have not been?" the CFO of a financial company instantaneously replied, "I like to be ahead of everybody else. If you don't have that drive, you're not the one to make strategy—it won't be strong or good enough."

The Polish manufacturing COO emphasized that in order to be successful in making strategy, "You must be determined to win, have a fighting spirit." He explained, "Making good strategy—it's about figuring out how to win—this compelling need to get things right, perfect, or win. It's mandatory to good strategy making. Without it, you're simply making plans."

New strategies emerge from both competition and confrontation, necessities for learning to think strategically. Without competition and confrontation, strategy will not proceed. Dialogue, discussion, and debate are all required communication techniques the successful strategists used for leveraging competitive and confrontational situations.

In response to a question about what has allowed him to be successful in making strategy when others have not been, the American CEO of the technology company exclaimed:

The stakes are too high to not win. You've got to win. You'd better be able to take risks, be extremely well informed, and always build in backups. (pause) And you'd better win. (grin) Sometimes it doesn't seem like work—it's more like a game (laughter)—and we want to win. We must win!

The German manufacturing executive succinctly stated, "I like to win. I like the challenge of the game. And when you run one of the world's best textile companies, you must win, or you lose. It's simple."

A Japanese financial executive sheepishly confessed, "I am very stubborn, (laughter) or at least everyone says this about me—so maybe it's true. It must be this way if I want to make good strategy. I don't lose!"

A compelling desire to win can reframe reality. This made Lady Macbeth the most powerful woman of Scotland. She created the future because she alone demonstrated the greatest desire, and everyone in Shakespeare's *Macbeth* followed her agenda before their own.

Desire to win was a strong undercurrent in the successful strategists' descriptions of learning to think strategically. This was one area where they seemed to make a definitive case for black or white—either they win or they lose. I could argue that having an intense desire to win allowed these executives to gravitate toward a highly competitive environment and even to contribute and perpetuate its competitiveness; it may also have enabled them to excel and thrive in a competitive environment. The desire to win was perceived by the executives as a motivator. It tied all of the other attributes together by becoming the reason for learning—to make a winning strategy.

24

Interplay of the Five Attributes

The combination of this particular set of five attributes supports critical reflection, which is the central process of dive learning that is required in the informal strategic learning model presented in Part III. The three-stage informal learning model, consisting of preparation, experience, and reevaluation stages, and the five attributes are connected. Different combinations of the five attributes, in a simultaneous interplay, are used during each of the three stages: preparation, experience, and reevaluation.

I would argue that the set of five attributes establishes a mental precondition conducive to engaging in reflective processes or that the routine use of the reflective process model fosters the set of five attributes. I might also deduce that in response to certain strategic thinking tasks, challenges, or undertakings—a particular set of attributes is, in fact, required for strategic thinking. Because so much of strategic thinking occurs informally, I argue that all of the foregoing may well contribute to developing strategic thinking.

Paying attention to and developing the combination of the five attributes is as important as the informal process we use in learning to think strategically. A compelling and fierce desire to win propels the reflective process. A vivid and active imagination generates curiosity and creativity in the reflective process. The quest for broad perspective is enhanced by both a desire to win and imagination, offering the individual a perpetual array of new possibilities that requires continuous testing. The ability to juggle, to constructively deal with many conflicting things at once, invites challenge and tension to the reflective process, especially when it is combined with the ability to constructively deal with things one has no control over. Although the specific combination of these attributes is different for each person and each strategic thinking circumstance, they are all essential to learning to think strategically.

In a surprising way, the five attributes can be both a source of challenge in the strategic thinking process and a venue to overcome challenge. As a source of challenge, this combination of five attributes presents the potential for feeling obsessed and overwhelmed.

For example, the Japanese financial CEO explained that in his quest to achieve a broader perspective, he felt overwhelmed and desperate by having to attend to so many things over which he had no control. He expressed tremendous feelings of angst when attempting to balance competing feelings of trying, on the one hand, to unleash his creativity and at the same time to rein in his imagination. He expressed distress at having to monitor his nearly compulsive desire to win. Yet he ascribed not a negative connotation to the descriptors he used (i.e., "frustration," "overwhelmed," "distressed") but, instead, a positive connotation—he became animated and energized as he recalled numerous such experiences.

Instead of his succumbing to the pressure, the interplay among these attributes created motivation and challenge that, in fact, propelled him forward in the pursuit of making strategy. The executives regarded situations that could easily have been considered detrimental to making strategy as an opportunity to exercise imagination. They frequently used reflection in action to reframe the circumstance as an opportunity for a win. In this sense, being able to engage the attribute of imagination functioned as a motivator because the executives could create options and alternatives to gain a competitive advantage. According to their descriptions, the executives regarded having their imagination challenged as a kind of sport or game that was fueled by their desire to win.

In a discussion about learning within a challenging context, M. W. McCall, M. M. Lombardo, and A. M. Morrison of the Center for Creative Leadership note: "Development occurs to some degree in even the most hostile environments, so the issue is one of channeling, controlling, and enhancing whatever positive is already happening."[5]

Communication Techniques for Attribute Integration

The deeper-level, or dive, learning domain is used extensively to connect the attributes to one another. Storytelling, dialogue, and debate were communicative learning techniques favored by the successful strategists, not only to inspire creativity and to stimulate their imagination, but to build, sustain, and connect the other attributes. Storytelling created a means by which they could deal with things over which they had no control and provided a reference point for the testing of subsequent experiences and as a means of sharing information. Interestingly, stories in the form of parables and analogies were commonly described as a way of transferring strategic learning across contexts.

Their storytelling was reflective in nature, so, instead of just exchanging facts, the strategists indicated that they received more knowledge by putting the information into a context—a story. They tended to use this technique to challenge their assumptions and reflect both in and on action. This is congruent with a comment by informal learning experts Victoria Marsick and Marie Volpe: "Informal learning often depends on chance encounters and random events and circumstances. Only afterward do people construct a logical story to explain their learning to themselves and others."[6]

Stories may serve as an impetus to gathering and testing data. For example, a small factual detail is brought to light in the telling of a story, making the listener realize that this detail could be crucial. This prompts an inquiry for more information from a variety of sources. Or a story may serve to broaden and deepen the data by providing context. A German manufacturing executive noted, "We just like to come together and talk about what we read—it seems we all read different things—and of course we also read the same publications. And we tell stories, a lot of stories about different scenarios.—It's better than just talking all the time. I think storytelling elevates my thinking."

Curiously, storytelling was also used as a kind of testing tool by the strategists. They noticed that stories change with the telling, although the facts of the circumstances on which the story is based may remain constant. Have you ever noticed how the story of a major success your business had changes depending on when the story is told (within minutes of an announcement, six months later, or 12 years later), who the audience is (your kids, a recruiter, a new hire, your rival), how often it has been told (the more it is told, the more it is tested), and who told it? The first telling of any story is likely to be quite different in its description of details, the sequence, the pace, and so on than subsequent versions of the same story.

This ability to continually add layers of context is an inherent strength of storytelling, and because stories change all the time, it allows the strategists to continually use their imagination to combine information and try out various scenarios with colleagues. The hypothetical scenarios served to engage them in reflection in action. As executives presented a story, they got a flurry of reactions, questions, and new data that challenged the original story. Reflection occurred, followed by revisions to the story; subsequently, either part of the story was retold or a brand new story was shared. More questioning occurred, followed by still more information and data and eventually more reflection and revisions.

Storytelling also appeared to be used continually to refine the executives' thinking about strategy making. By drawing on each other's thinking and hearing their stories, the executives were able to frame and reframe situations by putting things into a broader perspective and therefore view situations, variables, and options differently. In this sense, they appeared to use what L. G. Bolman and T. Deal call a *symbolic frame*,[7] which is effective in ambiguous or uncertain circumstances where roles, relationships, and goals are unclear.

The executives in the study were acutely aware that they were tasked with making global strategy within a chaotic environment, and storytelling seemed to allow them to create symbols to diminish the unpredictability. As Columbia University professors Victoria Marsick and Marie Volpe explain, "The symbolic frame considers the roles of myths, symbols, stories, . . . actors, rituals, ceremonies, humor, play, and metaphors in organizational life."[8] The strategists in this study perceived a disorderly and confused environment as a challenge to advance their strategic agenda, and storytelling served as an effective communication technique for clarification and unification to this end.

In conclusion, the combination of the five attributes is as important as the informal process we use in learning to think strategically. A compelling and fierce *desire to win* propels the reflective process. A vivid and active *imagination* generates curiosity and creativity in the reflective process. The quest for *broad perspective* is enhanced by both a desire to win and imagination, offering the individual a perpetual array of new possibilities that require continuous testing. And the ability to *juggle*, to constructively deal with many things at once, invites challenge and tension to the reflective process when it is combined with the ability to constructively deal with things one has *no control* over. The specific combination of attributes involved is not the same every time, but the interplay of these attributes is consistently used when we engage in strategic thinking.

While I believe that companies interested in developing a pipeline, or human infrastructure, of strategic thinkers should be a learning organization, the question is, learning to what end? The end is not the learning itself, nor is it in the innovative strategy alone; the end is in the full realization of the strategic idea. While execution is essential, execution is not the end of the strategic value chain process.

25

Adaptation as a Strategic Expectation

If the aim of good strategic thinking is to create a strategy that is sustainable, innovative, and competitive, by definition it also needs to be adaptive. Therefore, any development initiative must be focused on strengthening our intuitive ability to be aware of our intuition repertoire, identify our patterns and frames, and build a habit of critical reflection. This builds adaptive capacity on which we can draw over and over.

> *Strategic adaptation is most often about recovery or trying to survive a crisis that has suddenly appeared and threatens the strategy.*

The idea of adaptability is not news. As noted in Chapter 2, complexity theory sees strategic thinking as being first and foremost about adaptation. And if we recall the ancient Greek notion of strategy, it also made implicit reference to the need for adaptive and flexible capability in order to deal with polarities, uncertainties, complexities, and contradictions inherent in strategy.

Strategic adaptation consists of building on what has been established before while exploring new possibilities in the present. Strategic adaptation, unfortunately, is not all about creative fun. Research shows that strategic adaptation is most often about recovery or trying to survive a crisis that has suddenly appeared and threatens the strategy. This is consistent with transformative learning in the deepest level of the dive domain (see Part IV).

In reference to the start of strategic thinking, a Japanese executive explained: "To start, you must have a purpose. Sometimes I start because I'm afraid of something, many times I suppose it's this (laughter). And you understand that being afraid is a problem. So in some sense perhaps I start with a problem, and then I just move to different places to look at the problem."

And the technology company COO explicitly stated:

> *I think I learn as much from things that hurt me as from things that help me—probably more if I take the time to think. It's like you have a net you drag through life. You bring along all your "collectibles," your experiences, with you. And there are times when they'll help you and times when they'll get in your way. Those are the times you can learn the most from. They're your experiences, and it's up to you what you do with them.*

The inclusion of reflection in action and reflection on action had become a conscious habit over the years for many of the executives I interviewed— something they learned and valued from their experience. They seemed to be aware of, expect, and trust the chaos, tension, and unexpected elements and did not feel compelled to control the disorder. Instead, they seemed to accept the anxiety as part of the challenge and expressed both satisfaction and motivation in using reflection in action. Through their experience they found it to be part of the successful process of learning to think strategically.

The executives in the study, as so many in my practice, have the ability and confidence to turn an obstacle into a challenge and a challenge into a win. They have learned to facilitate their own learning by reflecting and reframing a challenge until it becomes a strategic opportunity for them. I continue to be fascinated by accounts of this adaptive process from executives engaged in strategic thinking—a continuous and dynamic interplay of the five attributes and the three-stage informal learning process at work.

For example, all three of the executives from a Polish manufacturing company mentioned government interference as a contextual hindrance. They referred with disdain to the degree of involvement of the government, the bureaucracy, the perception that the government's intention was to provide interference rather than support for businesses, the slow pace at which the government moved, and their past experience with governmental punitive powers.

All three of the Polish executives also indicated that the government was an "unknown" element, a "factor beyond their control," and an impassioned "source of fire" that appeared to fuel their sense of determination, which suggested that they learned incidentally to transform the negative factor of government into an element of challenge. At first, the government appeared to be an impediment to their strategic thinking, but it actually served as a motivator by creating a sense of challenge, which was an incentive to their learning. Although the government activities were cited as a negative factor, the executives seemed to regard it as something they could not control and, therefore, a challenge, rather than a real impediment to learning.

The Hong Kong technology executive explained factors that contribute to his being a successful strategy maker: "I think it's a combination of who I am and my luck, honestly. I'm basically a very driven and hardworking guy. I need to really like or be fascinated by what I'm doing—even as a kid I never just did what somebody told me. (laughter) And I like to pretend different things inside my mind. I don't give up easily. (laughter) That's probably a good trait, at least most of the time."

An adaptive strategist is able to respond rapidly and effectively to unexpected events and can quickly shift from a planned sequence of actions to an alternative that is more appropriate.[9]

Something I have noticed from my own practice that was supported by the findings of the study underlying this book is that successful strategists do not explicitly mention "mistakes" as being part of their learning. Nor do they respond to probes about the role of "mistakes" in their learning to think strategically. Surprising at first, a closer look revealed that the strategists in the study acknowledged their mistakes, but they didn't call them mistakes *per se* or distinguish mistakes from experimentation or trial and error. Their descriptions implied that they incorporated learning from these experiences into their continuous cycle of critical reflective processes. In other words, they automatically included, reflected on, and revised mistakes during the experience and reevaluation stages of the informal learning process. They also used dialogue and storytelling as techniques to test and to preempt mistakes and to adapt in order to move forward.

One of the financial executives brushed aside the word *mistake* yet went on to explain:

I don't really think about mistakes, or I'd just get stuck . . . gotta move forward. It's more like I'm adjusting to things all the time. When things don't work out, that moment becomes part of the new future. It's strange. When this happens we look again at the data and then we pull apart the analysis. This is the part I really like because I think in a different way. It's the tough part, but I always learn from it. We imagine all these possibilities and make up a lot of stories. Telling stories is good, you know, because they help you understand what went wrong. And we talk about all kinds of things we have to try. This kind of thing happens all the time; it's just part of learning to make adjustments and it's hard to explain. There are lots of these adjustments that need to be made to strategy, lots of things go wrong. But they're not really mistakes—they're just part of the process.

I notice that successful strategists with whom I work invariably have a strong sense of self-reliance. They don't dwell on negatives or obstacles—they expect them and perceive them as challenges and as learning initiatives. Mistakes allow them to refocus their attention and force them to see things differently.

An overreliance on detailed plans and regimented procedures crowds out adaptive potential.

Adaptation is similar in some respects to improvisation. We cannot plan an improvisation—we assess the situation and react. Intuition is essential for improvisation. In strategy making, we rely on intuition to decide when to adapt and to determine the degree to which a situation is deteriorating. We rely on our intuition to decide how to adapt, which routine or action script we should use to adjust. Furthermore, we need intuition to decide whether or not to trust our adaptation, because the changes we want to make may result in subsequent, worse problems.

Details Can Doom Adaptation

In my practice, I frequently find that, although country and regional business heads are tasked with strategic responsibilities and are highly committed to developing local strategic thinkers, they nonetheless tend to cancel opportunities for strategic adaptation by creating an overreliance on excruciatingly detailed plans and procedures among their senior managers. Research has shown that an overreliance on detailed plans and regimented proce-dures crowds out adaptive potential.[10] An overdependence on plans and pro-cedures becomes an impediment and runs counter to developing strategic thinking.

In contrast to strategic thinkers, strategic planners often aim to specify every specific detail, leaving nothing to chance. Unfortunately, the more details there are, the harder it is to adapt and the more fragile the plans become. Such a strategic plan becomes susceptible to actually diverging or derailing from the anticipated outcome.

In their book *Managing the Unexpected*, Karl Weick and Kathleen Sutcliffe discuss three ways that detailed plans can stifle adaptability.[11] First, plans make us insensitive to the anomalies that tell us it is time to adapt, because plans describe what is relevant and what is not. Anything that is irrelevant to the plan doesn't get much attention. Second, plans may include contingency actions for coping with difficulties, but these contingencies were drawn up in advance and are usually void of context, the constraints, and any new oppor-tunities that tend to crop up the moment the plan is being implemented. And third, plans are designed to have us repeat "optimized" patterns of activity. But high-reliability organizations cope with unexpected events by adapting to circumstances rather than by depending on plans.

Adaptation is not simply building a new strategic plan to replace an old one. Rather, it means modifying a plan that is in progress via a strategic thinking process — it's difficult to catch a bird in flight. The plans we develop most often need to be improved and modified as we learn in action, because businesses compete in a grossly complex, constantly changing, uncertain global context that is saturated with incomplete and inaccurate information. Adapting strategy is much more difficult than planning strategy because there are innumerable variables, both known and unknown. We need to be strategically adaptive to deal with such a chaotic and unpredictable environment.

In my practice, I notice that executives often stumble over the paradox that the greater the uncertainty we face when making strategy, the more advantage there is to managing that uncertainty by planning to adapt. In other words, paying attention to our hunches, or our common sense, is what is needed. We tend to know intuitively that the more uncertain and unpredictable our strate-gic environment, the more useless our detailed plans tend to be. At the same time, prudent security measures require that we have extraordinarily detailed and well-rehearsed plans that can be executed in a nearly automatic manner; for this, we need to practice technical drills without error and to understand information. Strategic thinking is not about the creation of a static plan but, rather, about setting a dynamic thinking process in motion. An important part of facilitating strategic thinking capacity is to create the expectation of adaptation.

Strategic planning is not the antithesis of strategic thinking; rather, it is complementary to it and needs to be balanced within the overall strategy-making process.

The idea of *bounded rationality* was first introduced by Herbert Simon, who won a Nobel prize in 1978 for his work on decision making and problem solving. His idea is that there are too many facts and too many combinations of facts for us to make any important decision by simply gathering and analyzing all the facts.[12] He found that the more complex the decision, the faster the complications add up and the more it becomes necessary to "know" how to make a decision in ways other than through cognitive sequential analysis.

We need a method that allows us to make effective decisions in these all-too-familiar strategic situations. Technical analysis and computer models can help, but only by providing a sophisticated synopsis or consolidated information. Given that most global strategy is created under these complex circumstances, the decisions we make are connected to many conditions that lack metrics yet weigh heavily on the overall strategic risk quotient. Therefore, when we consider learning to think strategically, we must pay attention to honing our intuitive skills in order to balance our analytical skills.

Strategic planning is not the antithesis of strategic thinking; rather, it is complementary to it and needs to be balanced within the overall strategy-making process. Meticulous planning is an imperative to the implementation phase of strategy. Instead of a pointless debate about which is right—intuition or analysis—we can see that both are necessary. The real challenge is not whether to trust intuition, but how to strengthen it to make it more trustworthy. One way to support the development of strategic thinking is to offer strategists tools and exercises for enhanced intuitive decision making. Furthermore, if we expect to adapt our strategy, we tacitly accept the unpredictability of it and openly try to work with it, instead of trying to outplan it.

Strategic adaptation, however, is not always a good idea, and improvisation is not inherently beneficial to strategic thinking. A well-developed intuition allows us to "know" when to change a plan and when to leave it alone. Our intuition functions as our internal red flag, giving us a sense of the benefits from taking action and alerting us to the unintended consequences that arise from making adaptations. Our ability to adapt is only as good as our intuition, which is based on our experience.

WHAT CAN WE DO TO IMPROVE STRATEGIC THINKING?

Engaging in Informal Learning Approaches: Strengthening the Five Attributes and Critical Reflective Processes

I have never let my schooling interfere with my education.

Mark Twain (1835–1910), American author

26

Developing the Five
Essential Attributes

This part does not include a list of how-to exercises and activities. Rather, I am recommending things that work for clients in my consulting practice to support the long-term sustainable development of strategic thinking, things that are heavily reliant on informal learning yet easily adaptable to formal workshops and lectures that are more structured. I invite readers to use the information in this book as a source to create their own developmental ideas, to experiment, and to modify current approaches.

The overall recommendations I put forth in this part focus on strengthening the five essential attributes discussed in Part IX (imagination, broad perspective, juggle, no control over, and desire to win) and on developing critical reflection as discussed in Parts IV, V, and VI. These recommendations enable rigorous practice of the combined five attributes and critical reflection, thus allowing strategists to link learning in their expanded life experience to a global business strategy context.

Chapter 26 discusses the role the arts can play in developing strategic thinking. Chapter 27 describes three practical ways to address development of critical reflective processes: "and" thinking, action learning, and lateral thinking. Chapter 28 presents a list of suggestions for individuals, learning facilitators, business schools, and organizations.

If we assume, as many organizations do, that human capital is the only true competitive global strategic advantage, and if we also assume that the global reality, in which we make strategy, promises only to become more complex and challenging, then common sense dictates that we address strengthening and expanding the strategic thinking capacity within organizations as a long-term business development investment. The technical rational approach to strategic planning addresses only the analytical aspect of the matter, leaving strategic thinking open to chance and interpretation.

If businesses are to remain largely technical operations, most organizations are fairly well equipped with excellent resources for strategic planning. But if organizations are expected to be competitive within the realm of growing complexities, contradictions, and change, and if business schools are to be perceived as something more than just expensive technical schools, most are far from being prepared.

With regard to strategy, organizations are beginning to recognize the gap between what they need (strategic thinkers) and what many are continuing to develop by default (strategic planners). If businesses are to remain largely technical operations, most organizations are fairly well equipped with excellent resources for strategic planning. But if organizations are expected to be competitive within the realm of growing complexities, contradictions, and change, and if business schools are to be perceived as something more than just expensive technical schools, most are far from being prepared. If this situation is to change for the better, businesses and business schools need to engage in some significant frame shattering and reframing regarding their approach toward strategy development.

While there are many things that can be done to strengthen strategic thinking, I recommend a somewhat unconventional approach of emphasizing experience in the arts and humanities as well as critical reflective processes in the strategy development approaches used by organizations and for business school curricula. This, in combination with the continued emphasis on analysis, logic, and linear thinking, can offer a potentially comprehensive and practical approach to addressing strategic thinking needs of an organization.

This first subsection explores the basic theme of participation in artistic endeavors as a recommendation for learning to think strategically. Odd as it may sound on the surface, such participation can support learning to think strategically, because the arts offer infinite scope and depth, are descriptive rather than prescriptive in nature, are inclusive of all five of the critical attributes, require the use of critical reflection, and allow endless application of strategic thinking, depending on time and circumstance.

The Arts to the Rescue

So what does participation and experience in artistic endeavors bring to the development of strategic thinking? It has nothing to do with artistic talent *per se*; the aim is not to achieve fame and fortune as an artistic master but, rather, to develop the five attributes and critical reflective processes necessary for strategic thinking. An arts experience "opens the doors of perception," as poet William Blake wrote in *The Marriage of Heaven and Hell.*

While an expansive life experience may include a multitude of activities that broaden our horizon and open new vistas, one of the most comprehensive and powerful strategic thinking influences I have experienced in my own business life and in working with clients is through extensive participation in the arts. Learning to think strategically is strengthened not merely from participating in an art; it must be linked with critical reflection in order to be beneficial.

Traditionally, strategy development has focused primarily on economics, finance, and analytical thinking. Emotion, imagination, intuition, and reflective processes have largely been invisible to strategy development, yet they are essential to creating and adapting the making of meaning within the strategic thinking process. When clients are focused on learning to think strategically, I highly recommend active participation in any of the arts because it contributes to the development of all five attributes (imagination, broad perspective, juggle, no control, and desire to win), requires critical reflective processes, and broadens their experience repertoire.

We can acquire firsthand learning through the experience of doing photography, painting, writing, singing, dancing, playing an instrument, and so on. We can also learn through secondhand experience—what the early 20th century philosopher William James called "knowledge about" the arts and humanities, for example, by listening to an orchestra, watching a dance, reading a novel, or seeing a play. Naturally, what we read, hear, see, and feel about the play, novel, painting, or dance performance contributes to our "knowledge about," which often triggers our deeply held beliefs. We find ourselves taking sides with a particular character and passionately defending or vilifying the actions of another. Experiencing the arts is a great way to surface the assumptions and become aware of the convictions on which we take strategic action and make decisions.

When either first- or secondhand artistic experience is coupled with critical reflection components such as critical inquiry, reflection, and dialogue (which can unfold nicely in a bar over drinks), personal interpretations and assumptions can be tested and new alternatives brought to light. This is what happens as we create alternative endings when we disagree or are disappointed with an unsatisfactory ending. Through critical reflection we test and challenge our assumptions and try to imagine other possibilities.

Nonlinear, a-rational thinking, divergent and convergent thinking, critical dialogue, and critical reflection — all come into play when we become engaged in an arts experience. With drama, a novel, or a film, there is often a visceral feeling that compels us to take a particular position. Engaging in critical reflection and critical dialogue about the assumptions we hold regarding these incidents is a great way to build analogies and to facilitate the transfer the learning of such an experience to strategy problems. The content of the drama or novel need not be business related, because it is the process reflection and premise reflection and metaphoric conversion that are essential to transferring the artistic experience across contexts.

An arts encounter can become a metaphor for a business strategy experience (and vice versa) if critical reflection and critical dialogue follow it.

Participation in an art form not only exposes us to new patterns through heightened sensory stimulation and imagination, but it experientially engages both the affective and cognitive learning dimensions that are needed to think strategically. Experiencing the arts (either in "doing" or in "knowledge about") requires us to use both the surface and the deeper learning domains. These artistic experiences allow us to practice essential aspects of strategic thinking without really "thinking" about it. Mental agility and imagination are strengthened as we look for parallels and patterns within a business context.

Furthermore, we learn to deal with paradox and contradiction as inherent features of the arts and are nudged into using critical inquiry and critical reflective processes as a way of making meaning. Our feelings lead to questions that require a cognitive response, and soon an iterative pattern between the cognitive and affective is set in motion.

An arts encounter can become a metaphor for a business strategy experience (and vice versa) if critical reflection and critical dialogue follow it. It is through critical reflective processes that the learning acquired from participation in the arts transfers to strategic thinking. Believe it or not, I find that my clients generally "get it" very quickly. The practice of transfer of learning from one context to another presents us with one of the most impelling learning experiences — it develops strategic innovation, sustainability, and adaptability like nothing else!

Benefits of Engaging in the Arts

Based on work with corporate executives in my consulting practice, I find there are innumerable strategic thinking benefits that come from actively engaging in the arts or other creative endeavors on a continual basis. Through engagement in the arts, we experience and practice broadening our perspective, making connections, seeing unusual relations, and thinking in new ways — precisely what is needed for learning to think strategically! Participation in the arts supports the development of the five attributes (imagination, broad perspective, juggle, no control, desire to win) by providing opportunities to do the following.

- Expand perspective
  We see, hear, feel different interpretations of the same data; balance individual and group roles; experience the impact of elemental changes in structure, form, texture, dynamics, distortion, diminution, and exaggeration; experience historical and cultural contexts on the interpretation of data. For example, although the musical notes printed on a page are fixed, they can be interpreted in many different ways. We recognize a tune, yet it is different each time because of the instrumentation, the tempo, the acoustics, our mood, and so forth. The smile of Mona Lisa remains the same, beautiful and fixed over the centuries; yet it changes with each viewing.
- Deal with many competing things at once
  We pay attention to the mastery of technique and simultaneously focus on the overall form, the structure of a piece, changing emotions, and creativity. We learn to juggle many things at once, focusing and shifting our attention with ease.
- Engage imagination
  The arts foster creativity and infinite possibilities. We see new relationships and connections between things and as a result of our decisions, actions, and responses.

- Experience tension
  An affective dimension is inherent in the arts. We have a feeling that generates an intense reaction that requires a release. Pride or humility accompanies an awareness of our habits, performance, or creations.
- Pay attention to things we can't control
  We understand that we can't control every specific aspect of the final movement of an orchestral performance—only our part. We can't control the physical properties of clay—they are what they are. Nor can we control the rotational capacity of the human hip or ankle. Yet we pay close attention to these things over which we have no control in order to work with them.
- Develop emotional awareness
  We experience a wide range of emotions when viewing a photograph or listening to a brass quintet—from disgust, revulsion, pain, aggression, and sadness to happiness, pleasure, eroticism, and ecstasy.
- Deal with paradox
  We deal with the finished and the incomplete; repetition and free form; continuity and deviation; prescription and creation; structure and experimentation; sameness and surprise.
- Accept incomplete information
  A creation is never truly a completed work. Just as successful strategy is always past tense, a successful performance is only a moment in time passed and is never finished.
- Take a risk
  Learning something new requires commitment and risk. We place ourselves in the vulnerable position of being a nonexpert, a novice, and possibly being judged incompetent.
- Learn discipline
  Regular practice is required for improvement. Practice requires discipline, sacrifice, precision, sequence, repetition, drill, and consistency. Discipline is required to balance technique versus feelings, which is required for artistic mastery.
- Appreciate practice
  Practice requires feedback and determination. We learn to appreciate a distinct sense of time (no shortcuts), movement toward something we strongly desire, nonlinear progress, and a combination of thinking and feeling.
- Learn the creative process through technique
  Creation doesn't just happen; learning the technical rudiments is necessary to create.

Although I am a big proponent of fostering informal learning, I also adamantly support the intermittent use of highly structured formal learning as a means of supporting informal learning. For example, formal learning from workshops, presentations, and provocative lectures can focus on "learning about" artistic information (e.g., topics such as form exaggeration and figure distortion in abstract painting). Strategists may eventually then transfer the learning across contexts and identify parallels and metaphors in their respective strategic environment. The emphasis is not on artistic perfection, but on strengthening strategic thinking ability.

Likewise, formal learning sessions on "learning about" critical reflective processes (e.g., critical inquiry or the role of intuition) can be another very useful step to fostering informal learning to think strategically. Formal skills practice sessions can effectively focus on "doing" critical processing techniques, such as drilling critical questions or practicing listening techniques.

27

Developing Critical
Reflective Processes

The skillful use of critical reflective processing (critical reflection, critical dialogue, and critical inquiry) is another way to address the development of the five attributes that are necessary for learning to think strategically: imagination, broad perspective, juggle, no control, and desire to win. I want to underscore that critical reflection does not necessarily lead to strategic thinking, but it is an essential component. In other words, the approaches suggested here may foster critical reflection, but they do not necessarily lead to changed perspectives in practice.

This chapter comprises three sections. The first discusses how reflective processes strengthen the five attributes. The second section explores "and" thinking. The third section presents a brief overview of two learning process approaches—action learning and lateral thinking—as ways to support the development of critical reflective processes and, in turn, the five attributes.

Critical Reflective Processes Strengthen the Five Attributes

As we have seen throughout the book, the five attributes overlap and are interdependent. Rather than addressing each of the five attributes separately, I find it more practical and realistic to look at how critical reflective processes can strengthen the combination of the five attributes.

How do critical reflective processes strengthen the five attributes? Active participation in any creative and artistic pursuit requires the use of critical reflective processes in order to make a meaningful connection to strategic thinking. Therefore, when we incorporate critical reflective processes in our arts experience, the combination of the five attributes naturally gets strengthened through the following.

- Macro–Micro connection
  We constantly vacillate between macro- and microperceptions, experiencing the relationship between the part and the whole. We also experience the consequences of having a single perspective and the benefits of taking a broad perspective.
- Focus
  We practice concentration when the focal point continually changes. We also learn to pay attention to different cues and signals, such as the use of amplification and minimization, accents, or silence, to gain or refocus attention. Additionally, we learn to focus on the appropriate domain of learning required at a given moment. The instrumental, surf domain requires a skills response, while the deeper, dive domain requires a more intuitive feeling level—practicing focus enables us eventually to make this a tacit ability.
- Reflection in action
  Through practice and repetition, we refine reflection and reaction. There is no endpoint in an artistic endeavor because reflection and experience are continually at work. We constantly ask, How else? What else? When else? Who else?
- Surprise
  We experience surprise as a means of shifting our focus. Our pattern recognition is altered and we shift or divert our attention. Our affective learning dimension is heightened—we laugh, gasp, gulp, or cringe as a response to a dance movement, a costume, or a line in a play.
- Intuition
  We learn to trust our intuition through using it and reflecting on it. This happens naturally in the arts—as we acquire experience through practice, feedback, and repetition, we develop our intuition and become confident at using it.
- Affective awareness
  We experience the subtleties and variances of emotions and the impact emotion has on an arts experience or performance. We also become aware of feelings attached to reactions that an artistic experience invokes.
- Integration
  We synthesize and integrate the affective domain with the cognitive domain, the analytic with the intuitive, and the instrumental with the deeper learning domain.

- Systems thinking
  We figure out the influence and impact of the relationships between performer, audience, technicians, media, the business operations, teachers, the composer, and so on.
- Learning transfer
  We transfer this artistic learning to strategic thinking — one experience becomes a metaphor for the other, which facilitates pattern recognition, framing, shattering, and reframing.

As we see from this list, the use of critical reflective processes (critical reflection, inquiry, and dialogue) supports the development of the five attributes necessary for learning to think strategically. Another way to do this is through the creation of scenarios, possibilities, and alternatives to problems. Surprisingly, we often resist examining strategic alternatives thoroughly because it can lead to confusion or ambivalence. Asking questions about alternatives seems like common sense, but it is rarely done in a disciplined and open manner at traditional strategy meetings because political expediency and same-frame thinking tend to get in the way.

Critical reflection, inquiry, and dialogue also develop the five attributes, in that they sharpen reflection in action and reflection on action. Critical reflective processing also helps bring in diverse perspectives and divergent opinions on strategic issues. When reflection in and on action is repeated enough times and the results are successful, it becomes second nature, and we ultimately trust the intuitive judgment that comes from our frequent experience — a huge advantage for learning to think strategically.

"And" Thinking

Critical reflection, inquiry, and dialogue are also useful to improve our ability to make sense of opposites, contradictions, polarities, and paradoxes in a way that generates new ideas and new possibilities. I call this ability, quite appropriately, "and" thinking — making new meaning of this *and* that. As we know, much of global strategy making requires an ability to deal with contradictory information and paradoxes. Making strategy that is adaptive does not afford us the time for a long process of elimination until we finally get it down to just "this" and eliminate "that."

"And" thinking requires making meaning of "both."

"And" thinking is part of our contemporary strategy-making reality. It is a major variance to the technical rational "this-or-that" approach to problem solving and decision making that is traditionally taught in strategy courses. "And" thinking can be an especially difficult way of thinking, because it runs counter to the notion of technical rationality that relies on a scientific process of elimination. While the aim of the scientific process is to reduce to a single best, strategic thinking opts for a process that is adaptive and generative. "And" thinking requires making meaning of "both." It requires that we temporarily suspend judgment and invite new possibilities that may seem exaggerated and ridiculous. I find that once executives begin to practice "and" thinking, they invariably report that their confidence in creating new possibilities for solutions improves considerably.

Most often I find American strategists would rather take a risk of being wrong all the way than to live with the tension of ambivalence that is inherent in "and" thinking.

Curiously, in my work with strategists in many countries, I have noticed that Americans in particular often prefer extremes to ambivalence when it comes to strategic thinking. My American clients often insist on a this-or-that decision very early in the strategy-making process. Some of the common underlying assumptions that begin to surface through inquiry and dialogue include: fence-riding is bad, wrong, and weak; good strategists can or should be able to control everything; and, there is only one best way.

I have noticed that Americans like the expedience that comes with being definitive in the moment: pick or choose, this or that, either–or. Most often I find American strategists would rather take a risk of being wrong all the way than to live with the tension of ambivalence that is inherent in "and" thinking. However, what is required for global strategic thinking is being comfortable with the inherent tension of dealing with complex circumstances that include opposites, contradictions, and paradoxes in order to be able to shatter and reframe.

We are making strategy in an increasingly paradoxical and uncertain world, and the business world therefore should be thought of as a paradoxical network of global *and* local, general *and* specific, modern *and* postmodern environments. It also consists of fragmentation *and* globalization, heterogeneity *and* uniformity, passive consumption *and* active customization, individualism *and* tribalism, and the old *and* the new. Furthermore, we need to understand, acknowledge, and pay attention to developing both affective *and* cognitive, rationality *and* intuition, dialogue *and* debate, inquiry *and* reflection, and convergence *and* divergence. Strategic thinking requires cooperation and competition, collaboration and confrontation as different approaches to the same means of challenge and testing.

A word of clarification here. I do not want to suggest the use of "and" thinking as a compromise, because compromise weakens the strategic decision on both sides. Rather, we want to strengthen the strategic decision by looking at new connections that are forced through the use of "and" thinking.

> *The very idea of forcing two opposing or contradictory ideas or opinions into a single thought or concept can create tremendous tension and imbalance — to the point of outbursts and mental shutdowns. "And" thinking can also lead to innovative breakthroughs because of the rich and deep reflection, critical inquiry, and critical dialogue that work with the tension.*

Chaos theory warns that the closer we get to thinking we understand a pattern and believing we can control it, the more likely we are to be surprised and frustrated when it turns out to be quite different from what we imagined. For strategists it is imperative to practice thinking that facilitates dealing with contradictions. Daily life regularly reminds us that our minds and our businesses are not always systems in balance. If we allow our mind to play regularly with highly unlikely possibilities in relation to some current pattern or trend, then the future will not come as a devastating surprise. We will have a large repertoire of experience with such possibilities, which increases the likelihood of adapting.

"And" thinking is about making seemingly unrelated connections with the intent of generating new possibilities. The very idea of forcing two opposing or contradictory ideas or opinions into a single thought or concept can create tremendous tension and imbalance — to the point of outbursts and mental shutdowns. "And" thinking can also lead to innovative breakthroughs because of the opportunity for rich and deep reflection, critical inquiry, and critical dialogue that work with the tension. It is imperative that we learn this kind of "and" thinking if we want innovative and adaptive strategic thinking. An ability to deal with incomplete information teaches us to trust our instincts, intuition, and self-confidence.

As emphasized throughout the book, thinking strategically requires a very different learning process than planning strategically. The two can be complementary—strategic planning and strategic thinking need to be framed not as opposing either–or choices but, rather, as a new frame.

Two Learning Processes: Action Learning and Lateral Thinking

Two learning processes that I encourage anyone interested in strategic thinking to use to develop critical reflective processes are action learning and lateral thinking. I recommend these in particular because they develop critical reflective processes, they are flexible and integrative, and they can be either highly structured and formal or very informal.

Action Learning

Action learning (AL) is essentially an approach that consists of learning and action. While AL programs vary considerably, according to action learning expert Michael Marquardt of George Washington University they all comprise six components: problem, group, questions, action, learning, and coach.[1]

Strategic development programs in corporations and universities are intended to assist managers and executives in making better strategy. Although a few programs may help achieve this goal, most do not. Learning to think strategically is not something learned overnight or through listening to strategy gurus. It requires emotional (affective) and intellectual (cognitive) learning, the inclusion of life experiences, the sum of the five attributes, and being adept at using critical reflective processes. In an effort to change strategic thinking, feedback, confrontation, and reflection are imperatives. This can sometimes be overwhelming, unwitting, or frightening.

Reg Revans introduced the concept of action learning in the 1940s in the United Kingdom.[2] Since then, there have been many interpretations and variations of its application. In a nutshell, AL is a systematic and structured approach to developing cognitive and affective discipline, skills, and thinking habits—essentials for learning to think strategically, because it assists with learning transfer across contexts.

With regard to strategic thinking, AL integrates informal and formal learning and is an excellent way to establish individual and organizational use of the deeper learning domain for strategic problem solving and decision making. Once initial problems are formulated, there is ample room for uncovering patterns of thinking, inferences, and so on. Though the strategic thinking process is complex and dynamic, its components can be structured to a certain extent. AL encourages participants to experiment and make discoveries about their own learning as they embark on solving strategy problems. Furthermore, it also develops a cadre of people who have the capacity to use reflective processes in strategic thinking.

Linear and logical critical thinking can be included as a structured part of an AL process as a means of balancing the nonlinear and creative nature of the five essential attributes. Critical thinking establishes a logical chain of reasoning that is useful to unravel assumptions and to test new frames and ways of thinking. In critical thinking a pattern of reasoning, starting with the basic construct of a reason → conclusion, is established and elaborated on. The process moves toward complexities, such as the construction and deconstruction of an argument, developing and testing hypotheses, analyzing assumptions, evaluating inferences and causal explanations. Fluency and confidence in using critical thinking are necessary for shifting back and forth between dialogue, discussion, and debate as well as for testing rational validity of ideas generated using a-rational thinking.

The implementation of AL can vary significantly depending on a company's specific goals, time frames, and individuals involved. What is important is that strategic imperatives be translated into business initiatives that drive action learning.

Lateral Thinking

Lateral thinking (LT) is an approach to strengthening the strategic thinking attributes of imagination, broad perspective, and juggling. According to the originator of lateral thinking, Edward De Bono, "Lateral thinking is both an attitude and a method of using information."[3] LT is a kind of nonlinear, a-rational thinking that is concerned with changing patterns. Instead of taking a pattern and then developing it, as happens with vertical thinking, LT aims to restructure the pattern by putting things together in a different way. By its very nature, it is compatible with and supportive of developing adaptive, innovative, and sustainable strategy.

De Bono further notes that in using lateral thinking "one acknowledges the usefulness of a pattern, but instead of regarding it as inevitable, one regards it as only one way of putting things together. This attitude challenges the assumption that what is a convenient pattern at the moment is the only possible pattern."[4] Since successful strategy is always past tense, LT is enormously relevant and important for learning to think strategically because it emphasizes movement and future.

De Bono contrasts two terms: *vertical thinking* and *lateral thinking*. While acknowledging that lateral and vertical thinking are complementary, he differentiates the two by noting that vertical thinking is selective, meaning that it excludes other ways of thinking about accomplishing tasks. This vertical method is a derivative of technical rationality. By contrast, lateral thinking is generative and openly seeks to include other ways of approaching things. With vertical thinking we select the most promising approach to a problem. The intent of LT is to generate as many alternative approaches as possible. This supports the kind of mental process needed for strategic thinking.

> *Lateral thinking enhances the effectiveness*
> *of vertical thinking by offering it more to*
> *select from.*

In his well-known book *Lateral Thinking*, De Bono explains the necessity of withholding judgment when using lateral thinking as being threefold: "to arrange information in a way which would never have come about in the normal course of events; to hold an arrangement of information without judging it; and to protect from dismissal an arrangement of information which has already been judged as impossible."[5] The ability to suspend judgment is one of the most basic principles of LT, and it is also one of the fundamental points of difference from vertical thinking.

With regard to strategic thinking, LT is useful for generating ideas, while vertical thinking is useful for developing and implementing ideas. Lateral thinking enhances the effectiveness of vertical thinking by offering it more to select from. The implications for using LT to strengthen the five attributes are obvious, but it is necessary for strategists and facilitators of learning to clarify whether the situation calls for developing strategic planning or strategic thinking—that is, vertical or lateral thinking.

28

Suggestions for Learning to Think Strategically

This final chapter consists of four subsections, each focusing on suggestions for a particular group: individuals, learning facilitators, business schools, and businesses.

Suggestions for Individuals

There are several things that individuals can do to support the development of strategic thinking. First and foremost, participate in any creative art form, even if you're not "that type." It is not about whether you take up piano lessons or painting, carpentry or cooking, but that you are doing it. Enjoy whatever creative endeavor you choose. It is also beneficial to partner with a good coach or mentor who can guide you through reflective processes (critical dialogue, critical inquiry, critical reflection) until it becomes a habit; this supports the transfer of learning to a strategy context.

Additionally, keep a journal about your experience—your progress, reactions, observations, what you are doing and your feelings, what is easy, what is a struggle, what are you noticing about yourself and your progress. I also suggest that you use the five attributes as a guide for your journal reflections and questions. Draw parallels (literally and figuratively) about what you are noticing and experiencing in your artistic pursuit and about what you observe and think about strategy. Dialogue about your journal notes with colleagues, a coach, friends, or a teacher. Last, switch art forms (e.g., from photography to playing guitar), and pay attention to similarities across the arts and creative pursuits as a way to build a repertoire of metaphoric learning.

When critical reflective processes are introduced, I find that the reaction of aspiring strategists is often apprehensive. They generally have a sense that critical reflective processes are probably good for someone they know—but not appropriate for them! The executives are often ambivalent about seeking challenge and routine testing of current thinking because it is usually not part of the organizational culture. They are concerned about receiving support from others and are aware that colleagues may not approve of the potential reframing and proposed alternative actions. Again, they tend to like the concept but would prefer to forego the experience!

I find that offering strategists some knowledge of the surf and dive learning domains provides them with a choice and control as to the level of thinking they may wish to use in meetings. Furthermore, providing practice sessions for critical reflective processes can reduce the resistance and alleviate some of the anxiety associated with the strategic learning process.

Following is a list of additional suggestions for individuals who wish to start to develop a habit of learning to think strategically with or without formal support.

SUGGESTIONS FOR INDIVIDUALS

- Instead of saying no, ask a question.
- Ask questions that move from the surf to the dive level of thinking.
- Record as many of your thoughts, feelings, and new questions as possible in a journal or log. This is a useful and insightful way to begin to identify patterns, uncover assumptions, and highlight traps in your thinking.
- Take time to write down the feelings attached to your thinking. Over time, journal entries offer data to back up your intuitive sense of a pattern or trend. This gives you confidence in your judgment.
- Reflect about things that provoke questions or strong feelings.
- Draw or design your strategy ideas instead of writing them. Use color or shape codes for themes.
- Diversify and upgrade the kinds of verbal engagement you use. Alternate among dialogue, discussion, inquiry, and debate.
- Write or tell parables and analogies that illustrate your assumptions and beliefs about strategy issues.

■ Invite listeners and questioners who don't know the background, the content, or the politics of a strategic issue to offer a new perspective.

■ Scrutinize the content, the process, and the premise of a strategy matter separately; then look at connections between and among them.

■ Avoid a quick-fix approach to problems. Instead, hold back and suspend judgment. Deliberately poke around until you find a surprise. Then inquire and reflect on that surprise.

■ Show-and-tell the perspectives and the patterns you see in data: what they mean, might mean, why and why not. Pointing out patterns can greatly accelerate the discovery process in strategy thinking, because sometimes it is hard to imagine patterns you haven't seen or don't know what to pay attention to. It is actually helpful and efficient to the creative process to use show-and-tell for expanding the range of visibility.

■ Slow down in order to speed up later. Relax and play and reflect.

■ Identify role models who practice strategic thinking. Ask them to articulate their thinking, feelings, and experiences of the learning process.

■ Partner with an internal, external, peer, or team coach for any of the action learning activities to practice dialogue and to practice critical inquiry.

Traps That Impede the Development of Critical Reflective Processes

While everyone can strengthen critical reflective processes to some degree, some personal traps can impede our ability to develop critical reflective processes. They are not matters of our stupidity or pathology. Rather, they come from the way our mind handles information and the resultant habits our mind has formed. If we are not on guard, our habits of mind can unknowingly become any one of the following personal traps that hinder our ability to learn to think strategically.

Immediate Gratifiers

These are the people who want strategic results—now! They are all about action, with no time, experience, or appreciation for the thinking that underlies and improves strategic action. Once we begin to lose our ability to imagine or create, we cannot envision the future, and strategic thinking capacity vanishes.

Know-It-Alls

These people tend to make instant judgments based on frozen same-frame thinking. They believe it is this way because they say it's this way or because it's the only way they know. This kind of thinking is largely based on fear and an inability to think using critical reflective processes. Challenge and testing is "wrong" and feels threatening. Know-it-all thinking stops dialogue. It freezes us into place and leads us to ignore information that supports other positions. When trapped in this mind-set, change often occurs only when it is forced on us by failure or crisis.

Experts

Highly expert people sometimes make up their minds so quickly that they overlook critical flaws in the process. Experts minds are like computers that can scan vast amounts of data with few interruptions. But because of their vast experience and familiarity, experts often fail to consider elements that should be factors in their decisions. Sometimes someone who lacks specific expertise and thinks more slowly can have an unexpected advantage. Such a person may follow a more careful thinking process—noticing more signals, weighing all the factors involved, noticing where data are missing, or spotting paths of questioning that have not been taken.

Satisfieds

These people are satisfied and content and see no reason to change. This kind of resistance to change is based on a rationale that if we want to preserve our privileged place in a particular corporate or social niche—the one that let me in regardless of whom it shut out—then critical thinking or critical reflection is a threat to our sense of self and our position. We sometimes need to be reminded that discomfort, imbalance, and discontent are powerful motivators for learning and for change.

Conformists

Similar to the satisfieds, conformists show up in corporations and organizations that have a club mentality. Once we decide that our group is superior, our mind focuses only on who is one of us and who is not—and what actions, objects, or attire make that distinction clear. Symbolism overrides thinking. Rituals and conformity can be useful in times of economic stability because they allow an organization to create bonds and feelings of solidarity. But when change is required, the rigidity of conformist thinking makes it impossible for the group to detect the signals of change and to envision a new future. This has disastrous implications for developing strategic thinkers and highlights the need for diversity in strategy meetings.

Simplifiers

As situations become more complex and contradictory, a common approach to making sense is to oversimplify. Because we feel overwhelmed, we sometimes falsely believe that all complex and contradictory things can be simplified. We deny the real complexity because we do not know how to make meaning of these competing and contradictory things. The temptation for simplification in a chaotic and fast-paced environment is tremendous, and we often become vulnerable to shortcuts and quick fixes.

If we want to strengthen our ability to think strategically, we need to be aware of any existing mental models we have that may be a trap to our thinking. This can be best accomplished through continuously expanding our experience base, practicing with a skillful and artful coach, colleagues, or friends who support the use of critical inquiry, critical dialogue, and critical reflection.

Suggestions for Facilitators of Learning

So what can we do to support the readiness of executives who wish or need to learn to think strategically? For those responsible for facilitating learning the best support can be the following.

- Offering information about the learning process used for strategic thinking, the role of informal learning, intuition, learning domains, transfer, and the role of critical reflective processes.
- Distinguishing between learning strategic thinking and learning strategic planning.
- Encouraging sufficient space and time to reflect.
- Practicing inquiry and dialogue so that learners feel confident and gain experience in using questions, active listening, and dialogue.
- Ensuring that learners are involved in strategy making, for this is the best place to practice reflection in and on their action.
- Trusting that executives and managers can and do have meaningful learning experiences that transfer and contribute to strategic thinking.

Most often these experiences have nothing to do with work or structured formal learning.

Roles for Learning Facilitators

The ability to do many things at once has become a way of life. Technology does an increasing number of remarkable things—to the point of confusion. We humans are being pressured into achieving performance standards of technology and designing technology that imitates human performance. Over time, this influence confuses strategic thinking by posing the recurring strategic question of what is the right thing to do. As we attempt to facilitate learning to think strategically the following three points are useful to remember.

1. Successful strategy is always past tense; therefore, take an adaptive stance and assume that things will continue to change. Keep moving mentally!
2. Successful strategic thinking requires agility in using both sides of the strategy coin: the linear, logical, analytic side and the nonlinear, a-rational, intuitive, imaginative side. Because the linear, logical side is already deeply entrenched in traditional learning and organizational development practice, sharpen the focus on the nonlinear, a-rational, intuitive side.
3. Successful strategy is adaptable, sustainable, innovative, and winning. This requires developing the five attributes (imagination, broad perspective, juggle, no control, desire to win) and using the learning process to ensure these.

So what does all this mean for organizational learning facilitators? It opens opportunities to assume any or a combination of the following three roles.

- Key strategist
  Partner at all levels of organizational strategy meetings by contributing content data and offering a specific perspective. A chief learning officer, in particular, has an organizational responsibility to speak directly to the individual development and social contribution strategy dimensions and to bring challenge into the culture in an effort to create a pipeline of strategic thinkers within the organization.
- Concept creator
  Advocate for a process that radically changes the way in which strategy is made. Instead of discussing whether to use an inside-out/outside-in approach or a top-down/bottom-up strategy or structure/infrastructure, advocate instead for a holistic, inclusive, adaptive, nonlinear, a-

rational strategy thinking approach as a genuine concept re-creation that can lead to a sustainable and innovative strategy. This can be linked to a linear, logical, rational planning approach.

■ Process facilitator
Partner in a supporting role with the chief learning officer and organizational learning specialists who support executives and line managers to challenge, revise, and test the data and their thinking throughout the strategy-making process. Consider integrating the five key attributes into the selection criteria and development plans of high-potential candidates.

The following suggestions offer additional ways for facilitators of strategic learning to support and strengthen the cognitive and affective skills required for strategic thinking.

■ Give permission to people to act as the contrarian during strategy meetings. Rotate until everyone feels comfortable playing this role with everyone else during every meeting. Establish pride and respect in playing the contrarian role.

■ Invite provocative or antagonistic speakers, and urge them to shake up your thinking with fresh perspectives and challenges. Bring in outside speakers with good thinking habits but from worlds that are unfamiliar and very different from your own. Listen, reflect, and dialogue about corporate, competitors, public, political, educational, social, ethnic, and religious issues and perspectives.

■ Use storytelling as a documentation and deployment mechanism. It enables very complex concepts and results to be transferred readily.

■ Draw on and respect nonwork experiences. Learning occurs throughout all activities of the organization, not just the classroom or within working hours or the confines of the workplace. Doing and action are frequently rewarded, to the exclusion of deeper thinking that requires time and critical reflection and inquiry.

■ Look, listen, and record the many informal opportunities for learning.

■ Think of ways to repeat the things that worked.

■ Rotate people in and out of various groups—allow plenty of opportunity for people to inquire and to dialogue.

■ Formally teach techniques to question and to respond and to debate, discuss, and dialogue.

■ Explicitly recognize and appreciate executives who endorse and practice informal development efforts that focus on reflective processes, in order to foster awareness and identify role models. This helps create an every-day environment that is conducive to informal learning.

Finally, by enabling everyone within the organization to learn a disciplined approach to strengthen the five essential attributes and to develop critical reflective capacity, we can ensure that what emerges will at least be an informed, innovative, and sustainable strategic pipeline of sorts, even if there is no clearly articulated strategy from the top.

Suggestions for Business School Curricula

The strength of business school curricula is that they are essentially a model of pragmatism and technical rationality. This is also their weakness. The reality of the global business environment in which strategy is made, however, has outgrown this model. If business schools wish to move strategic thinking beyond a hope and a prayer, then the definition of strategy within curricula needs to be expanded to include learning to think strategically, rather than being limited to learning strategic planning.

Reading and analyzing poetry, dramas, paintings, dance, and music are great ways to learn about basic human nature — and human nature as it intersects with products and services is, after all, what strategy making is all about. Becoming engrossed in a novel or play or being moved by a particular piece of music is a powerful experience. When we recognize that the situations we encounter have been previously experienced, recorded in some form, and reflected on by countless generations in various countries, our perspective begins to broaden, our pattern recognition focuses or sharpens, and our curiosity grows.

We begin to connect our current situation to that in the play, poem, music, dance, or picture through metaphorical and analogical thinking. We gain insight through stories, paintings, and dramas from which to reflect and diverge. Through critical dialogue we continually transfer learning and come to understand how others have dealt with uncertainties, conflict, injustice, paradoxes, contradictions, and risk. This learning process belongs in business school conversations.

Learning is one of the very few business situations in which the process is more important than the result.

Learning is about striving for balance and finding our bearings. The same goes with making strategy. Learning is one of the very few business situations in which the process is more important than the result. Learning is the competitive factor that differentiates strategic thinking from strategic planning, namely because of its generative and sustainable nature. Therefore, we want to continually place ourselves in a state of imbalance in order to test and challenge our ability to learn.

I am not recommending the inclusion of art or music appreciation courses in business curricula; nor is there any reason to eliminate the analytic content in existing courses. Rather, I recommend that attention be given to the flip side of the strategy coin. The five essential attributes and critical reflective processes need to be developed either through informal means or by using an instructional approach of either integration or isolation.

There are two common schools of thought about how to strengthen critical reflective processes. One is that critical reflective processes happen naturally; the second is that they need to be structured. I believe it is important to support the former with the latter as a means to accelerate strategic thinking. Business schools should set an expectation for the use of critical reflective processes and also group the processes into segments that can be practiced (e.g., listening, intuition, inquiry, lateral thinking, reflection, and dialogue) in a structured format using either an integrated or an isolated instructional approach.

An integrated approach might include incorporating such things as exercises in design, drawing, storytelling, metaphoric writing, and intuition into the content of existing strategy courses. On the other hand, an isolated instructional approach might require a seminar allotted to critical inquiry or a workshop on design or storytelling.

Although newly minted MBAs are often extremely adept at thinking within an analytical frame, it seems to me that they are not nearly as adept when required to shift modes. I notice, across the globe, MBAs often lack critical reflective processes needed to transfer, shatter, and reframe—precisely what is needed for innovative and adaptive strategic thinking. They are in a quagmire when it comes to strategic thinking, unable to identify what their habits and patterns are and unable to draw from and transfer experience across contexts. Without this, it is impossible to imagine and generate truly innovative strategy. Although many young MBAs have impressive life histories, their inability to critically reflect and to transfer learning across contexts diminishes their contribution to the strategy game.

I notice that when MBAs enter businesses and organizations, they typically have a fixed-frame mentality regarding problem solving and decision making. They have learned (very thoroughly) one way to examine a problem and often falsely assume that there is a best solution for each problem. While this is useful for operational matters and simple problems, it is often counterproductive as support for the learning process needed in strategic thinking. Therefore, business schools also need to acknowledge and persistently work with both the surf and the dive learning domains across the curriculum, rather than focusing almost exclusively on the surface domain of instrumental transactional learning, which lends itself to analytical kinds of courses.

In referencing the history of strategy, we can see the tremendous and long-lasting impact that the technical rational way of thinking has had on business school curricula. With regard to strategic thinking, they are locked into a singular, outdated, analytical mode of thinking that emphasizes frameworks that were in vogue during the industrial revolution. The focus continues with the top-of-the-triangle, logical, rational thinking and objective representation taking absolute precedence over anything else. No wonder executives are disappointed with the inability of experienced managers and young MBAs to think strategically—they have simply not been taught. These highly linear, logical, rational skills need to be balanced and blended with learning that requires divergent, open-ended, creative, broadening, and generalized thinking abilities that are less finite and less concrete and include an emphasis on the affective as well as cognitive learning domains.

Business curricula have erred by overreducing and overspecializing courses and content to a degree of counterintent in the realm of strategy. In an effort to make things efficient, schools have gone overboard and across-the-board with measurement, analysis, convergence, and debate. This overemphasis has created unrealistic and false expectations about the nature of strategy and about the degree of complexity and dynamism of strategy making in the real world—thus deviating from intention and impeding the possibility for success when it comes to strategy.

Furthermore, the traditional business school curriculum has been detrimental to the learning required for strategic thinking. Strategic thinking essentially draws on learning processes that we have all but dismissed, discredited, or forgotten: elements of discipline, patience, time, and critical thinking, dialectical thinking, and dialogue capability. These are equally important to honing logic and analytic skills that we have singularly addressed over the past seven decades. It is impossible to hyperthink. There is no such thing (contrary to the implied messages being sent). We need to experience the very real process involved in reflection and creativity—speed is only achieved via experience.

Suggestions for Organizations

Much of what we have just said can also be applied to companies and other organizations. Within many companies, the development of strategic thinking among employees is singularly focused on developing a set of planning and analytic skills. Furthermore, many organizations believe that strategic thinking resides in a few chosen executives. But strategic thinking is far more complex than developing a skill set. It involves a high degree of cognitive and affective abilities, and it requires attention to developing creativity, reflectivity, and dialogue, not merely behavioral or skill development.

Organizations should focus on the application of engagement in creative endeavors to strengthen strategic thinking (not on the artistic achievements). Organizational funding for the experiences can make teachers, classes, directories, partnerships, and resources available and accessible. Furthermore, companies should develop a vocabulary and a habit of talking about learning transfer across contexts, for vocabulary facilitates meaningful dialogue, which enhances the transfer process. Additionally, organizations can support the transfer of learning by using coaches to support the development of critical reflective processes.

Corporate strategic development programs also need to emphasize analysis and intuition and to identify problems and decisions that require this-and-that thinking. Executives should take time to explain the thinking they use to combine two coexisting options into a new and preferable alternative. This requires a willingness to be open to exploring new possibilities by bringing novel, provocative, and even unlikely or controversial ideas in and out of focus constantly.

Organizations also need to allow practice time to dialogue during strategic meetings, especially regarding contradictory issues. The aim of such dialogue should be on practicing "and" thinking as a means of developing imagination, broad perspective, and adaptability. Dialogue about problems and factors that may require rational decisions should be differentiated from those that may require an a-rational approach. Explore the tension these two approaches create and how this tension is a useful source for making new connections and innovations.

Following is a list of recommendations for organizations to support strategic thinking.

SUGGESTIONS FOR ORGANIZATIONS

- Shatter the tip-of-the-triangle model of strategy making. Instead, draw and develop from all levels, all functions, and all locales of the organization.
- Clarify the organizational intent by differentiating strategic planning from strategic thinking.
- Encourage and support activities such as participation in the arts and creative life experiences in order to develop the five attributes and critical reflective processes. Alternate experiences in the arts with structured dialogue and critical reflective skill development sessions.
- Support and encourage learning processes such as action learning and lateral thinking as a means of strengthening the five attributes and transferring experience to a business strategy context.
- Institutionalize time for reflection. Senior executives should explicitly articulate the value and relation between time, reflection, experience, and learning. Reflection can and usually does happen outside of work. What is important is that reflection be acknowledged and established as an expectation, supported with ideas of what it looks like, and that it then be processed and incorporated into strategy thinking.
- Support an awareness of intuition in order to develop experience and trust among executives as they use it as part of the strategic thinking process.
- Talk about discoveries and situations where critical reflective thinking contributes to strategic decisions. This is a great way of helping people learn to pay attention to it.
- Don't overestimate the impact of formal learning, just because it is an organizational habit or because it is convenient to quantify.
- Explicitly recognize informal learning as being valuable to the corporate culture.
- Don't become obsessed with measuring everything. Trust that powerful and significant learning can occur outside the four walls of organizational control.
- Organize "think tanks" across the organization and around the globe (live or virtual). The purpose is to develop a pipeline of strategic thinkers by strengthening the five attributes and critical reflective processes, not to solve problems. "Think tanks" can become forums to practice and

experiment with processes and an opportunity for senior executives to model and further develop strategic thinking.

- Include junior and mid-level managers in discussions about the strategic learning process. This serves as a role-modeling opportunity to learn informally through experience. Junior managers should have access to the experienced senior executives as a learning resource, and they should be supported with adequate time for reflection. This can be a great strategic pipeline builder.
- Establish critical dialogue and inquiry as a management expectation.
- Build challenge and testing into the organizational culture through senior leadership modeling.
- Move lessons learned from the surf domain to the deeper, dive domain. Don't just share transactional, instrumental, surface thinking about what went wrong, what changed, and the results. Include process and premise reflection to encourage the affective learning dimension.
- Expand the in-company group with whom executives regularly conduct informal dialogue and storytelling. Omit the big, showy, overprepared storytelling productions and, instead, use storytelling and critical dialogue as an everyday alternative to bullet points and sound bites. The listening required can create enormous tension, which encourages and enriches reflection.

Summary

Throughout this book, starting with the ancient Greek concept of strategy, which assumed an unresolvable tension and mutuality between chaos and ordered cosmos, encouraged a balance and integration of opposing and contradictory perspectives, or *metos*, we followed the swinging pendulum toward technical rationality and its obsession with the linear scientific approach to strategy making. We have now arrived at a crossroads on our journey in search of the Holy Grail of strategic learning.

The ancient Greek idea of a strategic context was surprisingly similar to the context in which we currently find ourselves making strategy—uncertainties, rapidly changing and incomplete information, things we cannot control, and dealing with paradoxes and contradictions. This requires a strong propensity for critical reflection, critical inquiry, dialogue, and the five attributes. By adopting an expanded notion of Greek strategy, we realize an image of strategy that is generative, innovative, sustainable, and adaptable in nature. These, then, must be the focus of our strategic development initiatives. Business schools, companies, consulting firms, and learning facilitators all need to understand and support the learning process required for strategic thinking in order to develop it as a complement to strategic planning.

By its very nature, strategy is dynamic; therefore, successful strategy is always past tense. Competitive organizations understand that learning to think strategically is a business imperative. Learning to think strategically is not easy—it requires abilities that are not generally taught in formal, traditional strategy courses but, rather, are learned informally. Strategic thinking requires experience and time for critical reflection, inquiry, dialogue, and commitment to developing the five attributes.

After centuries of traveling the long and winding roads, practitioners of strategy and scholars alike have to acknowledge the uncanny similarities between the current challenges of our global strategy making and that of the ancient Greeks. Although our present-day global strategy context is in so many ways qualitatively and quantitatively different from that of the ancient Greeks, it is nevertheless as unpredictable, rapidly changing, and full of contradictions and paradoxes as at the dawn of Western civilization. While our learning repertoire is perhaps more expansive than that of our predecessors, common sense suggests that we can benefit from the knowledge of many centuries and can build on and learn from the lessons of the past. As is often the case, the new way turns out to be just a well-forgotten past way.

Hopefully, this book has generated questions in the minds of readers that will facilitate practical, original, and informal ways of learning to think strategically—ways that acknowledge and build on the strengths of the learning legacies of the past.

Notes

Part I: How Did We Get to This Point?

1. *Webster's Third New International Dictionary of the English Language Unabridged*, 2256.
2. Cummings and Wilson, *Images of Strategy*, 6.
3. Cummings and Wilson, *Images of Strategy*, 6.
4. Cummings and Wilson, *Images of Strategy*, 6.
5. Cummings and Wilson, *Images of Strategy*, 9.
6. Chandler, *Scale and Scope*.
7. Chandler, *Scale and Scope*.
8. Botticelli, "Competition and Business Strategy in Historical Perspective."
9. Sloan, A., Jr., *My Years with General Motors*.
10. Andrews, *The Concept of Corporate Strategy*, 23.
11. Selznick, *Leadership in Administration*, 67–74.
12. Selznick, *Leadership in Administration*, 91–107.
13. Chandler, *Strategy and Structure*, 42.
14. "Competition and Business Strategy in Historical Perspective." Harvard Business School 9-798-010, rev. Dec. 11, 1997, 3.
15. Cummings and Wilson, *Images of Strategy*, 17.
16. Cummings and Wilson, *Images of Strategy*, 16.
17. Mintzberg, Ahlstrand, and Lampel, *Strategy Safari*, 57.
18. Henderson, *The Logic of Business Strategy*, 10.
19. Gluck and Kaufman, "Using the Strategic Planning Framework," 3–4.
20. Conley, *Experience Curves as a Planning Tool*, 15.
21. DeKluyver, *Strategic Thinking*, 3.
22. Prahalad and Hamel, "The Core Competence of the Corporation," 80–91.
23. Mintzberg and Lampel, "Reflecting on the Strategy Process," 23–24.
24. Cummings and Wilson, *Images of Strategy*, 16–17.

25. Mintzberg, Ahlstrand, and Lampel, *Strategy Safari*.
26. Mintzberg, Ahlstrand, and Lampel, *Strategy Safari*.
27. Pietersen, *Reinventing Strategy*, 51.
28. Mintzberg, Ahlstrand, and Lampel, *Strategy Safari*.
29. Revans, *The Origin and Growth of Action Learning*.

Part II: How Do We Learn to Think Strategically?

1. Marsick and Watkins, *Informal and Incidental Learning in the Workplace*, 7.
2. Marsick and Watkins, *Informal and Incidental Learning in the Workplace*, 12.
3. Marsick and Watkins, *Informal and Incidental Learning in the Workplace*.
4. Jarvis, *Adult Learning in the Social Context*, 70.
5. Sloan, J. *Case Study of How Nine Executives Learn Informally to Develop Strategy in a Global Context*.
6. Jarvis, *Adult Learning in the Social Context*.
7. Mezirow, *Fostering Critical Reflection in Adulthood*.
8. Mezirow, *Fostering Critical Reflection in Adulthood*.
9. Mintzberg, *The Rise and Fall of Strategic Planning*.
10. Schon, *The Reflective Practitioner*, 50.

Part III: What Does Learning to Think Strategically Look Like?

1. Sloan, J. *Case Study of How Nine Executives Learn Informally to Develop Strategy in a Global Context*.
2. Boud, D. and Walker, D. *Barriers to Reflection on Experience*, Bristol (PA: The Society for Research into Higher Education & Open University Press, 1933).
3. Boud and Walker, *Barriers to Reflection on Experience*, 72.
4. Dewey, *Experience and Education*.
5. Kolb, *Experiential Learning*.
6. Marsick and Watkins, *Informal and Incidental Learning in the Workplace*.
7. Dewey, *Experience and Education*.
8. Mezirow, *Transformative Dimensions of Adult Learning*, 100.
9. Argryis, Putnam, and McLain Smith, *Action Science*.
10. Schon, *Educating the Reflective Practitioner*.
11. Mezirow, "A Transformative Theory of Adult Learning."
12. Mezirow, *Transformative Dimensions of Adult Learning*, 104.
13. Brookfield, *Understanding and Facilitating Adult Learning*, 91.
14. Marsick and Watkins, *Informal and Incidental Learning in the Workplace*, 74.
15. Sloan, J. *Case Study of How Nine Executives Learn Informally to Develop Strategy in a Global Context*.

Part IV: What Kind of Learning Is Required to Think Strategically?

1. Hilgard and Bower, *Theories of Learning.*
2. Nonaka and Takeuchi, *The Knowledge-Creating Company*, 58–59.
3. James, W. *Pragmatism.*
4. Yorks, *Strategic Human Resource Development*, 41.
5. Cell, *Learning to Learn from Experience.*
6. Mezirow, *Learning as Transformation.*
7. Mezirow, "A Transformative Theory of Adult Learning," 49.
8. Mezirow, "A Transformative Theory of Adult Learning," 58.
9. Mezirow, "A Transformative Theory of Adult Learning," 49.
10. Mezirow, "A Transformative Theory of Adult Learning," 49.
11. Mezirow, *Transformative Dimensions of Adult Learning*, 87.
12. Mezirow, "A Transformative Theory of Adult Learning," 49.

Part V: How Can We Talk About All This?

1. *Merriam-Webster's Collegiate Dictionary, Tenth Edition.*
2. Cross and Israelit, *Strategic Learning in a Knowledge Economy*, 235.
3. Dixon, *Perspectives on Dialogue.*
4. *Merriam-Webster's Collegiate Dictionary, Tenth Edition.*
5. *Merriam-Webster's Collegiate Dictionary, Tenth Edition.*
6. Cross and Israelit, *Strategic Learning in a Knowledge Economy*, 232.
7. Cross and Israelit, *Strategic Learning in a Knowledge Economy*, 233.
8. Cross and Israelit, *Strategic Learning in a Knowledge Economy*, 234.
9. Bender, *Operation Excellence.*

Part VI: Why Do We Learn Strategic Thinking This Way?

1. Klein, *The Power of Intuition*, 5.
2. Dreyfus and Dreyfus, *Mind over Machine*, xiv.
3. Dreyfus and Dreyfus, *Mind over Machine*, xiv.
4. Schon, *Educating the Reflective Practitioner*, 24.
5. Von Krogh, Ichijo, and Nonaka, *Enabling Knowledge Creation*, 74.
6. Von Krogh, Ichijo, and Nonaka, *Enabling Knowledge Creation*, 77.
7. Von Krogh, Ichijo, and Nonaka, *Enabling Knowledge Creation.*
8. Klein, *The Power of Intuition.*
9. DeBono, *Lateral Thinking*, 42.

10. Mezirow, *Transformative Dimensions of Adult Learning*, 87.
11. Schon, *The Reflective Practitioner*, 241.
12. Schon, *The Reflective Practitioner*, 68.
13. Mezirow, *Transformative Dimensions of Adult Learning*, 104.
14. Schon, *The Reflective Practitioner*.
15. Mezirow, *Transformative Dimensions of Adult Learning*.
16. Klein, *The Power of Intuition*, 70.

Part VII: What About the Numbers?

1. Klein, *The Power of Intuition*, 66.
2. Klein, *The Power of Intuition*, 67–70.
3. Argyris and Schon, *Organizational Learning II*.

Part VIII: What Does Culture Have to Do With Strategic Thinking?

1. Alyahya and Vengroff, "Human Capital Utilization, Empowerment, and Organizational Effectiveness in the Middle East," 6.
2. Hofstede, *Culture's Consequences*.
3. Trompenaars and Hampden-Turner, *The Seven Cultures of Capitalism*.
4. Gundling, *Working GlobeSmart*.

Part IX: Is Anybody Born with This "Know-how"?

1. Sloan, J., *Case Study of How Nine Executives Learn Informally to Develop Strategy in a Global Context*.
2. Klein, *The Power of Intuition*, 151.
3. Sloan, J., *Case Study of How Nine Executives Learn Informally to Develop Strategy in a Global Context*.
4. Boud and Garrick, in *Understanding Learning at Work*, 221.
5. McCall, Lombardo, and Morrison, *The Lessons of Experience*, 161.
6. Marsick and Volpe, *Informal Learning on the Job*, 7.
7. Bolman and Deal, *Reframing Organizations*.
8. Marsick and Volpe, *Informal Learning on the Job*, 85.
9. Sloan, J., *Case Study of How Nine Executives Learn Informally to Develop Strategy in a Global Context*.
10. Sloan, J., *Case Study of How Nine Executives Learn Informally to Develop Strategy in a Global Context*.

11. Weick and Sutcliffe, *Managing the Unexpected*.
12. Klein, *The Power of Intuition*.

Part X: What Can We Do to Improve Strategic Thinking?

1. Marquardt, *Action Learning Solving Problems and Building Leaders in Real Time*.
2. Revans, *The Origin and Growth of Action Learning*.
3. DeBono, *Lateral Thinking*, 52.
4. DeBono, *Lateral Thinking*, 52.
5. DeBono, *Lateral Thinking*, 229.

Bibliography

Abualjadail, M. "Problems Affecting Productivity of Public and Private Sector Employees in Saudi Arabia." Doctoral dissertation, University of La Verne, La Verne, CA 1990.

Ahiauzu, A. I. "The African Thought System and the Work Behavior of the African Industrial Main." *International Studies of Management & Organization* 16 (1986): 37–58.

Alexander, D. L. "The Effect Level the Hierarchy and Functional Areas Have on the Extent Mintzberg's Roles As Required by Managerial Jobs," *Academy of Management* (1979): 186–189.

Ali, A., and Swiercz, P. "The Relationship Between Managerial Decision Making and Work Satisfaction in Saudi Arabia." In E. Kaynack and Erdener (eds.), *International Business in the Middle East*. New York: Walter deGruyter, 1986, pp. 137–149.

Alkahtani, A. "Involvement of Employees and Their Personal Characteristics in Saudi Construction Companies." *International Journal of Commerce & Management* 10 (2000): 67–78.

Al-Tweam, N. I. "Attitudes of Saudi Public Bureaucrats: A Study in Administrative Responsibility and Control of the Bureaucracy." Doctoral dissertation, The Library of the Saudi Arabian Cultural Mission, Washington, DC, 1995.

Alyahya, K., and Vengroff, R. "Human Capital Utilization, Empowerment, and Organizational Effectiveness in the Middle East: A Comparative Perspective." University of Connecticut and Harvard University: Global Development Studies paper, 2004.

Amidon, D. *The Innovation Superhighway: Harnessing Intellectual Capital for Sustainable Collaborative Advantage*. Woburn, MA: Butterworth-Heinemann, 2003.

Andrews, K. R. *The Concept of Corporate Strategy*, rev. ed. Homewood, IL: Richard D. Irwin, 1971.

Ansoff, H. E. *Corporate Strategy*. New York: McGraw-Hill, 1965.

Arbelaez, Harvey, and Milman, Glaudio. "The Business Environment of Latin American and the Caribbean." *International Journal of Public Administration* 23 (2000): 1253–1268.

Argyris, C. *Knowledge for Action.* San Francisco: Jossey-Bass, 1993.

Argyris, C. *Reasoning, Learning, and Actions: Individuals and Organizational.* San Francisco: Jossey-Bass, 1982.

Argyris, C., Putnam, R., and McLain Smith, D. *Action Science.* San Francisco: Jossey-Bass, 1985.

Argyris, C., and Schon, D. *Organizational Learning: A Theory of Action Perspective.* Reading, MA: Addison-Wesley, 1978.

Argyris, C., and Schon, D. *Organizational Learning II: Theory, Method, and Practice.* Reading, MA: Addison-Wesley, 1996.

Argyris, C., and Schon, D. *Theory in Practice: Increasing Professional Effectiveness.* San Francisco: Jossey-Bass, 1974.

Bandura, A. *Social Foundations of Thought and Action: A Cognitive Social Theory.* Englewood, NJ: Prentice-Hall, 1986.

Barney, J. B. "Firm Resources and Sustained Competitive Advantage." *Journal of Management* 17 (1991): 99–120.

Bender, M. *Operation Excellence: Succeeding in Business and Life — The U.S. Military Way,* 1st ed., New York: AMACOM, 2004.

Bjur, Wesley E., and Zomorrodian, A. "Towards Indigenous Theories of Administration." *International Review of Administrative Sciences* 52 (1986): 393–420.

Bleeke, J., and Ernst, D. *Collaborating to Compete Using Strategic Alliances and Acquisitions in the Global Marketplace.* San Francisco: Jossey-Bass, 1993.

Bolman, L. G., and Deal, T. *Reframing Organizations: Artistry, Choice, and Leadership,* 2nd ed., San Francisco: Jossey-Bass, 1997.

Bottger, P., Hallein, I., and Yetton, P. "A Cross-National Study of Leadership: Participation as a Function of Problem Structure and Leader Power." *Journal of Management Studies* (1985, July): 359–368.

Botticelli, P. "Competition and Business Strategy in Historical Perspective." Draft paper prepared for President and Fellows of Harvard College. Harvard Business School Publishing, December 1997.

Boucouvalas, M. "Consciousness and Learning: New and Renewed Approaches." *New Directions for Adult and Continuing Education* 57 (Spring 1993): 57–69.

Boud, D., and Garrick, J. Quote by Weil, S.W., and McGill, I. in *Understanding Learning at Work.* New York: Routledge, 1999.

Boud, D., Keogh, R., and Walker, D. *Reflection: Turning Experience into Learning.* New York: Nichols, 1985.

Boud, D., and Walker, D. "Barriers to Reflection on Experience." In Boud, D., Cohen, R., and Walker, D., *Using Experience for Learning.* Bristol, PA: The Society for Research into Higher Education & Open University Press, 1993.

Brockett, R. G., and Hiemstra, R. *Self-Direction in Adult Learning: Perspectives on Theory, Research, and Practice.* New York: Routledge, 1991.

Brodbeck, Felix, et al. "Cultural Variation of Leadership Prototypes Across 22 European Countries." *Journal of Occupational and Organizational Psychology*, 73 (2000, March).

Brookfield, S. *Learning Democracy: E. Lindeman on Adult Education and Social Change.* London: Croom Helm, 1987.

Brookfield, S. "Tales from the Dark Side: A Phenomenography of Adult Critical Reflection." *Proceedings of the Adult Education Research Conference*, no. 35. Knoxville: The University of Tennessee, May 1994.

Brookfield, S. *Understanding and Facilitating Adult Learning.* San Francisco: Jossey-Bass, 1986.

Burgelman, R. A. "A Process Model of Strategic Business Exit: Implications for an Evolutionary Perspective on Strategy." *Strategic Management Journal* 17 (1996): 193–214.

Cell, E. *Learning to Learn from Experience.* Albany: State University of New York Press, 1984.

Cell, E. *Organizational Life: Learning to be Self-Directed.* Lanhan, MI: University Press of America, 1998.

Chandler, A. D. *Scale and Scope: The Dynamics of Industrial Capitalism.* Cambridge, MA: Harvard University Press, 1990.

Chandler, A. D. *Strategy and Structure: Chapters in the History of the Industrial Enterprise.* Cambridge, MA: MIT Press, 1962.

Chase, R., and Aquilano, N. *Production and Operations Management,* 6th ed. Homewood, IL: Richard D. Irwin, 1992.

Chene, A. "The Concept of Autonomy in Adult Education: A Philosophical Discussion." *Adult Education Quarterly* 34 (1983): 38–47.

Collins, J. M. *Military Strategy: Principles, Practices, and Historical Perspectives.* Dulles, VA: Potomac Books, 2001.

Conley, P. *Experience Curves as a Planning Tool.* Boston Consulting Group pamphlet, 1970.

Courtney, H., Kirkland, J., and Viguerie, P. "Strategy Under Uncertainty." *Harvard Business Review* (November–December 1997): 66–79.

Cranton, P. *Understanding and Promoting Transformative Learning.* San Francisco: Jossey-Bass, 1994.

Cross, R., and Israelit, S. *Strategic Learning in a Knowledge Economy: Individual, Collective, and Organizational Learning Process.* Woburn, MA: Butterworth-Heinemann, 2000.

Cseh, M. "Contextual Learning of Owner-Managers of Small, Successful Romanian Companies." *Contextual Learning Issues.* Academy of Human Resource Development (HRD) Conference Proceedings, 1999.

Cummings, S., and Wilson, D. *Images of Strategy.* Malden, MA: Blackwell, 2003.

Daniels, K., and Bailey, A. "Strategy Development Process and Participation in Decision Making: Predictors of Role Stressors and Job Satisfaction." *Journal of Applied Management Studies* 8 (1999): 27–45.

Davenport, Thomas. *Human Capital: What It Is and Why People Invest in It.* San Francisco: Jossey-Bass, 1999.

DeBono, E. *Lateral Thinking.* New York: Harper & Row, 1970.

DeKluyver, C. A. *Strategic Thinking: An Executive Perspective.* Upper Saddle River, NJ: Prentice-Hall, 2000.

Dewey, J. *Art as Experience.* New York: Pondview Books, 1934.

Dewey, J. *Experience and Education.* New York: Collier Books, 1938.

Dixon, N. M. *Perspectives on Dialogue.* Greensboro, NC: Center for Creative Leadership, in-house publication, 1996.

Dotlich, D., and Noel, J. *Action Learning: How the World's Top Companies Are Re-Creating Their Leaders and Themselves.* San Francisco: Jossey-Bass, 1998.

Doz, Y., and Prahalad, C. K. "Headquarters Influence and Strategic Control in MNC's." *Sloan Management Review* (1982, Fall): 15–29.

Dreyfus, H. L., and Dreyfus, S. E. *Mind over Machine: The Power of Human Intuitive Expertise in the Era of the Computer.* New York: Free Press, 1986.

Duke Corporate Education. *Translating Strategy into Action.* Chicago, IL: Dearborn Trade Publishing, 2005.

Edmonson, A., and Moingeon, B. *When to Learn How and When to Learn Why: Appropriate Organization Learning as a Source of Competitive Advantage.* London: Sage Publications, 1996.

Fisher, A. *Critical Thinking.* United Kingdom: Cambridge University Press, 2001.

Flanagan, J. C. "The Critical Incident Technique." *Psychological Bulletin* 51 (1954): 327–358.

Fry, R., and Kolb, D. "Experiential Learning Theory and Learning Experience in Liberal Arts Education." In Steven E. Brooks and James E. Althof (eds.). *Enriching the Liberal Arts Through Experiential Learning.* San Francisco: Jossey-Bass, 1979.

Georgescu, P. *The Source of Success: Five Enduring Principles at the Heart of Real Leadership.* San Francisco: Jossey-Bass, 2005.

Gilbert, X., and Strebel, P. "Developing Competitve Advantage." In J. B. Quinn, H. Mintzberg, and R. James (eds.). *The Strategy Process.* Englewood Cliffs, NJ: Prentice Hall, 1988.

Gluck, F. W., and Kaufman, S. P. "Using the Strategic Planning Framework." McKinsey internal document: *Readings in Strategy*, 3–4 (1979).

Greeno, J. G. "A Perspective on Thinking." *American Psychologist* 44 (1989): 134–141.

Greenwald, B., and Kahn, J. *Competition DeMystified.* New York: Portfolio, 2005.

Griffin, R. W., and Pustav, M. W. *International Business: A Managerial Perspective.* Reading, MA: Addison-Wesley, 1996.

Gundling, E. *Working GlobeSmart.* Palo Alto, CA: Davies-Black, 2003.

Hamel, G. "Strategy as Revolution." *Harvard Business Review* (1996, July–August): 70–71.

Hamel, G., and Prahalad, C. K. *Competing for the Future.* Cambridge, MA: Harvard Business School Press, 1994.

Hamermesh, R. G. *Making Strategy Work: How Senior Managers Produce Results.* New York: John Wiley, 1986.

Harris, J. *The Learning Paradox.* Toronto, Canada: Macmillan, 1998.

Hellgren, B., and Melin, L. "The Role of Strategists: Ways-of-thinking in Strategic Change Processes." In J. Hendry, G. Johnson, & J. Newton (eds.). *Strategic Thinking: Leadership and the Management of Change.* Chichester, UK: John Wiley, 1993, pp. 47–68.

Henderson, B. D. *Henderson on Corporate Strategy.* Cambridge, MA: Abt Books, 1979.

Henderson, B. D. *The Logic of Business Strategy.* Cambridge, MA: Ballinger, 1984.

Hilgard, E. R., and Bower, G. H. *Theories of Learning.* New York: Appleton-Century-Crofts, 1966.

Hofstede, G. *Culture's Consequences.* Beverly Hills, CA: Sage, 1980.

James, J. *Thinking in the Future Tense.* New York: Simon & Schuster, 1997.

James, W. *Pragmatism.* New York: Longmans and Green, 1925.

Jarvis, P. *Adult Learning in the Social Context.* New York: Croom Helm, 1987, p. 70.

Johnson, G. "Managing Strategic Change — Strategy, Culture, and Action." *Long-Range Planning* 25, P. Sadler (ed.). Oxford: Pergamon Press, 1995 pp. 28–36.

Kanter, R. M. *World Class: Thriving Locally in the Global Economy.* New York: Simon & Schuster, 1995.

Kim, Soonhee. "Participative Management and Job Satisfaction: Lessons for Management Leadership." *Public Administration Review* 62 (2002): 231–242.

Kim, W. C., and Mauborgne, R. *Blue Ocean Strategy.* Boston: Harvard Business School Press, 2005.

Klein, G. *The Power of Intuition.* New York: Currency Books, Doubleday, 2003.

Knox, A. *Helping Adults Learn.* San Francisco: Jossey-Bass, 1986.

Kolb, D. *Experiential Learning: Experience as the Source of Learning and Development.* Englewood Cliffs, NJ: Prentice-Hall, 1984.

Kouzes, J., and Posner, B. *The Leadership Challenge*, 3rd ed., San Francisco: Jossey-Bass, 2002.

Leonard-Barton, D. "Core Capabilities and Core Rigidities: A Paradox in Managing New Product Development." *Strategic Management Journal* 11 (1992): 111–125.

Lincoln, Y. D. *The Making of a Constructivist.* Newbury Park, CA: Sage, 1990.

Lippitt, L. *Preferred Futuring.* San Francisco: Berrett-Koehler, 1998.

Loehle, C. *Thinking Strategically.* United Kingdom: Cambridge University Press, 1996.

Lorange, P. *Corporate Planning: An Executive Viewpoint.* Englewood Cliffs, NJ: Prentice Hall, 1977.

Marquardt, M. *Action Learning Solving Problems and Building Leaders in Real Time.* Palo Alto, CA: Davies-Black, 2004.

Marsick, V. J., and Sauquet, A. *Learning Through Reflection.* San Francisco: Jossey-Bass, 1999.

Marsick, V. J., and Volpe, M. (eds.). *Informal Learning on the Job. Advances in Developing Human Resources, no. 3.* San Francisco: Academy of Human Resource Development/Berrett-Kohler Communications, 1999.

Marsick, V. J., and Watkins, K. E. *Informal and Incidental Learning in the Workplace.* London: Routledge, 1990.

Matejka, K., and Murphy, A. *Making Change Happen on Time on Target on Budget.* Mountain View, CA: Davies-Black, 2005.

McCall, M. W., Lombardo, M. M., and Morrison, A. M. *The Lessons of Experience.* Ashland, MA: Lexington Books, 1988.

Merriam-Webster's Collegiate Dictionary, Tenth Edition. Springfield, MA: Merriam-Webster, 2001.

Mezirow, J. "A Transformative Theory of Adult Learning." In M. Welton (ed.), *In Defense of the Lifeworld: Critical Perspectives on Adult Learning.* Albany, NY: SUNY Press, 1995.

Mezirow, J. *Fostering Critical Reflection in Adulthood.* San Francisco: Jossey-Bass, 1994.

Mezirow, J. *Learning as Transformation: Critical Perspectives on a Theory in Progress.* San Francisco: Jossey-Bass, 2000.

Mezirow, J. *Transformative Dimensions of Adult Learning.* San Francisco: Jossey-Bass, 1991.

Mintzberg, H. "An Emerging Strategy of 'Direct' Research." *Administrative Science Quarterly* 24 (December 1979): 582–589.

Mintzberg, H. "Patterns in Strategy Formation." *Management Science* 24 (1978): 934–948.

Mintzberg, H. "The Design School: Reconsidering the Basic Premises of Strategic Management." *Strategic Management Journal* 11 (1990): 171–195.

Mintzberg, H. *The Rise and Fall of Strategic Planning.* New York: Free Press, 1994.

Mintzberg, H., Ahlstrand, B., and Lampel, J. *Strategy Safari: A Guided Tour Through the Wilds of Strategic Management.* New York: Free Press, 1998.

Mintzberg, H., and Lampel, J. "Reflecting on The Strategy Process." *Sloan Management Review* [special issue] 40 (Spring 1999): 23–24.

Montgomery, John. "Probing Managerial Behavior: Image and Reality in Southern Africa." Paper prepared for the Annual Meeting of the African Studies Association, Madison, WI, October 26–November 1, 1986.

Mumford, A. *Learning at the Top.* New York: McGraw-Hill, 1995.

Nelson, R. R., and Winter, S. G. *An Evolutionary Theory of Economic Change.* Cambridge, MA: Harvard University Press, 1982.

Nonaka, I., and Takeuchi, H. *The Knowledge-Creating Company: How Japanese Companies Create the Dynamics of Innovation.* New York: Oxford University Press, 1995.

Pietersen, W. *Reinventing Strategy: Using Strategic Learning to Create and Sustain Breakthrough Performance.* John Wiley & Sons, 2002.

Polanyi, M. *Personal Knowledge: Towards a Post-Critical Philosophy.* Chicago: University of Chicago Press, 1958.

Polanyi, M. *The Tacit Dimension.* New York: Doubleday, 1967.

Porter, M. E. "The Contributions of Industrial Organizations to Strategic Management." *Academy of Management Review* 6 (1981): 609–620.

Porter, M. E. "What Is Strategy?" *Harvard Business Review* (November–December 1996): 61–78.

Prahalad, C. K., and Hamel, G. "The Core Competence of the Corporation." *Harvard Business Review* (March–April 1993): 80–91.

Quinn, J. B. *Strategies for Change: Logistical Incrementalism.* Homewood, IL: Irwin, 1980.

Rangan, S., and Yoshina, M. *Strategic Alliances.* Boston: Harvard Business School Press, 1995.

Revans, R. W. *The Origin and Growth of Action Learning.* London: Chartwell Bratt, 1982.

Rodrigues, C. A. *International Management.* St. Paul, MN: West, 1996.

Rothe, K., and Ricks, D. A. "Goal Configuration in a Global Industry Context." *Strategic Management Journal* 15 (1994): 103–120.

Rothwell, W. J. *The Action Learning Guidebook.* San Francisco: Jossey-Bass/Pfeiffer, 1990.

Rubin H., and Rubin, I. *Qualitative Interviewing: The Art of Hearing Data.* Thousand Oaks, CA: Sage, 1995.

Schneider, S., and DeMeyer, A. "Interpreting and Responding to Strategic Issues: The Impact of National Culture." *Strategic Management Journal* 12 (1991): 307–320.

Schoeffler, S., Buzzel, R. D., and Heany, D. F. "Impact of Strategic Planning on Profit Performance." *Harvard Business Review* 54 (March–April 1974): 137–145.

Schon, D. *Educating the Reflective Practitioner.* San Francisco: Jossey-Bass, 1987.

Schon, D. *The Reflective Practitioner.* New York: Basic Books, 1983.

Scribner, S. *Thinking in Action: Some Characteristics of Practical Thought. Origins of Competence.* Cambridge, UK: Cambridge University Press, 1986.

Selznick, P. *Leadership in Administration: A Sociological Interpretation.* Evanston, IL: Row, Peterson, 1957.

Senge, P. M. *The Fifth Discipline.* New York: Doubleday, 1990.

Singley, M. K., and Anderson, J. R. *The Transfer of Cognitive Skill.* Cambridge, MA: Harvard University Press, 1989.

Sloan, A., Jr. *My Years with General Motors.* New York: Doubleday, 1963.

Sloan, J. *Case Study of How Nine Executives Learn Informally to Develop Strategy in a Global Context.* Doctoral dissertation, New York, Teachers College, Columbia University, 2002.

Sloane, P. *Lateral Thinking Skills.* Sterling, VA: Kogan Page, 2003.

Spitzer, Q., and Evans, R. *Heads, You Win!* New York: Fireside Book, Simon & Schuster, 1997.

Stacey, R. *Managing Chaos: Dynamic Business Strategies in an Unpredictable World.* London: Kogan Page, 1992.

Taleb, N. *Fooled by Randomness.* New York: Random House, 2004.

Taylor, F. *Principles of Scientific Management.* New York: Norton, 1967.

Teece, D. J., Pisano, P., and Shuen, A. "Dynamic Capabilities and Strategic Management." Mimeo, June 1992, pp. 12–13.

Trapp, R., and Benoit, P. J. "An Interpretive Perspective on Argumentation: A Research Editorial." *The Western Journal of Speech Communication* 51 (1987): 417–430.

Trompenaars, A., and Hampden-Turner, C. *The Seven Cultures of Capitalism.* New York: Doubleday, 1993.

Von Krogh, G., Ichijo, K., and Nonaka, I. *Enabling Knowledge Creation.* New York: Oxford University Press, 2000.

Von Neumann, J., and Morgenstern, O. *Theory of Games and Economic Behavior.* Princeton, NJ: Elgen Books, 1944.

Vygotsky, L. S. *Thought and Language.* Cambridge, MA: MIT Press, 1987.

Webster's Third New International Dictionary of the English Language Unabridged. Springfield, MA: Merriam-Webster, 1993.

Weick, K. *Sensemaking in Organizations.* Thousand Oaks, CA: Sage, 1995.

Weick, K., and Sutcliffe, K. M. *Managing the Unexpected: Assuring High Performance in an Age of Complexity.* San Francisco: Jossey-Bass, 2001.

Weil, S. W., and McGill, I. *Making Sense of Experiential Learning: Diversity in Theory and Practice.* Buckingham, UK: SRHE and the Open University Press, 1989.

Wick, C. W., and Leon, S. *The Learning Edge: How Smart Managers and Smart Companies Stay Ahead.* New York: McGraw-Hill, 1993.

Yorks, L. *Strategic Human Resource Development.* Mason, OH: Thomson, South-Western, 2005.

Zander, R. Stone, and Zander, B. *The Art of Possibility.* Penguin Books, 2002.

Zuboff, S. *In the Age of the Smart Machine.* New York: Basic Books, 1988.

Index

In this index *f* following a page number indicates a figure found in the text and *t* indicates a table.

collaboration, dialogue and inquiry in, 104–105, 116–117
communication. *See also* dialogue
  attribute integration techniques, 217–220
  convergent, 206
  divergent, 110, 205
  storytelling technique, 19–20, 218–220
  strategic conversation, xix–xx
  successful strategists use of, 104–105, 108, 215, 218–220
communicative domain of learning, 88–89
competence, distinctive, 9
competitive affective element, 53–54, 66, 213
complexity theory, 20–21
compromise, 243
conformists, 250–251
consulting firms, history of, 12
content reflection, 68, 154
conversation, strategic, xix–xx
Corporate Strategy (Ansoff), 11
corporations, successful. *See under* strategy, corporate
cosmos, 5–6, 72
creativity
  arts involvement and, 233–237, 240–241, 247
  in business, 206–208
  factors encouraging, 21
  intuition versus, 206
culture, corporate. *See also* strategy, corporate
  conformists, 250–251
  corp-think mentality, 138
  for developing strategic thinkers, 125
  hierarchical, 8, 21, 186–189, 191–193
  same-frame thinking in, 138, 207–208, 250
  satisfieds in, 250
  understanding frames in, 89

culture, impact on
  frame change, 90, 193–194, 197
  information sharing, 191–192
  learning, 53, 55–56, 150x, 187
  pattern recognition, 142–143, 182–184, 188–189, 193
  strategic learning, 125, 183, 186, 194–197
  strategic thinking, 181–189, 193, 196–197
  strategy making, 184–185
Culture's Consequences (Hofstede), 185
Cummings, Stephen, 6

Darwinian adaptation, 20, 21, 24
data (metrics)
  defined, 78
  information's relationship to, 78, 110
  limitations and strengths of, 166
data analysis
  intuition integrated in decision making, 163–168, 175–177, 176*t*
  limitations of, 226
  storytelling and, 219
data-dialogue cycle, 110, 111*f*
Deal, T., 220
debate in strategic learning, 103–107, 106*f*, 112
de Bono, Edward, 146, 245–246
decision making, strategic
  ambivalence in, 242
  bounded rationality in, 226
  complacency in, 150–151, 158–160
  intuition and, 132–134, 139
    analysis integration with, 175–177, 176*t*
    rationality integration with, 171–173, 172*f*
  pattern recognition in, 139–142
  tacit knowledge in, 134–136
  technical rational approach to, 242
  traditional model, 169–171, 176
  uncertainty in, 170–171

About the Author

Julia Sloan is a global executive development consultant working with leading international corporations operating in both emerging and developed markets.

With more than a decade of expatriate corporate experience, Julia has lived and continues to work extensively in Asia, Eastern Europe, the Middle East, Africa, and the United States.

Her research interests include strategic thinking in relation to learning theory and social-cultural theory. She has lectured at Columbia University, Massachusetts Institute of Technology and also Tokyo University, Nanjing University, and India Institute of Management. In addition to working in the corporate sector, Julia has also consulted for the United Nations, The World Bank, and UN Peacekeeping Operations.

Julia regularly presents at international business conferences and has addressed organizations including MITI (Japan's Ministry of International Trade and Industry), ASEAN (Association of South East Asian Nations), JETRO (Japan Export and Trade Organization), and the Ministry of Commerce in Thailand, India, and China. She has also testified before an array of international trade commissions.

Currently residing in New York, Julia holds a doctorate from Columbia University in organizational leadership development. Julia can be contacted via email at: sloanconsult@aol.com